# The Love of the Trinity

# The Love of the Trinity

By the
Right Rev.
Arthur F. Winnington Ingram, D.D.
Lord Bishop of London

WIPF & STOCK · Eugene, Oregon

Wipf and Stock Publishers
199 W 8th Ave, Suite 3
Eugene, OR 97401

The Love of the Trinity
By Winnington-Ingram, Arthur F.
Softcover ISBN-13: 978-1-7252-9650-3
Hardcover ISBN-13: 978-1-7252-9651-0
eBook ISBN-13: 978-1-7252-9652-7
Publication date 1/5/2021
Previously published by
The Young Churchmen Co., 1908

This edition is a scanned facsimile of
the original edition published in 1908.

# Preface

ON this loveliest of May days I send forth this little volume, the preparation of which has absorbed every available hour of my Easter holiday. As I write these words, with the birds singing all round me and all the trees springing to life, I can only breathe a prayer that it may help some poor soul to live and love again, and believe in the "Love of the TRINITY." Religion was meant, I feel sure, to be a very bright and happy thing, and no one ought to be happier than a believing Christian. The sermon which seemed to have helped so many in this volume was preached on the text, "The GOD of Hope fill you with all joy and peace in believing, that ye may abound in hope through the power of the HOLY GHOST"; and nothing in life is truer than the short statement of the Apostle, "We are saved by hope."

But I must again remind the reader of this book, as I have in the prefaces to the "Mission of the SPIRIT" and "The Call of the FATHER," of the peculiar nature of it. It is the verbatim report of a real Mission, with real souls to be saved and helped, and real difficulties to be answered. Hence, everything obviously had to be sacrificed to the work in hand. If a question was asked again, it must be

## *Preface*

answered again. It was no good to say that it had been answered in Clerkenwell, if it was a difficulty to a soul in Marylebone.

Although a large number followed round the Mission every week, half the church each time was full of new people, and this will explain also why repentance, confession, and faith had to be preached and urged in each church.

No effort, it is obvious, must be spared to prevent a single soul being left in its sins or in the darkness of despair, and hence an argument must be used again, an illustration repeated, or a story retold, if there was a chance of it helping anyone in the church.

In spite, however, of the difficulty of passing from church to church, it will be seen that it has not been impossible for the Mission to follow a course of instruction.

The love of the HOLY TRINITY has been shown to us in many more ways than it was possible to state, but few will deny that in selecting (1) Co-operation with Human Prayer, (2) the Incarnation, (3) the Atonement, (4) the Church and Sacraments, and (5) the Resurrection, we have selected five outstanding manifestations of that love. The addresses in Westminster Abbey were undertaken as part of the Central London Mission at the special request of the Dean, and personally I shall never forget the hush of that crowded congregation which assembled daily at one o'clock, nor the upturned faces of the men who had special seats reserved round the pulpit.

Besides these services, a special effort was made each week for the men of the district which the

## *Preface*

Mission had reached, and the last section of the book contains the addresses given, mainly to men. although on one or two occasions women were admitted to the gallery.

One address, on "Purity," was delivered to men only, and although care was taken to speak in a way which was free from anything which might not be heard or read by any boy or young man, yet, as a book when it is printed may fall into the hands of anyone, it has been thought best to omit this address here, and print it as a separate paper.

One of the most interesting gatherings of men during the Mission was held in St. Michael's, Cornhill, in the middle of the day, and was attended by five hundred of the leading men of the City of London, headed by the Lord Mayor and the Sheriffs; and another gathering which has in it the promise of a great development in the future was the meeting for old public-school and University men which was held at London House. The addresses given at both these gatherings will be found in the last section of the book.

With regard to the Mission as a whole, the reverent congregations which filled each church; the tide of intercession for the sick, the troubled, the tempted, and the heartbroken, which went up to GOD at every service; the great number of individual souls who were brought to begin a new life at one or other of the services—all served to make me spend Eastertide in thanking GOD for blessing such a humble, and, as I feel, such an inadequate effort. All through it the ordinary work of the diocese has had to be carried on, and there have been left only a few minutes for

## *Preface*

the sermon or meditation which had to be prepared for the evening service ; but GOD is very good, and *does* desire to make His children believe that He loves them, and to receive their love in return, and therefore takes very simple words and uses them to speak His message. May the same words, as they now stand written, make it " May Day " to some souls still in the winter of despair or unbelief !

A. F. LONDON.

FEAST OF ST. PHILIP AND
 ST. JAMES, 1908.

# Contents

| | PAGE |
|---|---|
| PREFACE | iii |

### TWO INTRODUCTORY ADDRESSES

| | |
|---|---|
| I. SPIRITUAL WONDER | 3 |
| II. "WITNESSES OF THESE THINGS" | 13 |

### THE MESSAGE OF THE MISSION

| | |
|---|---|
| I. THE LOVE OF THE TRINITY | 27 |
|     ANSWERS TO QUESTIONS | 40 |
| II. THE RESPONSE TO THE LOVE OF THE TRINITY | 47 |
|     ANSWERS TO QUESTIONS | 57 |
| III. THE PEACE OF GOD | 66 |
|     ANSWERS TO QUESTIONS | 75 |
| IV. THE LOVE OF THE TRINITY IN CO-OPERATION WITH HUMAN PRAYER | 86 |
| V. TRUE RESIGNATION | 100 |
|     ANSWERS TO QUESTIONS | 107 |
| VI. THE LOVE OF THE TRINITY IN THE INCARNATION | 112 |
|     ANSWERS TO QUESTIONS | 123 |

## Contents

| | PAGE |
|---|---|
| VII. THE GROWTH OF THE CHRIST-LIFE WITHIN US | 134 |
| VIII. THE LOVE OF THE TRINITY IN THE ATONEMENT | 145 |
| ANSWERS TO QUESTIONS | 155 |
| IX. HOW CAN WE BE FORGIVEN? | 162 |
| ANSWERS TO QUESTIONS | 172 |
| X. THE LOVE OF THE TRINITY IN CHURCH AND SACRAMENTS | 176 |
| ANSWERS TO QUESTIONS | 184 |
| XI. GLORY TO GOD | 190 |
| XII. THE LOVE OF THE TRINITY IN THE RESURRECTION | 201 |

### ADDRESSES IN WESTMINSTER ABBEY

| | |
|---|---|
| I. WHAT AM I? | 211 |
| II. WHY AM I HERE? | 219 |
| III. WHAT DOES GOD THINK OF ME? | 229 |
| IV. WHERE AM I GOING | 237 |

### ADDRESSES TO MEN

| | |
|---|---|
| I. AN ADDRESS TO OLD PUBLIC SCHOOL AND UNIVERSITY MEN AT LONDON HOUSE | 247 |
| II. THE PROBLEM OF LONDON | 260 |
| III. FAITH | 268 |
| IV. HOPE | 287 |
| V. WORK | 303 |
| VI. PRAISE | 316 |

TWO INTRODUCTORY ADDRESSES

# I

# ST. PAUL'S, COVENT GARDEN

*THURSDAY AFTERNOON*

ADDRESS TO ONE THOUSAND BUSINESS MEN AND WOMEN

## SPIRITUAL WONDER

" Blessed are the eyes which see the things that ye see: for I tell you, that many prophets and kings have desired to see those things which ye see, and have not seen them; and to hear those things which ye hear, and have not heard them."—ST. LUKE x. 23, 24.

MY Mission effort in Central London, which begins to-day, has received an unexpected consecration to me, in the death to-day—for it will be the death, I feel certain—of one of the most faithful parish priests of Central London.* I have just come from holding his hand and whispering in his ears as he dies the comfort of the Christian faith; and I feel myself that as I preach to you—for there is nothing like the presence of the dying to make you feel whether a thing is real or not—the sight of that faithful priest dying in Central London gives a consecration to the whole Mission.

* The Rev. G. F. Holden, Vicar of All Saints', Margaret Street, who died in the afternoon of the day when this sermon was preached.

## *Spiritual Wonder*

And perhaps you may ask why it is that the Bishop of London adds on forty or fifty sermons in six weeks to his work. Well, it is simply out of care for you, my brothers and sisters—nothing else in the world. I know your lives, and I want to help you; I want to help your faith. I know there are numbers in doubt, in difficulties, tied and bound by some sin, and I want in this Mission to Central London simply to put myself at your disposal, to come and preach to you, to answer your questions from the very beginning, and see if, by GOD'S help in answer to our prayers, there may not be many of my brothers and sisters drawn nearer to the great FATHER. Of course, I can only give the Mission message day by day. I must take one thing at a time. In twenty minutes I cannot expect to preach the whole Gospel to you.

My first subject is what I call " Spiritual Wonder." Philosophy begins in wonder, we are told, and certainly when wonder dies out of our religion the power of religion is gone. When you look into the history of our Christian religion, it all begins in a spirit of wonder. It is wonder that makes the angels cry: " Glory to GOD in the highest, and on earth peace, goodwill toward men." What they saw stirred the whole of Heaven to the deepest wonder. The Holy Mother of our LORD with wonder " pondered all these things in her heart." The disciples, as they followed JESUS towards Jerusalem, were amazed. When St. Paul was converted—and what a help it is to us, that conversion of St. Paul! What strong evidence must have turned that strong intellectual man, and led him to become a humble, believing Christian! —when he was converted, he burst out into an

*Spiritual Wonder*

expression of wonder : " O the depth of the riches both of the wisdom and knowledge of GOD ; how unsearchable are His judgments, and His ways past finding out !" And when with the eye of faith we look into the other world, and try and listen to what it is that is stirring Heaven, we find still that it is wonder— " Worthy is the Lamb that was slain to receive glory, and honour, and power; for Thou wast slain, and hast redeemed us unto GOD by Thy blood."

Now, the point that I want to put before you is this : that religion has lost its power when it becomes a dull thing, a dull accessory to life instead of the turning motive of the whole of life. When the Light of the World has faded " into the light of common day," when prayer has ceased to be the great romance of the day, when preaching has ceased to be the proclaiming of the most exciting message the world has ever heard, then preaching has lost its power, and prayer has lost its power, and religion has lost its power. And the question—the first question—that I come to ask every one of you in this Mission is this: Ought we to have lost our wonder in religion ? Ought it to have faded into the light of common day ? Is it less wonderful to-day than it was two thousand years ago ? Have we lost it ? and if we have lost it, how are we to get it back ?

I ask first, then, *Ought religion to have lost its wonder for us to-day?* And I will take five things, five points in the Christian religion which are as true to-day as ever.

1. Take, first, that elementary truth of the Christian religion which really *is* the Christian religion, and that is the truth of the Incarnation. I am going to make

## *Spiritual Wonder*

it a special feature at the men's services during the Mission, to try to explain the difficulties of faith, and I shall hope to show that the Incarnation is the most natural thing in the world; that there is no reason, from anything we know in science—no reason from the point of view of reason itself—why GOD should not have revealed Himself to man, as the Christian religion teaches us. GOD had taken a great deal of trouble with the world. Here we are, at the head of creation, whether creation came about by evolution or not; and I say the more you read, the more you study science, and the more you read the writings of men like Sir Oliver Lodge speaking for science, the more you find that there is no reason why GOD should not reveal Himself to man in the person of His SON. My point is this—not to give you grounds of faith, which I will do another day—if it is true, if the SON of GOD really came down to this planet, and lived here, is it not the most wonderful thing in the world ? Just think of it like this. We are one of the stars in the Milky Way; if you get a little further from the earth (as you find described in a little book called " The Agnostic's Progress "), the earth becomes the size of the moon; and if you get a little further off it becomes like one of the distant stars; and if you go a little further off, it becomes an invisible star. Now, supposing we on this planet, at a distance from a star that we could just see, were told that the SON of GOD had come down and lived, and taught, and died, and risen again, and revealed GOD to the inhabitants of that star, I could imagine any thinking man— and it is only the unthinking man who does not realise the importance of these things—looking

## *Spiritual Wonder*

across to that distant star and saying, " Blessed are the eyes that see the things that ye see: for I tell you, many prophets and kings have desired to see those things which ye see, and have not seen them; and to hear those things which ye hear, and have not heard them." I can imagine his looking across to the star, and saying, " Happy, happy planet to have been told the secret of the ages which all the thinkers of the world wanted to know !" My brothers and sisters, we happen to be on that planet, and my appeal to you is this: Surely it is only the stupid, only the man who does not think and the woman who does not think, who does not say that, if the Christian religion is true, it is the most astonishing and wonderful thing in the world; that, at any rate, " wonderful " is the least thing that we can say about it ?

2. Or take the Atonement. There are some people who make themselves miserable because they do not understand the Atonement. I should be very miserable if I thought I could. If it was the SON of GOD Who, as we believe, lay upon the Cross, surely it must be a thing beyond anything that we can explain. As I said as I knelt by my dying friend just now, I thank GOD that we are not saved by any theory of the Atonement, but by the fact of it. And if you have seen, as I have, a young man in a Mission broken down with penitence for some sin, and then seen the look of peace which has come over his face when he believed he was pardoned; if you have heard, as I have, a girl cry out to GOD, " It is against Thee only I have sinned," and then at last seen her look of relief as I held up a picture of JESUS CHRIST on the Cross—if you have seen these sights, you have seen the comfort of the Cross.

## Spiritual Wonder

When we read, as we do to-day, of 160 children crushed to death in America, nothing would save my faith unless I believed that CHRIST came to share our sufferings. I could not love some rose-crowned Apollo who never dipped his finger in the world's anguish. CHRIST was a Man of Sorrows and acquainted with grief. It is the thought that GOD suffers Himself that carries me through the sight of those tortured babes. But while I see the comfort of the Cross, am I to be unhappy if I cannot understand everything? What I can do is to wonder at it. When St. Paul at last believed it, he knelt at the foot of the Cross, and said, "He loved me and gave Himself for me." That is what stirred St. Paul to the depths of his being, and what I want to put to you is that every one of you has been redeemed by the same Death; and I ask you to get time to put yourself before the same Cross, and ask what it means to you.

CHRIST asks you from the Cross:

> "This have I done for thee;
> What hast thou done for Me?"

The first sight that you will see, if you are called to die, as my friend is to-day, is the sight of JESUS Himself, with the marks of the nails in His hands and feet, now in His glorified Body; but how would you face Him if He looked at you and said, "How did My death affect you?" I would rather be the man who said, "It was too great for me to believe," than the man who said, "Yes, I believe it, but I forgot it."

3. Or again, take the doctrine of the TRINITY—GOD the FATHER, GOD the SON, and GOD the HOLY GHOST. We say it is true; we say that we believe that there is GOD the FATHER, GOD the SON, and

## Spiritual Wonder

GOD the HOLY GHOST. At the baptism of our LORD the FATHER speaks: "This is My beloved SON, in Whom I am well pleased"—and the HOLY GHOST descends in bodily form as a dove. There is no meaning in the New Testament passage in which our LORD says, "It is expedient for you that I go away, for if I go not away the Comforter will not come unto you," unless there is GOD the FATHER, GOD the SON, and GOD the HOLY GHOST. But is it not wonderful? Is it not a wonderful thing that we happy people should have explained to us what all the philosophers of the world wanted to know? If you read the old philosophers, as we had to do at Oxford, you find that the one central mystery was what is behind everything? what is behind this mysterious world? Here we are in a world of mysteries. We do not understand life, death, sleep; it is a world of mysteries, and it is only the thoughtless who do not see that. But what is behind it all? The reply is, GOD the FATHER, GOD the SON, and GOD the HOLY GHOST. And what we are meant to do is to wonder at the mystery. We are all meant, not to understand it, but to wonder at it. And when we realise that the whole plan of Redemption was the plan of the HOLY TRINITY, how GOD the FATHER sent His only SON, and the SON willingly and lovingly came only to do His will, and the HOLY GHOST came down with a mighty rushing wind and tongues of fire, and has never gone back, but is inspiring this Mission as much as ever He inspired the Christians in the days of the past—I ask you this one question: Ought we not to wonder, and ought we not to say, "Blessed are the eyes which see the things that ye see"?

## Spiritual Wonder

4. Or take prayer. If there is anything we feel sure about from the New Testament, it is that prayer is heard. That boy and girl, or your own little boy and girl at home, if they only kneel down and pray to GOD earnestly, do move the hands that move the universe. If there is one thing proved in this world, it is that prayer is a power. I was telling them in Wall Street only a short time ago a story which always touches me, of the little boy who was asked what he had in his hand, and said, "My kite." "How do you know it is your kite? You cannot see it." "No but I can feel it pull." We cannot all be wrong—clergy, working men, business men, and statesmen—we cannot all be wrong; we have felt it pull. If there is one certain thing, it is that prayer is a power in this world. But is it not a wonderful thing that your little lad can move the hands that move the universe? I say it is a marvellous thing; and I assert that prayer ought to be the most wonderful romance in the world. I would not dare to come and speak to you like this if I had not prayed first. And anyone who knows the glorious nature of prayer would not omit prayer any day—not offering merely some selfish prayer, but in communion with GOD trusting his life and the life of those he loves to the care of the all-powerful FATHER. And the more you respond to Him the more He can do for you. You cannot bring on your friend's son in business in the city unless the young man responds and is punctual; and JESUS can do no mighty work in a place if there is unbelief.

5. Or take, fifthly, Holy Communion. Now, I am no doubt speaking to many brought up in different ways,

*Spiritual Wonder*

but every Evangelical in my diocese as well as every High Churchman believes that in the Holy Communion JESUS the SON OF GOD comes to the soul in a special way, in a more special way than at any other moment of our lives. Every one believes that. I have been to the Russian church, and I have sometimes wondered whether, because of our simpler ritual and more frequent Communion, we are getting too much accustomed to the Holy Communion. But I put this point to you : If you believe that—and if you are instructed Christians you must believe it—is it not a marvellous thing that the eternal SON of GOD in the Holy Communion will take on Himself your troubles and worries and weaknesses, will put the Divine SPIRIT into you, and that you can go back refreshed with the Body and the Blood of CHRIST ? A good man used to receive the Holy Communion every day, and every day that he received it he received it with a more trembling awe and wonder. Now, have you lost that wonder ? Yes, you have lost it if you never on Sunday go to your church. Yes, you have lost it if you have given up your prayer and Bible reading. Yes, you have lost it if in your life, your business life, or your private life, you are not governed by the laws of GOD. If you believe that these laws are ennobling, you will at any rate try to make your lives noble.

How are we to get it back ? First, make time. Don't let business crowd out the whole of your spiritual life. It is quite right to do your best with your work. We all have to work from morning to night in London. But keep apart from your work those quieter times when you can

## *Spiritual Wonder*

think of these things. Get up a quarter of an hour earlier in Lent. Come back to your Communion, if you have left it. Study. I saw five unbelievers yesterday. They were unbelievers because they had never learnt the other side. Ask some one —your Rector, for instance—to recommend you books on the subject. Meditate on these matters, and go down on your knees and ask that your faith may live again. Examine yourself. Again and again I find that the man who comes to me in unbelief has had some moral reason for his unbelief; there is some moral defect in his vision. We do not see clearly if we have blurred our eyes by sin. " If thine eye be single, thy whole body shall be full of light; but if thine eye be evil, thy body shall be full of darkness." I do ask you on this second day of Lent to see whether in dishonesty, in some secret sin, in some private thing known to you and known to GOD, you are choking the avenue of Light.

Then, lastly, persevere. So many give up because they get tired of it, or because the whole thing becomes a far-off dream to them. We are not saved by our feelings, but by our faith. Come back to your faith, come back into the light, come back into the wonder of it all. It is the most glorious and wonderful thing in the world—the message I am going to preach in Central London. Come back like children into this wonderland in which the early Church began, and if you use this Lent aright, you will, I believe, spend your Easter Day with something like this thanksgiving:

> " When all Thy mercies, O my GOD,
>   My rising soul surveys,
> Transported with the view, I'm lost
>   In wonder, love, and praise."

## II

## HOLY TRINITY, MARYLEBONE

*SATURDAY AFTERNOON*

TO MISSION WORKERS BEFORE A TEN DAYS' MISSION
IN THE PARISH

"WITNESSES OF THESE THINGS"

"And ye are witnesses of these things."—ST. LUKE xxiv. 48.

IF we ask how it is that the world up to now has been converted—and we do well to remember that only one-third of the world is even nominally converted yet, and that is why the Church must be missionary right on to the end—when we ask how it has so far been converted, the answer is, "Through the witnesses"—not through the Apostles solely, not through the preachers, not through the ministry, not through the evangelists, but through the witnesses, "the unknown good who rest in GOD's still memory, folded deep."* If you take, for instance, the Apostles' time, it would have been a great thing to have heard St. John and St. Peter describe what they saw inside the tomb. Cannot you imagine how it would have inspired our faith to have heard them say, "We looked inside; we saw the linen clothes lying, and the

\* J. R. Lowell, "All Saints' Day."

## "*Witnesses of these Things*"

napkin still wrapped turban-like" (as the Greek means), " and lying in such a way that we saw that no human hand had taken the body away: it was the hand of GOD that had done it—we saw and believed"? It is quite clear from the story that there was something in what they saw, in the way the clothes lay in the tomb, which gave them faith at once. It would have been a great thing to have heard St. Thomas describe, as doubtless he did in many services in what we now call India, how he had seen the living CHRIST. "There He was; there were the marks of the Cross in His hands and feet and side, and He said, ' Reach hither thy hand, Thomas, and thrust it into My side '; but I was afraid to do it, but I saw it all." It would have been a great thing to have heard St. Paul describe his great conversion. But my point now is that it was not only the Apostles, or even mainly the Apostles, who converted their generation. It was the witnesses, the people whose names we do not know, the five hundred who had seen the risen CHRIST on the mountain, and who had gone back to their homes and said, " We saw Him ourselves on the mountain; in broad daylight we saw Him." Or, later on, the jailer would have told what he had seen—the wonderful things in prison; and those converted in Cæsar's household; and the soldiers in the legion. Unless the Apostles' work had been backed up by hundreds, and in time thousands, whose names we do not know, but who were silent, quiet, patient witness, we should never have seen the world converted, even as far as it is up to now.

And when we get on to the time after the Apostles

## "Witnesses of these Things"

it is exactly the same; it is still the witnesses. The name "witness" means martyr, and martyr means witness. And therefore it was not only Bishop Polycarp who said, "Fourscore years have I served my King, and He has never denied me, and I cannot deny Him now," but it was little Blandina of twelve who said, "I am a Christian, and nothing wrong like this is done among us;" and there were numbers of others whom we do not know, patient, brave witnesses right to the death. And if, passing over the ages, I come down to those great districts of East London and North London, and ask what it is that I am looking to—nay, what JESUS CHRIST is looking to—to convert such great districts of London, the answer is, "The witnesses." I honour the five hundred clergy who work and toil in East and North London; with all my heart I back them up; but what I trust to is the fifty thousand communicants, witnesses who in every place and in every workshop and in every street are bearing quiet, silent, brave, faithful witness to the truth. We should be nowhere without them; we look to the witnesses.

And therefore it is that there is no body of people whom, as CHRIST'S minister—His chief minister in London—I look in the face with greater happiness and joy than a body of people like yourselves, the chosen workers in this Mission. You are the chosen witnesses; you are the people on whom, under GOD, the Mission mainly depends. There will be the Missioners who will preach by the power of the SPIRIT, who will lead the Mission, but we cannot get thousands of souls for CHRIST unless every single one of you witnesses is a faithful witness also. And it comes

## "*Witnesses of these Things*"

with added force when we see that this is the object for which we were born. It is a very common thing to ask, " What is the object of life ? Why was I born ? For what cause came I into the world ?" And if anyone asked me that question, I should know no answer to give but the answer which JESUS CHRIST gave, as representing everybody ; it was not only for Himself, but He gave the answer which every one was meant to take on his lips : " To this end was I born, and for this cause came I into the world, that I should bear witness unto the truth." And therefore the happy thought for you is the glorious conviction that in coming out as a faithful, as a true witness in this Mission for CHRIST, you are fulfilling the purpose for which you were born. To this end were you born, and for this cause came you into the world, that you should bear witness to the truth. And we can never press this too much upon ourselves, that, however popular we may be, however clever, however much we may get on in the world, however rich we may be, however good business men we may be, or however successful women we may be in society, if we fail as witnesses, we fail altogether in life ; and that the real test of whether we are fulfilling the purpose of our being or not is whether we are faithful witnesses or not.

And therefore before you, as it were, start upon the actual work of the Mission, I want to face with you two things : first, how can you be witnesses now ? You say : " It would be easy enough if we had lived in His time and seen Him with our eyes "; but how can you be witnesses in your generation now, just every bit as really as the witnesses of old ? And,

## "Witnesses of these Things"

secondly, what are the chief hindrances to being good witnesses?

I. And, first, how can you be witnesses to-day just as really as those witnesses of old?

1. First of all, by your bearing, by your words, and by your life, you must be witnesses that you have the peace of GOD in your own hearts. I have seen a good deal of Mission literature, and have had to take part in many Missions, but a thing I have just seen in the Vicarage here has pleased me more than anything I have seen at any Mission, and that is the letter signed by ninety-four men to their fellow-men in this district; every one was told before he signed it that he must not sign it unless he had the peace of GOD in his own heart. It is to me a most hopeful augury for this Mission that the ninety-four men, knowing what it meant, sent that letter out boldly with their names attached, not minding their names being known round this district. I say, GOD bless those ninety-four faithful witnesses. And therefore, whether it is man or woman, the first way in which you can bear witness is by having—and it is soon found out by those who watch your life whether you have it or not —the peace of GOD in your own heart. And if there is anything in your life or in your heart which is spoiling the peace of GOD, get peace with GOD before the Mission goes further. You cannot win others to the peace of GOD—there will be a note of unreality in everything you say—unless you have confessed every sin to GOD, and are at peace with GOD yourselves, through JESUS CHRIST our LORD.

2. And then, secondly, you have to be witnesses to

## "*Witnesses of these Things*"

our heart-belief, and that is that JESUS CHRIST is as much alive as ever. You say it would have been so much easier if we had lived then; we could have understood being witnesses then. But JESUS CHRIST is the same yesterday, to-day, and for ever. And as you go about the Mission what you have to witness to is this: that there is Some One Whom, having not seen, you love, and Who you believe loves you with an everlasting love, and loves your friend or your brother, or the mate with whom you work. That is the second thing you have got to bear witness to. Let me tell you, if I may, a story which I should never have told if the man concerning whom I am going to tell it was still alive. He is lying dead in the next parish—the Vicar of All Saints', Margaret Street. I think it was about two or three years ago he wrote me a letter, and he said : " I have more money in this living than I had in the last place where I was. I find there are so many hundreds a year which I do not want for my board and lodging. If JESUS CHRIST were visibly alive to-day, I should give that money to Him; it all belongs to Him; it is His money. As I cannot actually place it in JESUS CHRIST's own hand, and you are His chief representative in this diocese, I hand it to you." And every penny that that faithful parish priest did not want to support himself— of course, it is the first duty of a man to pay for his lodging and clothes—he handed over to me every year to spend for JESUS CHRIST. He said: " Spend it as you like, but I would like the preference given to the educating of young men who cannot afford it for Holy Orders." I suppose perhaps £400 or £500 a year used to come regularly during these years into

## "*Witnesses of these Things*"

my hands to spend for JESUS CHRIST. Of course, he made the condition that no one should know it at the time, and I only tell it now as of a neighbour in the next parish, to give an example of what it is to a man simply to believe in JESUS CHRIST being as much alive to-day as He was then, and to believe in Him as a present living Person Whom he loved, and Who loved him and loved others. He took his stewardship literally and to the last penny he could afford he gave all to JESUS CHRIST. We may well press home upon ourselves this question, Are we witnesses like that ? Are we witnesses who take literally our religion, who do not believe that we belong to ourselves at all, but are bought with a price, and that in all our business and work there is Some One Whom, not having seen, we love, and Who we believe loves us with an everlasting love, and every soul He has redeemed. That is the way to be a witness, and that is what we have got to be witnesses to.

3. And then, again, we have got to witness, not only to the love and the sacrifice of JESUS CHRIST, but also to His Resurrection and Ascension. And I think I can see the sort of look of strength and solidity that there is in a man's face who believes with all his soul that JESUS CHRIST is risen from the dead. As I was with that dear friend whom I have mentioned,* just holding his hand for more than an hour as he died, there was a sort of hope and strength about the man which I had noticed often in speaking to him. A man who believes entirely in the victory of JESUS CHRIST is master over death. You believe that; I believe that. Then there ought to be as we move about the world

\* See p. 3.

## "*Witnesses of these Things*"

a sense of coming victory; we ought to have the power of men who are really conquerors through Him Who loves us; and we ought to go on this Mission with the sense that already the enemy is beaten, and we have only to enter into the land that has been already conquered for us. There ought to be a note of conquest and power in every one who believes in the Resurrection of JESUS CHRIST. "With great power gave they witness of the Resurrection of JESUS CHRIST from the dead."

4. And with that, and almost side by side with that, and issuing from it, we have to be witnesses to the power of the HOLY GHOST. What is a Mission? We believe that a Mission is a special outpouring of the HOLY GHOST in answer to united and sustained, continued prayer. We believe that the HOLY GHOST has never gone back, but that when He came down with a mighty rushing wind and tongues of fire He came to stay. There is no Ascension Day for GOD the HOLY GHOST, but, as we stir up the gift that is within us by the laying on of hands, and as we are again and again united in prayer, on our cold hearts and speaking through our dumb lips comes the HOLY GHOST. As you go round and knock at the doors in your district, and do not know what to say, you have only to send up a cry in your heart, and the HOLY GHOST will give you the word to say. And as you feel perhaps timid about it, the HOLY GHOST will give you the courage to bear your witness at the right moment and in the right way. The SPIRIT is the finger of GOD, and conveys what we may call tact, the sense of touch, that Divine, spiritual tact—if we may use such a word—to enable us to win others, so

## "*Witnesses of these Things*"

as to win and not repel them by our effort. We have to bear witness to that.

5. And then once more you have to bear witness to the Church which JESUS CHRIST founded. This is a Church Mission. It is not our own idea, it is CHRIST's idea, that He should form a Divine society, and should send that Divine society into the world. And all these beautiful things that we have in the Church—Baptism of children, Confirmation in later years, Holy Communion, the Creed—our battle-cry—these things are not of our invention at all. Loyalty to them is loyalty to JESUS CHRIST. When I am asked why I am not a Dissenter, I say, "Because I do not dissent." I do not dissent from Church orders. Bishops, priests, and deacons have always governed the Church. I do not dissent from the Church Creed; every syllable is founded upon the warrant of Holy Scripture. I do not dissent from the Church Sacraments, founded by the Lord of the Church. I believe that JESUS stands at the font Himself, and says, "Suffer little children to come unto Me, and forbid them not." I believe that JESUS Himself breathes on us in Confirmation, and says, "Receive ye the HOLY GHOST." I believe that JESUS Himself stands at the Holy Table, and says, "Here is the bread of life for you to eat and the wine for you to drink." These things are to bind us to CHRIST. Would He have instituted them if they were to separate us from Him ? They no more get between me and my LORD than the rope on the mountain-side gets between me and my guide. The rope binds me to him, if I use it aright. Therefore, by your faithful and earnest use of them, by the regularity with which

## "*Witnesses of these Things*"

you come to CHRIST'S Church, in the earnestness of your Communion, by the way you bring your children to be baptized, and come yourselves to be confirmed, and bring your friends, you bear witness that you believe in a living Church, founded by a living CHRIST.

II. And that brings me, in the second place, to consider what it is that stands in the way of being faithful witnesses. I believe it is the want of four things:

1. First, want of courage. It does want courage. It is not too easy to go down a district where perhaps in six out of seven houses there is no response, and to go on doing it, in spite of receiving possibly little welcome. That may be the case with some of you. But the whole point is that you can have courage, if you ask for it. And a Mission is a time to take your courage in both hands and bear witness. It does require courage in the workshop to say to the man next you: "Come to the Mission to-night, old friend; come to the church where I am so happy, and see whether you cannot be happy too." It may incur a sneer or a rebuff. Now is the time, the Mission is the time, to commit yourselves—commit yourselves, commit yourselves, as a great Missioner once said; and when once you have broken the ice with a man, it is easier to go on. Do not, then, let us have any want of courage. It is a splendid thing really to bear the Cross a little with our SAVIOUR. We do not want Him to be ashamed of us when He comes; yet He says, "If anyone is ashamed of Me and of My word, of him also shall the Son of Man be ashamed."

2. Secondly, there is want of faith. We have not got a vision ourselves; the vision has faded away;

## "*Witnesses of these Things*"

there is something between us and the living CHRIST. Look and see what that is. "If thine eye be single, thy whole body shall be full of light; but if thine eye be evil, thy whole body shall be full of darkness." Make a prayer to-night that the spiritual eye may be cleansed, that you may see these Heavenly things, and then bear witness of them with fresh faith. It is the man who sees who makes an impression when he speaks; we may well pray thus:

> "Oh, speak to me, that I may speak
> In living echoes of Thy love."

3. Thirdly, there is want of perseverance. You get discouraged; but the true witness goes on. Look out on the starry night. What are those stars doing up in the sky? What is the moon doing? The answer is, They are being faithful witnesses. The moon is called "the faithful witness in heaven." Those stars each light up a little bit of the world's darkness, patiently bearing witness year after year; and that is exactly what we have got to do—to bear witness here, and persevere until the end. Never mind if we see but little visible result. GOD asks our work, and not our success. Therefore, if any are losing their perseverance and are getting tired, let the Mission bring them back, and make them resolve, "There is no more glorious thing than being a witness, and, GOD helping me, I will bear witness to the end."

4. And the last want very often is want of prayer. We forget that we can do nothing of ourselves. GOD knows there are thousands and tens of thousands who are living in Central London whose wants are untouched at present by the Gospel. I look at it as

## "*Witnesses of these Things*"

the duty of a Bishop to be the chief witness in the diocese, and therefore I add forty or more sermons —I suppose there will be that number—between now and Easter in order to try and give a lead to the work of witness, and so stimulate the Mission-work of the diocese; and I ask your prayers for the effort. I can do nothing whatever of myself. I shall remember you in my prayers that you may be blessed in your effort. You are all part of the Central London District; we are all fellow-workers together; but do let our Mission, both inside and outside this parish, be begun, continued, and ended in GOD. Depend upon GOD; work and pray; pray—that is the secret of power.

And so as I have sent these Missioners forth on their work, I send you forth on yours. "Arise, shine, for thy light has come." The light which will enable you to be faithful witnesses has come; we live in the light of it; we have only to sun ourselves in the light of it. "Arise, shine, for thy light is come, and the glory of the LORD has risen upon you." Only with courage, with faith, with perseverance and prayer, be faithful witnesses, and you will draw thousands to GOD, and then because you have turned thousands to righteousness, you shall shine as the stars for evermore.

# THE MESSAGE OF THE MISSION

# ST. MARTIN'S-IN-THE-FIELDS

*SUNDAY EVENING*

## I

### THE LOVE OF THE TRINITY

"The grace of our LORD JESUS CHRIST, and the love of GOD, and the fellowship of the HOLY GHOST, be with you all."
—2 COR. xiii. 14 (Prayer-Book Version).

THIS is the most loving and affectionate Epistle of all St. Paul wrote, and the last word of it is to be the motto or the message of the Central London Mission.

You will remember that this is now the fourth Mission that GOD has allowed me, as your Bishop, to conduct in London. "JESUS of Nazareth passeth by"—that was the motto of the message of the West London Mission. "Not by might, nor by power, but by My SPIRIT, saith the LORD of Hosts"—that was the motto of the message of the North London Mission; and how we loved night after night to see those crowded churches, and how we loved to dwell on the HOLY GHOST the Comforter, the HOLY GHOST that convinceth of sin, the HOLY GHOST that followed on and brought back the wanderers. "The Call of the Father"—that was the gracious, loving message we had in East London. And you might well ask, you of Central London, what message

## The Love of the Trinity

there is left for you. " Hast Thou no blessing for us, O our FATHER ?" And my answer is that I have for you in Central London—who, perhaps, have in some ways the hardest struggle of all in the heat of all the temptations of this Central London life, and all the trials and difficulties of business—the most glorious message of all, and that is " The Love of the TRINITY." That is the message for Central London—from GOD the FATHER, GOD the SON, and GOD the HOLY GHOST—" The grace of our LORD JESUS CHRIST, and the Love of GOD the FATHER, and the fellowship of the HOLY GHOST." If that is not enough for Central London, what is ?

And you must know that our method is this. We take one point at a time. We do not hurry over anything. Each address is not a sermon about which in going away we are to say, " What a good, or what a bad, sermon that was !" That is not the idea of the Mission at all. The Mission is charged with reality ; it is like being in the presence of the dying. It reminds me of that sacred hour I spent with a dear priest who died last week—Mr. Holden. Could I have told a lie in his presence ? Could I have tried to be eloquent in his presence ? Everything faded before the certainty of the coming death and the felt presence of GOD. And so it is to-day. We are not assembled here to hear a sermon ; we are assembled here with the eternal welfare of every living soul hanging between life and death ; and therefore we do not hurry in the Mission at all. We take one thing at a time. We think over it till we have taken it in by GOD'S help, and we go on to the next ; and then we think over what is said on the Sunday, and you send

## The Love of the Trinity

me up the questions and difficulties, and what occurs to you about the message, that I may be in touch with all your souls and your minds; and I answer them on the Wednesday before I go on to the next church. By that means the Mission is not a mere series of sermons: it is heart to heart work; it is soul to soul work. And that is why GOD, I believe, has blessed those efforts so much, because they are so simple and so direct. There is no eloquence about it from one end to the other.

I. And the first thing that we have to hold on to and dwell upon until we are able to believe it, or frankly say we do not believe it, is the love of GOD the FATHER. Now, what I believe to be the solemn truth about each single one to whom I speak is this: that GOD the FATHER loves you with an everlasting love, as if there were not another living person in the world. You say, " How could He do that ? There are so many." It does not matter about there being so many. A finite person can only think of a small number of people at a time; an infinite person can give himself wholly to each one, and therefore the glorious thing is this: that you and I when we kneel down, or even when we are not kneeling down, have the whole of GOD to attend to us. And even if you have not said a prayer for years—and I know there are some in this church who have not been to church before for months and years; there are some in this church, I know, who have not prayed for years—in the name of the living GOD I tell you this: that He still loves you with an everlasting love.

You say, perhaps, " How has He shown it ? I

## The Love of the Trinity

should like to ask you that, Bishop—how has He shown it to me?" Well, first, because you are alive. If you ask why it is that any of us are alive—why there is life in the world at all—I know no answer at all but this: out of pure love, GOD wanted to spread happiness; being complete and perfect in Himself, He wanted to make so many more millions of people sun themselves in the sunshine of His own happiness. That is why I am alive—that is why you are alive. I know some people say, " I did not ask to be alive; I don't want to be alive." Now, do be honest. We never have any quibbles in these Missions. You know you are glad to be alive; you know that, in spite of all your troubles and trials, you would rather be alive than not alive; you would rather be alive than never have existed at all. And the fact that you are alive, and have the gift of life, is an evidence, and the first evidence, of the love of GOD.

And then we go a little further. Have you had such a miserable life? As a matter of fact, is it not true of the vast majority of you here that you have had a happy home—at any rate, to start with—that you have got a wife, or husband, or father, or mother, or child, or friend, who loves you, and who makes life to you very warm and happy? And I say if that is so, you have another evidence that GOD loves you.

Or come a little further. Look back over your life. Is it honest to say that you have not had signs that GOD the FATHER has been taking care of you, and looking after you? What about that illness from which you recovered? What about that trial which

## The Love of the Trinity

passed away ? I want you, as if you were looking GOD in the face—and, indeed, you are—to say whether it is not true when, on the authority of GOD Himself, I say that GOD the FATHER loves you. And what has been your response to the love of GOD the FATHER ? Is it possible, as you look back, that you have not spoken to GOD the FATHER for a year, or two years, or ten years ? Is it possible that, while He has been thinking of you, and trying to get friend after friend to help you and take His message to you, and has brought you to church to-night through some friend whom He has used, that you have returned all the time a cold, apathetic response to His love ? Or you have injured, possibly, one of His children whom you have seen—some weak one whom you have not spared, although it was GOD's child; or you have not taught the children He has entrusted to you at all. Is it not, then, the first thing to do to-night to say to GOD the FATHER, " Forgive me, and take me back"? I remember one of the most touching scenes I have witnessed was on the evening of the Feast of the Epiphany, when there was one brought to me who absolutely believed that GOD would not forgive her ; that she had offended GOD beyond all hope of reprieve and of return ; and I shall never forget the fifty minutes I spent with that soul. " GOD loves you "—I called her by her Christian name, in order to get through the gloom which was almost madness—" GOD loves you, GOD loves you in spite of everything " ; and it was not until after some forty minutes, I said : " I have come from GOD to tell you that He loves you, and has forgiven you," that at last the gloom passed away. Down upon her knees

## The Love of the Trinity

she sank, looked up in her FATHER'S face, and was His child again. You would not have known her to be the same person who rose from her knees that day when the light of forgiveness and the love of GOD had gone home at last; and there she is to-day back in her own home, back in the love that GOD had provided for her, saved, redeemed, forgiven. Happy soul! There is absolutely no limit to what might happen in this Mission. If what I said about the past is true—if it is true that GOD the FATHER loves you with an everlasting love, that He sent this very Mission for you, that He brought you here to hear it, then go down upon your knees, poor wandering soul, and for GOD'S sake do not turn away now. This may be the very last message that can come to you. We pass out of the world very quickly; one person dies every eight minutes day and night in this diocese. It may make all the difference between dying at peace with GOD and dying in misery if you respond to the love of GOD the FATHER now.

II. And then we pass on to consider the grace of our LORD JESUS CHRIST. Who was JESUS CHRIST? An historical character. "JESUS CHRIST," says Tacitus, the Roman historian, "was put to death in the reign of Tiberius, when Pontius Pilate was Procurator in Judæa." I mention that because I have actually found in these Missions such doubt as this, that from some sceptical conversation of friends, or some shallow article in a magazine, people have actually doubted whether JESUS CHRIST ever lived at all. We shall have plenty of time in this Mission to state the grounds for our faith, and I shall especially take that subject at some of the Men's services, as I did

## The Love of the Trinity

at St. Petersburg and Moscow. But the point is this: Who was JESUS CHRIST? A good man who lived so many years ago. Is that all? We look at His life, and we find that He is accepted to-day as the living ideal of Europe, as the ideal of every progressive nation of the world. John Stuart Mill said: "Live so that JESUS CHRIST would approve of your life;" and Mr. Lecky said: "The records of these short years have done more to regenerate mankind than all the disquisitions of philosophers and all the plans of statesmen." We listen to hear this ideal, this perfect character speak to us, and He says, "I am the light of the world;" and I remember that sentence brought out of the gallery at Lancaster Gate in the West End Mission a man who had not said a prayer for forty years—"I am the light of the world." He says further: "He that hath seen Me hath seen the FATHER; before Abraham was, I am; My FATHER and I are one thing." We follow His life photographed for us supernaturally and providentially in five brilliant pictures—St. Paul's Epistles and the four Gospels —and we see that it is impossible that this perfectly pure, perfectly loving, perfectly lovable character can be deceiving the world; and when He looks us in the face and says, "What think ye of CHRIST; whose Son is He?" we answer back with the cry of the ages: "Thou art the King of glory, O CHRIST; Thou art the everlasting SON of the FATHER."

And therefore the grace of our LORD JESUS CHRIST, as we go on, is beginning to be a great thing, greater than we thought; in other words, we come to the second tremendous truth of the Mission, that besides the love of GOD the FATHER fixing itself on us, as it

## The Love of the Trinity

were, and though sometimes veiled from us, as faithful to us as the great sun, there is and may be, and as a matter of fact must be, if we are using it, if we will have it, the grace of the SON OF GOD within us, the same power that enabled Him to raise Lazarus from the dead, the power that enabled Him to heal the sick, to restore sight to the blind, the same winning grace which made Him win everyone, so that they said, "See how we prevail nothing; all the world has gone after Him"—all that may be within us now. Is that nothing to you who are living in lonely lodgings? Is it nothing to you, young man, who have to go home from your work into such lodgings every night, and, as a young layman said once to me, have to say "No, no, no," every night of your life? Is it nothing to know that you may have, and as a matter of fact do have, the grace of our LORD JESUS CHRIST to stand firm with? Is it nothing to you who are working at one of those great business houses in Regent Street and Piccadilly, and find a tone in the place which drags you down, and find it very hard to live a true, virtuous woman's life in London—is it nothing to you to know that you may have in you, working through you, as if there was no one else for it to work through, the grace of our LORD JESUS CHRIST—that you can say, as St. Paul said, "I live, yet not I, but CHRIST liveth in me"? "I besought the LORD thrice that it might depart from me"—this thorn in the flesh—"and He said unto me, My grace is sufficient for thee, for My strength is made perfect in weakness." It was that which enabled the little child Blandina to bear her witness before thousands of soldiers; it was that that kept the martyrs steady as they stood on the frozen

## The Love of the Trinity

pond all night, and would not take the offer of the hot bath or the fires which they saw. " Oh, LORD JESUS," they cried, "forty warriors have come out to fight for Thee; grant that forty warriors may receive the crown." And when morning dawned forty dead bodies lay on the frozen pond, and forty warriors had received their crowns in Heaven. But it was the grace of our LORD JESUS CHRIST that did it; it was that which enabled those boys in Uganda to burn to death some twenty years ago; it was the grace of our LORD JESUS CHRIST that has made before my eyes boys and girls in East London year after year stand firm in their workshops, in their factories, and in their homes against a hail of temptation. "What can I do," said a poor girl once, "to stand firm in my factory when they persecute me every day for coming to the Mission?" "Say 'JESUS, help me,' under your breath," I said; and she came back and said: "Oh, Mr. Ingram, it is everything; I have said it, and I have not yielded since."

And therefore the second glorious truth in the Love of the TRINITY is that every single one of those tempted, tried souls, living out their little day here—what a little day it is!—in the hour of temptation and probation, have the grace of our LORD JESUS CHRIST, through Whom the saints and martyrs have conquered and won. Is that nothing? I say it is everything. Do not let us leave that till we believe it. How could I go on day after day with the burden of this diocese? Even for a day I would not dare to do it if I did not believe that I had, unworthy as I am, the grace of our LORD JESUS CHRIST every day to do it with. And what is mine is yours.

## The Love of the Trinity

III. Then, once again, you might have thought that this was enough for Heaven to do for you; but, I tell you, the love of GOD is wider than the limits of man's mind, and the heart of the Eternal is most wonderfully kind. And we find that, as the great heart and mind of the Godhead contemplated what more They could do for those children which had been created, there was still one more thing that could be done; and when the LORD JESUS CHRIST went back to Heaven—and for some unknown mysterious reason it could not happen till He did—then the great windows of Heaven opened again, and down through the open Heaven came GOD the HOLY GHOST with a rushing mighty wind and tongues of fire; and He has never gone back. He is still here, still inspiring every Mission, still helping every soul; and we may have, not only the love of GOD the FATHER, not only the grace of our LORD JESUS CHRIST, but the fellowship of the HOLY GHOST as the final token of the love of the Everlasting TRINITY.

> " And every virtue we possess,
> And every conquest won,
> And every thought of holiness,
> Are His alone."

What is your relation to the HOLY GHOST—the HOLY GHOST Who comes (and we are told quite plainly what He comes for)—Who comes to convince us of sin, Who comes to take of CHRIST and show Him to us, Who comes to cry, " Abba, FATHER," in our hearts, and to make us believe we are children of GOD again, and Who comes to convert us and also to strengthen us ? Read that beautiful book by the priest

## The Love of the Trinity

who has just been taken from us.* He wrote it for this Lent at my request, on "The HOLY GHOST the Comforter." Take it—it is his last gift to the Church —and read it, pray over it, and see if by Easter you do not realise, besides the love of GOD the FATHER and the grace of our LORD JESUS CHRIST—you, *you* individually, *you* who have not prayed for all these years, *you* who have not lifted a finger yet in return for all this, not one finger—that you may have the comfort and the strength also of GOD the HOLY GHOST. And then see whether on Easter Day, for the first time, perhaps, for years, you cannot join the Easter anthem " Glory be to the FATHER, and to the SON, and to the HOLY GHOST."

And now I have only four short last questions to ask. This is the eternal truth about you—some day you will know this is true, if you do not believe it now—GOD the FATHER loves you; GOD the SON redeemed you; and GOD the HOLY GHOST is trying to sanctify you. What has been your response? That is all we have to consider to-night. What has been your response in prayer? What are your prayers like? There is GOD the FATHER every morning listening, waiting for His child. GOD the SON kneels by our side to offer our intercessions and prayers, and sweep them into His. GOD the HOLY GHOST prays in us, ready to pray with groanings that cannot be uttered. What have you been doing if you have never prayed at all, if your prayers have been cold, dull, mechanical things, and you are glad they are over? Then let our prayer be : " O GOD the FATHER, GOD the SON, and GOD the HOLY GHOST, have mercy upon us—have

* The Rev. G. F. Holden, see p. 3

## The Love of the Trinity

mercy upon us for our carelessness and coldness and want of love. Help us to pray."

The second question is, What has your life been ? I do not know anything about any single one of you personally, but GOD the FATHER, GOD the SON, and GOD the HOLY GHOST know what your life has been ; and if, while the HOLY TRINITY have been trying to sanctify your soul and restore it and recreate it, you have been, with your little or great influence, against Them, and you have been against GOD, and decrying religion or despising the young for being religious, then go down on your knees at once and say : " O GOD the FATHER, GOD the SON, and GOD the HOLY GHOST, forgive me ; it was I who did it. I have fought against Thee."

The third question : What has your service been ? " Whom shall I send, and who will go for Us ?" That is the awful voice of the TRINITY calling for service. " Whom shall We send, and who will go for Us ?" And when the Ordination candidates come and are ordained in St. Paul's Cathedral next Sunday, that is in response to the call of the TRINITY. They have come out. " Here am I ; send me," they have said. But those who cannot be ordained must respond too. What has been your response from the point of view of service ? If you have done nothing—if there is not a living soul, as far as you know, who is the better for your life and service, then may GOD the FATHER, GOD the SON, and GOD the HOLY GHOST have mercy upon you ; and give you another chance, give you another year to work.

Fourthly and lastly, What has your worship been like ? We can almost hear in Heaven : " Holy, holy,

## *The Love of the Trinity*

holy, LORD GOD Almighty, which was, and is, and is to come : Holy, holy, holy." We are meant to be sending up adoring praises and worship on earth, warming our spirits every Sunday, at any rate, by taking part in the worship of Heaven. What is the worship of this church ? Is it always full on Sunday ? If not, why not ? And if our worship has been cold and dead, then may GOD the FATHER, GOD the SON, and GOD the HOLY GHOST have mercy for the fourth time on us ; and if we kneel down in that spirit to-night, we start the Mission with penitence. I was reading to the choir-boys at the Chapel Royal between their services to-day that beautiful story of the forgiven brigand. There was nothing that he had done right ; all his record was wrong, but he wept for his past life, and as the demons and the angels contended for his soul as he lay dying, and the demons thought they had conquered as they brought up wicked deed after wicked deed that he had done, and dared the angels to produce anything else, one angel took up the handkerchief which lay on his bed, heavy with tears, and cast it into the scale, and it weighed down all his sins. If our Mission begins in penitence it begins aright ; and we may end it in the blessed peace of having the grace of our LORD JESUS CHRIST, and the love of GOD, and the fellowship of the HOLY GHOST with us, now and for ever.

# St. Martin's-in-the-Fields

*WEDNESDAY EVENING*

## ANSWERS TO QUESTIONS

1. I have had a good many questions referring to what I said as to prayer being the romance of the day. I find that I saddened some people, not meaning to do it, because I seemed to hint that the good of prayer depended upon a state of feeling. Now, I do not mean that at all. My first questioner, one who has a hard life of it, and whom I should be most terribly sad to think I had depressed, is rather puzzled; he or she for two years has gone on praying, because a year or two ago I said in his or her hearing that we must not depend on feeling at all, but must go on praying.

### Is prayer a question of faith, not of feeling?

I say it again to-night, that many of the most earnest Christians are terribly tried for years by having no sensible enjoyment of their religion. They must never give up; nothing is worse than that. But, on the other hand, I still hold to what I have said, that prayer is the most wonderful romance of the day, whether you feel it or not, and we must by faith realise that it is. I put it to you again. If it is true that GOD the FATHER is listening, that GOD the SON is by our side, and that the HOLY SPIRIT will pray in us; if in the great plans of the Godhead our little prayer is made room for, and it matters to GOD whether we pray or not —then, I ask you, would it not be mocking us to say, " Ask, and ye shall receive ; seek, and ye shall find," if the prayer was not answered ? I ask the writer of this letter to say

## Answers to Questions

whether, if we have only five minutes to pray, and we have faith, it is not the great romance of the day. You will never do a greater thing during the whole day than what you do in that five minutes when you are in communion with GOD the FATHER, GOD the SON, and GOD the HOLY GHOST. It is, therefore, the great romance of the day. If it is true that we have access by one SPIRIT through JESUS CHRIST to the FATHER, then just think what prayer means. You, I, people of no merit at all, are admitted into the secrets of the Holy TRINITY. If that is so, then I say again it is the great romance of the day; but, on the other hand, there is no inconsistency—that is the way I would put it—if I say also, Go and pray, even if you have no warm feelings.

2. That really is also the answer to the next questioner, who feels that

**Prayer is never effectual except when there is some near crisis to trouble me. I am a communicant, but I do not seem to get any benefit from prayer. Why is this?**

This is the same old difficulty we have found in so many Missions—it is the difference between faith and feeling. We walk by faith, and not by feeling. What we have to train ourselves to do, I believe, is not to look for warm feelings, but simply to have faith to trust and believe and act, and then the feelings may take care of themselves. Therefore, I would say to the writer of this letter, Realise by faith what Prayer and Communion really are, because, as I have said, we are apt to get so accustomed to the Holy Communion that we lose sight of what it is. If it is really true that the SON of GOD Himself comes in a special way to us, and puts His strength within us, then I say the wonder of it is so great that the sense of wonder ought to be permanent. Go on, then, with the life of faith, and do not be deterred by lack of feeling.

3. Then the next is a personal question from another ques-

## Answers to Questions

tioner about the time when the questioner distrusted GOD at a crisis of her life, "and I want to know whether GOD has forgiven me."

**Do you think GOD has forgiven me for doubting at the time when I ought to have trusted Him more, and whether He loves me just as much?**

These Wednesday meetings are the after-meetings of the sermon on Sunday—that is the idea of them. Therefore, I assume, of course, that every one was here on Sunday night. Thus you will see that the answer to that question is the whole of the sermon of Sunday night,* which was that GOD the FATHER loves you with an everlasting love, that the grace of the LORD JESUS CHRIST is with you, and the fellowship of the HOLY GHOST is with you. If all that is true, then it follows as I said, if you have repented of that distrust, if you have come back, then the FATHER's home is open to you, you are forgiven, you are back in the FATHER's home again.

4. Then comes a more difficult question:

**If GOD tempts no man, why do we say, "Lead us not into temptation"?**

Of course, on the surface—I mean according to the words—there is a contradiction, a puzzle. We are told distinctly, "GOD tempteth no man. When a man is tempted, he is drawn away by his own lust and enticed"; and I may say here that, if there are any who are saying to themselves, "Oh, it is my family temper; I had such terribly difficult circumstances; my position was so difficult; my school was a bad one; my office was a bad one; the place where I work demoralises me," these are excuses which will not stand in the Day of Judgment. One lot may be more difficult than another, but we have to believe what is said in GOD's own book: "When a man is tempted, he is drawn away by his own lust and enticed." Every honest man and

\* See page 27.

## Answers to Questions

woman knows that he or she need not have done that thing. It is like the old story of Aaron and the calf. Aaron shaped the calf and put it in the fire, and when Moses came and taxed him with making a graven image, you remember what he said : " The people gave me all the earrings and offerings, and I simply cast them into the fire, and there came out this calf." But he did not say anything about taking the mould to mould it himself ; he disowned his own hand in it altogether. That is exactly what some of us do. If there is a young man who is a failure in life, who feels that he is an entire failure, he cannot begin by taking the right step, he cannot begin remaking his steps, better than by acknowledging, " It was I who did it ; I moulded myself. If I had not been so weak, if I had not been so foolish, if I had asked for the SPIRIT of GOD, I need not have done it." That is what penitence must be, the beginning of reform. It is not till we say, " I myself did it," and do not lay the blame on a brother, or sister, or father, or mother, or uncle—it is not until we admit this, that we can receive the grace of GOD to change our life. Aaron should have said, " I moulded the calf with my own hands, and I am responsible." It is certain, then, that GOD does not tempt us, but He does allow temptation to exist. It is a fallen world in which we are ; and therefore what I always myself understand by that prayer is, " Let not the trial be too hot for me ; let me not be led into temptation too hot for me ; guard me in my tempted life." That is what I think is meant when we pray that petition in the Lord's prayer.

5. Then I have a far more difficult question :

**Are we to believe in the actual presence of the Body and Blood of CHRIST in the Sacrament?**

I simply answer in the words of the Catechism : " The Body and Blood of CHRIST, which are verily and indeed taken and received by the faithful in the Lord's Supper." You cannot, after all, go beyond that ; you do not want to go any

## Answers to Questions

further. That is a clear statement, according to the tenets of the Church of England, as to what the Holy Communion is—as to trying to explain it, and puzzle it out and theorise and find out some definition, this has always led to heresy or a vague unbelief. Therefore, I believe that our Church is wise in using those simple words. " What is the inward sign and thing signified ?" " The Body and Blood of CHRIST, which are verily and indeed taken and received by the faithful in the Lord's Supper."

6. My next question is one from a teacher on teaching the Old Testament, especially to children.

**Should young children be taught that all the Old Testament stories are true? If so, how can it be explained at the same time that GOD is a GOD of love? Also, is it right for children to be taught, for example, that GOD allowed Jacob to be blessed, when they also know that it is wrong to deceive people?**

This is a great difficulty in bringing up children. I think we ought to tell them the difference in the evidence between the far-away stories in the Old Testament and the well-defined, clearly authenticated miracles, say, in the New Testament; there is a great difference in the evidence. But, on the other hand, if you are to teach the children at all, get the best books that have been published on the Old Testament, and see how strong the Old Testament story has come out from the fire of criticism. Teach them, for instance, as I have tried to explain to-day, the inner and very instructive meaning of that story about Moses and Aaron. The idea that the Old Testament is out of date is one of the greatest mistakes in the world. There are many books, of which one occurs to my mind. Canon Randolph, the Principal of Ely Theological College, has brought out a very beautiful little book upon the witness of the Old Testament to CHRIST. Read a book like that, or read a book like Geikie's " Hours with the Bible "—volumes which I used

## Answers to Questions

to find very useful in teaching the people in Bethnal Green. They will give you first-hand knowledge on the points. The more you know, the more you will see the value of the Old Testament.

With regard to Jacob—and this illustrates the point—if you look at the story of Jacob, you will see that he was greatly punished for his deceit. Over and over again he was deceived by his own son, just as David was. People say, " David was a man after GOD's own heart, and look what a dreadful thing he did !" Yes ; but read the story of David, and you will see it is one of the most telling lessons as to the way GOD punishes men. When people have punishment for their sins it is not a sign that GOD has forsaken them, but a sign that GOD is taking trouble over them. Punishment is often the thing that does them the most good. The Old Testament stories are most useful in this, that they show how GOD, by trouble and discipline, changes a man like Jacob, a deceitful young man at the beginning, into Israel, the Prince of GOD—changes him by discipline and grace. And it was because Jacob responded to this discipline, and showed himself capable of being turned, that he was blessed.

### 7. How is it that GOD allows 160 children in a school to be crushed to death, and partly burnt to death, in one day?

Let me just answer in a few words that question, because it is a difficulty to so many that GOD allows earthquakes, famines, and the wreck of ships. My belief is this: that GOD shows us in this way what a great responsibility He puts upon His viceroys. We are the viceroys of GOD in this world. When He made us men of free-will, He gave us also our brains to use, that we might discover His laws in Nature, and obey them. Therefore, it would not be consistent with His method of training reasonable self-governing people of free-will, fit to live with Him hereafter for ever—and that is the privilege and destiny of every soul

## Answers to Questions

here, to live with the HOLY TRINITY, to be companions of the HOLY TRNITY in eternity—it would not be consistent with that if He did not leave us with our brains and our common sense, our knowledge and our work, and the responsibility to a large extent of obeying or disobeying His laws. If, then, we build schools which are death-traps, if we go and live near volcanoes which are not dead volcanoes, if we put our hands in the fire, GOD will not interfere to prevent the laws of Nature taking their course. It is only by epidemics of cholera that we find out how to cure such epidemics. Think how much the mind of man has discovered since Charles Kingsley's days. You remember that he certainly advocated praying in the midst of pestilences; he would pray to GOD, but what he said was that there is no use in only praying. "Look to your drains as well," he said in his practical way. GOD, in training up people to be—well, I dare to say it—companions with Him for eternity, puts us in a place governed by certain laws. He expects us to learn and obey those laws of Nature as well as the moral laws which He gives. When we hear, therefore, of these calamities, we must remember that GOD is not apart from them. I can picture GOD taking up every one of those poor little children as they died and carrying them off in His eternal arms to be safe with Him, but He will not interfere to defeat or to alter the natural result of the carelessness of man.

# St. Martin's-in-the-Fields

*WEDNESDAY EVENING*

## II

## THE RESPONSE TO THE LOVE OF THE TRINITY

"The grace of our LORD JESUS CHRIST, and the love of GOD, and the fellowship of the HOLY GHOST, be with you all."
—2 COR. xiii. 14 (Prayer-Book Version).

WE have to face a very practical question: What is to be the response to the love of the TRINITY? I am going to assume that all of you have now tried to believe that GOD the FATHER loves you with an everlasting love, that there is within your reach—nay, within you, if you will have it, the grace of our LORD JESUS CHRIST. And you have thought over what that means; you believe, or have tried to believe, that you may have the fellowship of GOD the HOLY GHOST—that same HOLY GHOST Who came down, with tongues of fire and the sound of a rushing mighty wind, to comfort and purify and inspire. Now, the question is: What is to be the response to th:s love? Before we can make our response we must believe in its reality. Since I have seen you I believe that I have seen the power and love of the

## *The Response to the Love of the Trinity*

TRINITY lift a soul right out of what it would have been impossible for him to be lifted out of without the love of the TRINITY. I have seen a soul lifted right through a most dangerous operation, so that the man was as cool as he went into the operation—although he had been very nervous before it—as cool as if he were walking into a place of no danger whatever. I have no more doubt in my mind—no doubt whatever—that it was simply the power of GOD to which he trusted which lifted him out of himself. I went to-day eighty miles to try and help a man. I have seen this other man also being helped through terrible pain, deadly pain, by his trusting to the love of GOD. " I am not afraid of death ; I am not," he said, " afraid at all." He was lifted through the pain and weariness minute by minute and hour by hour by the love and power of the HOLY TRINITY. There is not the slightest doubt about it. But for that, a man who has perpetual pain must be fretful, must get irritable, can hardly go on calm and quiet and gentle. I have seen souls—not once, but over and over again—lifted through sorrow, lifted through intolerable sorrow—which you are quite certain they never could possibly have gone through without the help of GOD. I would like to appeal to you now. You may know nothing about pain or operations, or you may be able to look back on some such crises, when you know that GOD helped you through them ; but there must be surely some here who have been helped through sorrow and bereavement, anxiety and perplexity.

Again, I have seen souls helped not only through

## The Response to the Love of the Trinity

danger, fear, pain, and sorrow, but right through temptation—lifted high up, and right through it. I dare say I am speaking to some who know that they have been helped, or, at any rate, if they have not been, it was because they did not trust GOD the FATHER, GOD the SON, and GOD the HOLY GHOST. They see now that they would have gone through the temptation if they had had the grace of our LORD JESUS CHRIST, the love of GOD, and the fellowship of the HOLY GHOST. It is only those who believe in the reality of these things who will rise to the response which I am going to put before you—a fourfold response.

1. I believe that it is impossible for a man or woman who comes to believe in the love of the TRINITY not to pray, even if he or she have never prayed before. I believe that it is the first thing which must follow. If we do not believe, we shall not pray; but if we really believe for the first time, or have our old faith again renewed—that down from Heaven is outstretched the loving hand of GOD, that He has hold of us—not that we have hold of Him, and may perhaps let go, but that GOD has hold of us, and that no man can pluck us out of our FATHER's hand—then that soul is bound to pray, bound to turn and say, "I thank Thee, O GOD, for Thy protection, and for Thy love." It is like a little child who is quite sure of his mother's love, and kisses his mother. It is a natural thing, and he cannot help doing it. So there must be the response of the child in some sort of prayer. But what sort of prayer? I cannot but recommend all of you here to buy a penny book, which has just come out, by that great saint

## *The Response to the Love of the Trinity*

of GOD lately taken from us—Bishop Wilkinson, the Primus of the Scottish Church, and one of my own dearest friends. Just before he died he was asked to issue some old addresses of his on Prayer for a penny, because it was felt that we do not bring out our best literature cheap enough, and therefore an effort is made to bring out the best writers in penny books for the multitude. This is a book called "Our Private Prayers," by Bishop Wilkinson. You will find there, most beautifully put, how the first and most important part of prayer is thanking. And so it is bound to be, if we believe in the love of the TRINITY. The first thing is to thank before we do anything else. I believe that in our morning prayers, when the child of God has the right spirit, the first thing that the child says is: " I thank Thee for the rest and protection during the past night." Looking up and giving thanks— that, perhaps, is the greatest need that we have in our whole life; if we are to make prayer the great romance of life, as I have already said we are, then we must thank a great deal more. We ask for things, and we do not notice whether we have got them or not. We ought to thank GOD as an integral part of our praying.

I shall only say a few things about prayer now, because we shall take the work of the HOLY TRINITY in prayer as a separate subject. I have only time now to say, Take everything to GOD in prayer; " In all things let your requests be known unto Him." There is nothing too small, and yet at the same time, when you bring any request to GOD in this way do not say, if you do not get this particular request, " GOD has not heard me," because it may not be the thing for you. I heard of a man the other day who

## The Response to the Love of the Trinity

gave up prayer because he said that he prayed for a rise in Stocks again and again, and he had not got it. Well, perhaps a rise was precisely what was not the best thing for him. What GOD looks to, as He regards the eternal welfare of a man or woman, is what is best for them, as He tries to bring them on to their ultimate eternal good. Prayer is not to be used as a sort of juggling trick. People have not got into the atmosphere in which they have begun praying until they believe in the love of the TRINITY to do the very best for them according to their eternal welfare and their eternal peace.

The last thing I will say about prayer is, " Live day by day." I remember so well—and I have just told this in the preface which I have written to the little book by Bishop Wilkinson, and therefore I can say it in public now—that one day when I was walking in Scotland I said to him : " I cannot thank you enough for teaching me the lesson of ' day by day ' which comes out in the ' Laws of the Kingdom ' "—a book of his called " The Laws of the Kingdom," and one of the chapters is called " The Law of Day by Day." So he turned quickly to me and said : " Did I say that ?" I said : " Of course you said it ; there is a whole chapter in ' The Laws of the Kingdom ' on ' The Law of Day by Day.' " He did not say to me anything more that day, but next day he said to me : " It was curious, Bishop, your speaking to me about ' Day by Day.' I was so dreadfully worried yesterday about something, and it was the very thing that I wanted someone to say to me." So I repeated to him his own lesson just at the moment when he wanted it for himself. That is a great lesson to all of us with

## The Response to the Love of the Trinity

regard to our preaching and teaching others. You must not mind saying the simplest thing to people, even a thing which they have often said themselves, because, if said at the right moment when they want it, GOD uses it to help them. There may be some soul here who wants this message to-night : " Take your life day by day and hour by hour ; do not look too far ahead. If you are suffering, you have only to suffer that day. If you have an anxiety day by day, GOD undertakes to see you through it, but only day by day. " One of the great secrets of a happy, calm, and strong life is to pray day by day and to trust day by day. Our first response to the love of the TRINITY is in daily personal prayer.

2. Then, what is the next ? I believe that when men of the world get, perhaps with some reason, rather cynical about religion, it is due to our talking a great deal about praying—praying for other people and for ourselves ; but they do not see in our *lives* any response to the love of the TRINITY. Naturally they watch us far more closely, perhaps, than we have any idea of, and they look to see what is the response in the man's life, what difference his prayer makes to him. If they find us quite as irritable and unhappy in our trouble ; if they find us quite as careless about the questionable joke and perhaps the questionable story ; or if they find us just as selfish at home, just as particular about our little bit of comfort, just as much put out if we do not get exactly what we want, as some who do not pretend to any religion, we cannot wonder if they do not think very much of the Christian religion, and do not believe very much that we believe in the

## The Response to the Love of the Trinity

love of the TRINITY. We must face it, that the second response we must make to the love of the TRINITY is a life of a certain kind. What is that kind to be ? I think I notice that it must have three characteristics. First, it must be calm and strong. Anyone who really believes that GOD the FATHER'S arms are round him, that the grace of our LORD JESUS CHRIST is within him, and that he is in communion with the HOLY GHOST, must be far calmer than one who does not, because he has supernatural strength. Then, it must be pure. " He that hath this hope purifies himself even as GOD is pure." Therefore, if I am speaking to any who think they are religious, and would be very sorry if we were to say they were not, and who really imagine that they believe in the Christian religion—which is, of course, the love of the TRINITY in its completeness—then, I say, see that your heart is pure, that your life is pure. What are your thoughts like, your imaginations ? The HOLY SPIRIT cannot dwell with dark, foul imaginations. What is your life like, the part of your life that other people do not know—your thoughts, your words, and your actions ? There must be in your life an increasing and a sensitive purity if you believe in the love of the TRINITY. Do make that resolve to-night, if you make no other : I will purify myself even as GOD, even as CHRIST is pure ; I must, if I am to live in communion with the pure GOD, be pure. Then, again, it must be unselfish. Look how unselfish the Three Persons of the HOLY TRINITY are with regard to one another : one backs up the work of the other. GOD the FATHER sends GOD the SON : He gives up His only-begotten SON ;

## The Response to the Love of the Trinity

the only-begotten SON comes forth of His own free will; and then the HOLY SPIRIT comes down and cries " Abba, FATHER," supplementing the work of GOD the FATHER, bringing home the work of GOD the SON, all displaying loving unselfishness throughout. Is it possible to have a Church worker so jealous of another that she will not speak to her ? Is it possible to have jealousy among fellow-curates in a parish believing in the love of the TRINITY ? Is it possible to be selfish and peevish at heart and make every one uncomfortable if you really believe in the love of the unselfish TRINITY ? It is impossible, and when we are like that we have fallen below the true standard; we have fallen below the life that ought to be lived by those who respond to the love of the TRINITY.

3. Then, take a third point—service. Is it not a great thing to know that GOD the FATHER, GOD the SON, and GOD the HOLY GHOST cry to us for help from Heaven as they look down upon the masses in London ? " Whom shall We send, and who will go for Us ?" And then the great cry of humanity is: " Whom wilt Thou send, and who will come to us ?" It is an awful thing to think that the HOLY TRINITY have bound themselves—at any rate, they have planned; GOD forbid I should say that GOD limits Himself to anything—to work through men's ministry, and through women's ministry, on other men, women, and children—that He uses, in other words, human ministry in His work. And therefore to-day, among these thousands of people, if you listen, you hear the great cry come from the heart of the Godhead: " Whom

*The Response to the Love of the Trinity*

shall We send, and who will go for Us ?" And we are bound, if we believe in it, to answer in our little way: " Here am I ; send me." We cannot help it when we believe in it. There may be some young men who in the fullest sense make the answer, " Here we are; send us." There may be some who may come out for ordination, but the great mass of you cannot. You cannot become Sisters of Mercy, all of you women ; some might join the Deaconesses and Sisterhoods ; but you are nurses in hospitals, or your work is in the City ; you are typists up in the City ; you are workers in other ways. Therefore it is impossible for you to do that, all of you. Still, the great point is to say, " Here am I ; send me," all the same. There is something for everybody to do. The poor parishes want Sunday-school teachers. One day, after a great meeting in the East End of London, on the top of the tram as that great multitude went away, we secured the offers of numbers of women to teach in the Sunday-schools of East London. Or, again, the business men here are wanted after their own business is over to take over the finances of many parishes in London. There is an infinite variety of work for all if they will offer themselves. It is not that they offer to us at all ; if they make the offer to the HOLY TRINITY, GOD will show them how to use their lives ; and if they treat me as St. Paul treated Ananias—that is to say, went to him to be told what he was to do—I will try, GOD helping me, to guide anyone. I shall not be able probably to write myself, but I will take some means to guide all who write to some useful work for GOD.

4. Then there comes the fourth and the last

## The Response to the Love of the Trinity

response of *worship*. I say that every one who believes in the HOLY TRINITY must worship the TRINITY. You notice in the Athanasian hymn—sometimes called the " Athanasian Creed "—the expression used is " worship the TRINITY." The object of a soul's existence is to worship the TRINITY. Therefore, beyond praying and working, there ought to be this fourth response of worship, which must consist of wonder, love, and praise. I concluded the opening sermon with the words :

> " When all Thy mercies, O my GOD,
> My rising soul surveys,
> Transported with the view, I'm lost
> In wonder, love, and praise."

Those are the three integral parts of worship to those who believe in the love of the TRINITY. Now, cannot some of us to-night make that fourfold response to the love of the TRINITY ? Cannot we resolve at least, " I will pray to the TRINITY, and try and pray better than I have done ? I will live a life of which the HOLY TRINITY will approve ? ' We know that our fellowship is with the FATHER and with His SON JESUS CHRIST,' as St. John says. I will try and do something more ; I will try and serve, try and see what little service I can do, if the HOLY Trinity will accept my service. I will offer it to-night in thought and will ; I will be regular in my worship of the HOLY TRINITY ; I will try to worship with more wonder, love, and praise." If we all make that whole-hearted response, there will be joy in the eternal Home.

# ST. SEPULCHRE'S, HOLBORN

*WEDNESDAY EVENING*

## ANSWERS TO QUESTIONS

Some of these questions are from those who clearly have not had very much instruction on matters of faith; but I answer them because I want to help every soul. My experience is, that there are numbers of people kept from the joy and happiness of religion by difficulties which they never tell anyone, and which they perhaps never disclose at all; and again and again we find that these questions, asked by one, have really been the difficulty of another also, who thus hears the answer to a lifelong difficulty.

1. **If the second Person of the TRINITY, our LORD JESUS CHRIST, came to earth and dwelt among us, how was He indivisible, or the Unity of the TRINITY maintained throughout that period? Or, again, if, as we believe, there has yet been no ascension by GOD the HOLY GHOST, how can we worship the TRINITY in Unity in Heaven?**

The answer is that it is a spiritual Unity, absolutely undisturbed by what the action at any moment of one of the Three Persons of the TRINITY may be; that while GOD the SON was working His work of redemption here, He was not divided at all in spirit from GOD the FATHER, Who had sent Him forth, or from GOD the HOLY SPIRIT, in Whose power—as again and again we are told—He worked His miracles. Therefore, although, as I said at the beginning, this mystery of the HOLY TRINITY is above our comprehension, as it must be, and was

## Answers to Questions

meant to fill us with wonder, love and praise—which we take as the very keynote of this Mission—yet there is nothing in anything told us of the acts of either Person of the HOLY TRINITY in the New Testament inconsistent with an unbroken Unity all the time.

### 2. If GOD is just, why does He punish all for the sin of our first parents?

The difficulty is founded on a misunderstanding of what we are really taught. When we speak about original " sin " we mean that, as we follow up the history of humanity, up the stream of it, there is no place where we do not find a sense of sin. We find it even on a monument of the Pharaohs: a Pharaoh confesses to a sense of shame. Canon Curteis puts it very excellently in a book I am afraid now out of print—" Scientific Difficulties." He traces up this sense of sin and shame, and shows that it comes down from the *origo*, or source, of human history; hence the name *original* sin. It is a mistaken way, then, of putting it—that we are punished for the sin of our first parents. We have inherited a taint in our nature; we are members of a fallen humanity; it is a real flaw in us. That is why, of course, we at once baptize children, among other things, that there may be at once a force of grace and power to fight against that taint which the child has inherited as a member of a fallen race. The difficulty, then, as suggested is not one really that corresponds to the facts of the case or the teaching of the Church.

3. This question is one that comes up in many forms:

### When GOD is able, if He will, to work out everything for our good, why should the granting of our requests be attended by disaster?

As I have to say in answer to other questions, we must always remember—and this is the bed-rock lying behind difficulty after difficulty—GOD in one sense limited Himself when He made spirits with free will of their own: He

## Answers to Questions

bound Himself to work in a certain way. If He used His almighty power to make us good, He would break His own image in us. And therefore He tries to win, to persuade; He sends messengers to draw back and win back; but He cannot *force* back anyone, He cannot by His almighty power do things without winning the human will back. I was very much struck with a statement in that book called "An Agnostic's Progress," by Mr. Scott Palmer, that the first thing that brought him to believe in the reasonableness of the Christian faith was the doctrine of what he called the "self-limitation of GOD." It explained many things to him which he could not understand before. We shall see that it explains some of these difficulties which are suggested in other questions.

4. A questioner asks, in relation to my answer\* about the Body and Blood of CHRIST "verily and indeed taken and received by the faithful in the Lord's Supper":

**Would it not be correct, in regard to transubstantiation, to quote the prayer of the Communion Service: "Who made there, by His one oblation of Himself, a full, perfect and sufficient Sacrifice for the sins of the world"?**

Quite so; but that is another question. There are two aspects of the Holy Communion. There is the aspect of Communion to which the first question relates. There is also the aspect in which we are pleading the sacrifice in the Holy Communion. And, of course, the very prayer that has been quoted shows how utterly untrue it is to suppose that anybody imagines that in the Holy Communion the Sacrifice—the one Sacrifice—is repeated. What we do in the Holy Communion is to plead the Sacrifice. There was a useful little pamphlet by Archbishop Maclagan years ago which pointed out that, as Joseph's brethren held up the blood-stained coat to tell the father that Joseph was dead—

\* See p. 43.

## *Answers to Questions*

mutely held it up—so in the Holy Communion we show forth mutely the Passion, and ask GOD to

> " Look not on our misusings of Thy grace,
> Our prayer so languid and our faith so dim ;
> For lo ! between our sins and their reward
> We set the Passion of Thy SON our LORD."

And if people only understood that, half the divisions in the Church about the Holy Communion would vanish altogether. There is only one Sacrifice, and we plead that one Sacrifice when we say " For JESUS' sake " at the end of our prayers, or we mutely plead it in the Holy Communion.

5. Next come some difficulties which are keeping a young man back from Ordination. I am very anxious, not only for his sake, but for the sake of other young men who, perhaps, have not had the courage to send me their difficulties, to answer him as well as I can.

**The existence of grinding poverty seems to be incompatible with the existence of an omnipotent and all-loving GOD. I can understand that trouble may develop character, but starvation cannot. It seems that by one act of will GOD can at once solve the whole social problem.**

This is precisely what I have already said that GOD will not do. I have said that one of the most touching things was the way in which the HOLY TRINITY ask for help from mankind. " Whom shall We send, and who will go for Us ?" And those who are ordained and sent out are the answer to the appeal of GOD and the cry of humanity. The cry of mankind is, " Whom wilt Thou send, and who will come to us ?" I was stating a most fundamental truth about the dealings of GOD with man. The glorious thing is that He asks our help. To solve the social problem is exactly what He has asked us to do with Him ; we are fellow-workers with GOD. When I was down in East London my greatest inspiration was the thought that, with all the difficulties of poverty and

## Answers to Questions

starvation to face, anyhow, we were there doing our best. I felt in the thick of it as part of GOD's answer, doing my little best with others to relieve it, and to make a better state of things. The real answer, then, to your difficulty, which I feel as deeply as you do, is to respond to GOD's call. All things being equal, and you ready for it, go down and be a slum priest, and be GOD's answer to the suffering world; do not hold aloof from it and criticise GOD, but say "Here am I; send me." This is the situation; the HOLY TRINITY cry for help to carry out the work; you are the answer if you will be.

6. Next comes a question which I tried in my long address on Faith* to answer in a way which I cannot now attempt again.

**The apparent and superficial improbability of Christianity perplexes me very much. Can you transmit thought over millions and millions of miles in a moment in prayer?**

But who told you it had to go so far? "GOD is about our path and bed every moment, and knoweth all our ways." It is a misunderstanding that our prayer has to go millions of miles. GOD is very near us. People forget that He is in the Church, moving up and down in His Church; the HOLY SPIRIT is within us; as Tennyson says:

> "Nearer He is than breathing,
> And closer than hands and feet."

Therefore, the whole idea of GOD being miles and miles away is utterly wrong. GOD is surrounding us. If only we believe that, Christianity is not prima facie so improbable. To me it is very probable that GOD, Who has taken so much trouble with the world, should want to reveal Himself to it. Even if we believe in evolution, as I do largely myself, GOD has taken infinite trouble with the world, and here we are,

* See p. 268.

living, moving people, with hearts and consciences and minds. Supposing that one of us had made a thousand to say nothing of millions of people so interesting, so lovable as mankind, should not we want to reveal ourselves to them? To my mind there would be nothing that GOD would have wanted more than to have revealed Himself to mankind, to have made His children love Him, to explain what He was like, and what they were to do. It is incredible that He should take so much trouble with mankind and then leave them. The more, then, you realise how deeply interested GOD is in every soul, the more you will be inclined to believe in the Christian religion, which tells you what He did to show this love. To believe in the love of the TRINITY drives you to believe in the Incarnation and the Descent of the HOLY SPIRIT.

### 7. Can you account for the divided state of Christendom?

I quite agree that there is nothing which is a greater trial to one's faith than the divisions of Christendom, because quite clearly CHRIST prayed that His Church might be one, and so visibly one that the world might believe that the FATHER sent Him. Therefore it is extremely trying to see Christians attacking one another, to see want of brotherliness, to see the three great divisions in the Church—the Eastern, Roman, and the Anglican—and besides them a large body of Christians, excellent people in their lives and their work, who would not say that they belong to either of the three. But I come round to this: my faith in the SPIRIT of peace and the love of GOD is strong enough to stand that. I say that we have got, in the power of the SPIRIT, to pray for the peace of the Church over and over again, and to work for it. As I look back on history, I believe with all my soul that the Church of England has two things in its hands which are some day going to contribute largely towards the peace and the visible unity of Christendom again—the historic orders and the open Bible. How do you suppose that the great Nonconformist bodies

## Answers to Questions

will ever rally under any Church which has not an open Bible ? How are the Greek or the Roman Churches ever to unite with any Church which has lost its historic orders ? Thank GOD, we have them both.

8. Then comes an old difficulty :

**Why did GOD create men and spirits who He knew would eventually be damned?**

I am not told myself, I am not told by my Church, I am not told in the Bible, that there are going to be a great multitude certainly damned. I do not find any single soul described by the Church as certainly damned. On the contrary, when our LORD was asked the question, " LORD, are there few that be saved ?" He said, " Strive to enter in at the strait gate." He would not lay down anything about it. Therefore, it seems to me that over and over again people have many difficulties which they need not have. The point is, have *you* got a chance ? If you have, then others have as well ; and, instead of worrying ourselves by theoretical difficulties as to how many souls are lost, whether they all have got a chance, why GOD created them, put all that aside, and strive to enter in at the strait gate, and to lead others into it ; try and bring other people into that state of mind which we call salvation, that soundness of mind and health which is a present salvation. That is what we want. I rise, then, from the perusal of this letter with the certainty that the clearly honest man who wrote it ought to " come to the help of the LORD against the mighty."

9. Then I come to a very interesting letter from an old clergyman relating to my answer about " Lead us not into temptation."

**Why should GOD "lead us into temptation"?**

I gave the answer\* in a sense in which I understood it : that the prayer was, " Let us not be tempted ; let no temptation be too strong for me or for any of you." But it is worth

\* See p. 42.

## *Answers to Questions*

noticing that we find the old version of the LORD'S Prayer as taught directly by our LORD in the language He spoke in the Nestorian Church of Chaldæa : ' Our FATHER, which art in Heaven ; we hallow Thy Name, that Thy kingdom may come," and so on ; " lead us out of temptation, and deliver us from the Evil One." I think that is clearly the meaning of the LORD'S Prayer. Therefore, it is interesting to know that in one version coming from the Nestorian Church of Chaldæa " Lead us out of temptation, and deliver us from the Evil One " is the form of the prayer.

10. **Do you think insanity is only for this life, and that after death a person who dies insane will be clothed in his right mind again ?**

I have no doubt whatever that diseases of mind and body will not go on into the other world. When I said the other day that five minutes after death you will be the same person, I meant the real person, but not the person who is disfigured by some form of insanity. If the life had been a good one, if he had the peace of GOD, that soul would be free from all mental defect and from all bodily defect in the other world.

11. Then comes another question which I have really answered practically before :

**If I am written in the book of fate with my name among the lost, what am I to do ?**

I should answer, How do you know your name is among the lost ? " GOD will have all men to be saved and come to the knowledge of the truth." Therefore, He will have you to be saved. Instead of sitting down in despair— " GOD will forgive thee all but thy despair "—saying your name is written among the lost, rise up and take with the hand of faith the loving present salvation offered you from GOD in this Mission. I was talking to a man once who asked whether a man's religious sense is not part of a man's original outfit. I do believe it is. I believe man is a praying animal. You may try as hard as you can to quench that nature, to

## Answers to Questions

"drive out nature with a pitchfork, but it will always return," as the Latin proverb says. There is many a man and woman in London trying to quench by doubts or carelessness the religious nature, but they cannot do it. We are born for Heaven, and born to pray. I say again, Do not try and fight against GOD, but let your real nature have its chance. No one is so much a true man or woman as when he or she is obeying that instinct and giving it full play.

**12. Should I be godmother when I am told that if I am I must not teach my godchild any definite Christian religion?**

No; certainly not. If you are not allowed to see that the child is taught the truths of Christianity, it would be a mockery to be godmother or godfather to it.

13. Then the last question, and one that goes far deeper than I can in a moment or two answer, is this:

**How are we to believe in the love of GOD when we see thousands of poor little children with no proper home, perhaps not knowing who their fathers are, born in this great London every year?**

My answer is that the contrast between the misery and unhappiness which surround their birth and their life, and the glorious happiness of tens of thousands of children whose parents have obeyed the laws of GOD, shows the difference between the results of obeying GOD's laws of righteousness and self-control and purity and the terrible results of disobeying them; and while the Christian Church, as she always has done from the beginning (when she gathered up the children that were left to die in the streets of Rome) to the present day, goes out and gathers up the waifs and strays in her loving arms for JESUS CHRIST, and rescues night after night the sinful, yet the very fact of the contrast between the misery of the one and the brightness and happiness of the other is a great attestation of the truth of the Ten Commandments.

# St. Sepulchre's, Holborn

*WEDNESDAY EVENING*

## III

### THE PEACE OF GOD

" The peace of GOD, which passeth all understanding, shall guard your hearts and your thoughts in CHRIST JESUS."
PHIL. iv. 7 (R.V.).

IS there such a thing as the peace of GOD which passeth all understanding ? It is a gift, at any rate, which we are clearly promised, if we will not refuse it ; it is the gift of the HOLY TRINITY, and is for us. But is there such a thing ? Of course, it is quite clear that JESUS CHRIST had it ; in the midst of all the tumult of the storm, He was asleep with His head on a pillow. But has any man—shall we say any mere man—had it ?

Take St. Paul : where was this apostolic benediction, which has rung for nearly two thousand years through the Church, written from ? From a prison ; given by a hunted man who did not know at any moment when he might be put to death, who had been in prison for a long time, who had been persecuted, and who had on him every day " the care of all the Churches." That always appeals to me. As the

## The Peace of God

troubles and worries of the Church in London pour upon me by every post, I think of St. Paul, who had on him the " care of all the Churches," and yet had the peace of GOD which passeth all understanding all the time. Or take St. Peter. I remember that when the Bishop of Lincoln was on his trial years ago I went to hear him preach. I remember over all these years the text which he took. He took the text about St. Peter when he was in prison : " And when they would have brought him forth, Peter was sleeping." There he was, expecting to be brought forth the very next day to almost certain death, but wrapped in the peace which passed all understanding ; peacefully Peter was found sleeping, as though he did not know that anything was going to happen to him at all, because his faith was strong enough to believe that he was in higher hands than his own all the time. Then, to come on down the ages, why should not we ask what happens to our own saints in our day ? We have the records of the saints long ago. We read how those saints died in peace, and that wonderful things happened at their death-beds. We have all read the passing of the Venerable Bede, one of the historians of the Church; but why should not we hear what happens to our saints as they pass away in our own Church to-day ? When I was in America one of my kindest hosts and most loving friends was Bishop Satterlee, Bishop of Washington. Many a time when 1 was in East London he used to come and cheer me on in my work, when he was on a visit to our country. When he laid the foundation-stone of the new Washington Cathedral—I was present at the service in a representative capacity, and the President of

## The Peace of God

the United States was also present, and over ten thousand people—there were such terrible clouds that it looked as if they were almost certain to burst upon us with torrents of rain. I remember that one of my brother Bishops said to me : " I know it must have been Satterlee's prayers that sent those clouds on, for to no one else would fine weather have been vouchsafed till the end of the service, when all those clouds were ready to pour down." It will show what they thought of him over there. To my utter surprise and grief, I was told the other day that he had died quite suddenly, and I think that this beautiful description by his chaplain of his death is something that should be part of the heritage of the Church, as much as the description of the passing of any saint that lived long ago : " As I entered the room bringing him the Holy Communion, I said, ' In the name of the FATHER, and of the SON, and of the HOLY GHOST,' and as I was about to deliver the bread, the Bishop said, ' Place it in my hands,' and I did. Then at the end of the sentence he said, ' Thanks be to GOD for His inestimable and unspeakable gift.' On my delivering the chalice into his hands, he said after the sentence, ' All praise be to GOD for His gift !' I saw that He was liable to pass away, and I lifted his hand that he might touch my head once more, and then I felt the pressure of his hand, and he said: 'GOD keep thee; GOD bless thee and protect thee, my son, my son ; and thank you for bringing me GOD'S precious gift.' His family were in the room, and received the Holy Communion. The Bishop slept for nearly three hours, and when he awakened, at 6.30, he said : ' With angels and arch-

## The Peace of God

angels and with all the company of Heaven we laud and magnify Thy glorious Name, evermore praising Thee, and saying, " Holy, Holy, Holy, LORD GOD of Hosts ; Heaven and earth are full of Thy glory. Glory be to Thee, O LORD most high !" ' Then he grew weaker and passed away, saying it was all right."

If, then, you ask me whether there is such a peace to-day in the hurry of American life, in the hurry of London life, as the peace of GOD which passeth all understanding, I ask you if that man did not have it. It is a real thing ; it is a real gift ; it is a thing you can almost touch, as it were ; you can touch it, at any rate, with your spiritual hand.

And the question is, Have we got it ? Have we received from the HOLY TRINITY the peace of GOD which passeth all understanding ? What will it do for us if we have it ? To answer the question will help us to find out whether we have it or not. What does the peace of GOD do ? We are told in this very verse it will " guard our hearts and our thoughts "— guard or garrison : that is what the word means. We were told the other day that so strong is our navy that every Englishman and every Englishwoman might sleep in peace because we were garrisoned so strongly ; and when I think over what St. Paul meant—and I preach to myself as much as to you—I should say that he meant something like this. There are four sentinels guarding the city, one at each corner to keep us in perfect safety whatever happens.

What are the four ? (1) The first is, " no man shall pluck us out of our FATHER'S hand." If that sentinel stands there, all nervous fear about what is

## The Peace of God

going to happen must vanish. If we believe that, while trial will no doubt come, and while we may have many losses, while we may lose those who are nearest and dearest to us, yet if both for us and for them the assurance " No man can pluck us out of our FATHER'S hand " be true, we have the first sentinel of peace standing there guarding the city.

(2) Take another : " If GOD be with us, who shall be against us ?" I look around London ; I see the forces of organized traffic in vice ; I see the thousands of poor little children ; I see the social problem looming in all its blackness, and I should be bound to have no peace if I did not believe that there is a sentinel at the second corner—" If GOD be for us, who can be against us ?"—if I did not believe that GOD was ten thousand times stronger than the devil, and that, if we come to the help of the LORD against the mighty, we are bound to win against the devil, and that in this battle which very often seems so uneven there is only one victory certain, and that is the victory of GOD—that GOD must win. We may delay the victory by our want of faith and sloth ; we may not take a share in it ; we may lose the deathless honour of being fellow-workers with GOD, but we cannot stop the final victory of GOD, because " if GOD be for us, who can be against us ?" Others will come more faithful than we, who will work more with GOD ; but if in the battle in our generation we take the pledge of love to GOD the FATHER, GOD the SON, and GOD the HOLY GHOST in our parishes, in our diocese, in our streets, we have the second sentinel guarding the city.

(3) Or take another : " All things work together for

## The Peace of God

good to them that love GOD." *All* things. Some of us here look back upon some trouble which seemed so bitter that it could not be meant to do us good; but I venture to say that that man or that woman sees to-day that it did work for good. Those who believe that it is a true promise that all things work together for good have got the third sentinel to guard their city.

(4) Or take the fourth: "Thou shalt keep him in perfect peace whose mind is stayed on Thee." Yes, however much abuse a man may have, however much he may be misunderstood by his friends in any course he deems it right to take, perhaps losing his best friend, his mind is still in perfect peace; if in his own conscience there is nothing between him and GOD, if he is doing what he believes to be the right thing at that particular time and in that particular business, this promise is a sentinel of priceless value. "Thou shalt keep him in perfect peace whose mind is stayed on Thee."

Now, does that help us to find out whether we have it? I do long, dear brothers and sisters—this Mission is not a thing to come to out of curiosity; it is a tremendous reality; it is like being in the presence of the dying—I long that not one of you should fail to obtain the peace of GOD. You may not get it completely now, but you may be on the way to it. What stops it? First of all, a bad conscience. There is all the difference in the world between sorrow and sin. In sorrow GOD the FATHER puts His arms around us, GOD the SON kneels by us, and GOD the HOLY GHOST comes down with healing touch and indescribable power, and gives us peace—

## The Peace of God

whence we do not know. But in sin there is all the difference. It stains and stings and festers, and there is no peace until it is got rid of. What I want to ask all of you is: Is there anything on your conscience which you will not face? If so, farewell peace; all the sentinels are gone; the city is not likely to be at peace, because it is at the mercy of the enemy. Therefore, I pray you, as you love your GOD, as you value your own happiness and usefulness in this world, to be at peace with GOD, through JESUS CHRIST. I always keep strictly to the Prayer Book as I preach these things. You can, by yourself, if you are earnest —right down earnest—confess your sin to GOD, and then listen to the message of forgiveness in the Communion Service, and hear the Absolution; you can receive peace by yourself. But if you cannot quiet your own conscience, then pull yourself together like a man, and ask some priest of GOD to help you back to peace, as the Prayer Book directs. But, one way or the other, you cannot be happy, and you cannot work, and you cannot live without the peace of GOD; you *must* have it.

Then comes, secondly, the want of faith. There are people who have confessed their sin, but they do not receive peace, because they forget that the hand of faith has to take the peace. Here it is waiting for them; they are forgiven; here is love and power and protection, and they will not take it; but it is just as much a duty to have faith as it is to have repentance. There may be some souls here who, so far as they know, have told out everything, and have nothing between them and GOD. Then lift up your hand like a child, and take the

## The Peace of God

peace waiting for you, and the peace of GOD shall garrison your heart and life.

Or consider worry. When JESUS CHRIST said, " Be anxious for nothing," the real word means, as we should say, " Do not worry ; take one day at a time." If all these things are true, then the great GOD has undertaken for us how long we are to live. If we are to go on with a life of happiness and work after death, and if we are in the hands of GOD, what does it matter, in the last resort, when and how we are going to die ? If we have grace to live, we shall have grace to die. One day at a time is all we are asked to live and to work. Therefore, instead of worrying, take one day at a time, and ask for peace for that day.

Then, once again, besides the confession and the means of peace, there are many who do not use the means of grace, which are the means also of daily peace. I may be speaking to some who never go to church, who hardly ever say their prayers, who did not open their Bible till this Mission. Is that the way to have peace, using ninety-nine out of a hundred parts of your life for yourself and leaving the hundredth to GOD ? No ; give free scope for all the forces that make for peace to come into your life. Make up that quarrel ; yes, go and make it up yourself ; do not say, " I will wait until the other person apologizes." Have the courage yourself to make peace ; use those means of peace which GOD has put before you, that the great peace of Heaven may come down upon you.

This peace is a present, a promised, and maybe a permanent thing; it is a gift from the love of the

## *The Peace of God*

TRINITY. O GOD the FATHER, grant it to each of us! O GOD the SON, through Thy merits and Thy redeeming work, we ask for it! O GOD the HOLY SPIRIT, bring it down to us from Heaven, and place it in every heart; fold us into the love of the FATHER, the SON, and the HOLY GHOST; fold us into the peace of Heaven.

# ST. JAMES'S, CLERKENWELL

*SUNDAY EVENING*

## ANSWERS TO QUESTIONS

1. **If we are to come to the Holy Communion at peace with all men, is it wrong to take the Sacrament if we cannot say truthfully that this is the case? There is some one who continually makes unhappy some one else whom I love, and I cannot forgive him. My blood boils; I am powerless to remedy the state of affairs.**

I should say that there was nothing in righteous indignation which makes a person unfit for the Holy Communion. We are meant to feel righteous indignation. Our LORD felt righteous indignation when He found His FATHER's house was being defiled. There is nothing, then, if that questioner is here, to prevent her coming because she feels righteously angry at her sister being unkindly and wickedly treated. But she ought to pray for the man as well as for her sister. She ought to have faith to pray that the man's heart may be turned. If we are told to pray for our enemies, then we must pray for one who is, for the time, our enemy, if he is hurting the one we love. Come, then, to the Holy Communion, but try and rise to the spirit which JESUS CHRIST displayed Himself upon the Cross.

2. I have a number of questions, as usual—and therefore I shall only be able to answer them very shortly—about GOD, and the existence of sin and evil.

**Is there a GOD at the head of this out-of-hand world? If we believed that, all questions would for ever go. Are**

we really deluded in thinking so? GOD in the Old Testament seems capricious, in the New Testament loving and gentle. Is there a GOD, one Creator, Who created sin? Surely some one could do something, and we calling ourselves Christians.

I put all those questions, which come from one questioner, together. We have answered them at every church, at every service. GOD did not create evil. He created spirits of free will, and, as I have said over and over again, the explanation is the necessary self-limitation of GOD in dealing with people who have free will. A thing cannot be and not be at the same time. You are either free or not free. If you are free to do good, you are free to do evil. What is described in the New Testament is GOD redeeming the world. He did not come down and force the free will of humanity. He redeemed humanity. He sent the good down through the very channels through which evil had come. All the Christians then in the army of GOD, all those who nurse and care for the sick in body, all those working in the slums, every Sunday-school teacher in London, are doing something; they are the answer to the questioner. "Surely some one can do something." It is GOD's people who have to act and work for Him. The very people who feel this most keenly, instead of criticising and doing nothing, ought to be the people offering themselves for the service of the Redeemer of mankind. It is a call to service. The more we feel the need of the love of the TRINITY, the more we ought to say, "Here we are; send us."

### 3. Why did GOD create sin? Surely He would see to what a pass it would bring man?

It is the same answer. The more you think about it, the more you see it must be so—that we must either be men or clocks. We used to discuss this question in East London every Sunday afternoon; and the more the working men thought it out, the more they saw that you must either be one thing or the other—either a puppet pulled by a strong

## Answers to Questions

power or a man of free will; and if you are a man of free will you must take the risk.

4. Then come two sets of questions criticising kindly what I said with regard to it being nowhere laid down that there are so many millions going to be damned. I say that the Church has never laid down for certain even that Judas Iscariot was lost; still less that our religion taught that the great majority of the human race would be certainly damned. That was asked before,* and I said that there was absolutely no justification for saying such a thing at all; on the other hand, there are most urgent warnings; our LORD JESUS CHRIST takes upon Himself the responsibility of giving the strongest warning. We look on Him as the most merciful Being in the world, and so He is. Therefore, we ought to attend all the more to the strong things which He does say. I believe this: that He saw the possibility of a soul being so completely turned the wrong way that it could not turn back. He speaks of " the worm that dieth not and the fire that is not quenched," and, although it is a metaphor, it must mean something. Therefore, I do not want, in preaching about the love of the TRINITY, to hide, for a single moment, the stern side of the Gospel. There is a very stern side, and JESUS CHRIST preached it Himself. It is quite true, as Dr. Pusey said, that no soul will ever be lost that has not had the FATHER throw His arms around him, and look into his face with looks of love, and has deliberately rejected Him. But there may be some soul that is doing that now. And the mission may be for the salvation of that soul that has gone on rejecting GOD, thinking that some day it will turn in another world, if not in this; and the stern side of the Gospel may be the very word that it wants. Every month, every week, every hour that it goes on makes turning more difficult, and perhaps impossible. Therefore, my questioners rightly remind me—although I need not say I had not forgotten it—that many would strive to enter in,

* See pp. 58 and 64.

## Answers to Questions

and should not be able. But what so often happens in people who quote the Bible is missing just the important word. "Agonize, struggle, to enter in the strait gate, for many shall *seek* to enter in"—that is another word—"and shall not be able." In other words, "the Kingdom of Heaven suffereth violence," as our LORD says in another place, "and the violent take it by force." Some seek to enter in the strait gate; they try to walk towards it, but what our LORD reminds us of is, that it must be a determined effort; that so strong are the attractions of vice, so easy and tempting is the broad way, that, in order to come into the narrow way, you are to make a determined effort to enter. "*Agonize* to enter in" is the literal translation of the Greek word. But that verse never says that so many are going to be eternally damned. It says that many will come up to the gate, will seek in a sort of half-hearted way to enter in, and will not be able. Therefore, we are to agonize to enter in with all our souls and with all our minds. Then the other verse quoted against me is, "Many are called, but few chosen." Yes, and if you look round London to-day you will see that this is a fact. How many in Clerkenwell have heard the bells ring but have not come? The preachers are preaching every Sunday; the clergy visit every house up and down the streets, but what is the percentage of those who assemble in this church out of the population every Sunday? Many are called, but few choose themselves to come. The verse then certainly states a fact, but I still hold that those verses quoted do not lay down the belief that the majority of the human race will be eternally lost.

5. **Since the coming of CHRIST and the preaching of the Gospel of love, love to GOD and to our FATHER, and also love to our enemies and forgiveness towards them, is it right that we should continue to sing some of the psalms, particularly the one "Let them go down quick into hell"?**

## Answers to Questions

This is a sensible question, and it must have very often struck people why we sing such a psalm, as we did to-night. The defence of it is that certain ancient saints had not learnt fully the Gospel of love. Even GOD can only get out of each age the goodness of which it is capable, and these saints of the Old Testament had not learnt yet the Gospel of forgiveness of enemies which, thank GOD, we have learnt from CHRIST ourselves. The writer of those psalms is identifying himself with GOD'S cause; and we must never use them in any spirit of personal resentment. They were written at a time when people were imperfectly taught. They had not the Christian spirit. We sing them as representing the spirit of a bygone age. But, at the same time, I must fairly tell you that I think it is well worth consideration in the Church as a whole whether we should continue to sing all those psalms in our service. I feel sometimes that the unlettered and the poor do not always understand the spirit in which we sing them, and sometimes such psalms do undoubtedly mislead their minds. Therefore, when it comes to the time for reconsideration of all our services, I think my voice will be on the side of leaving out of our public services some of what are called the "cursing psalms" which we sing to-day.

**6. Why is it said in Isaiah of the Great One, "He shall be called the Mighty GOD, the Everlasting FATHER, the Prince of Peace"? Does it mean that the FATHER became incarnate, or only the SON of GOD?**

If you take the mere words, the passage is somewhat puzzling. But, of course, the Everlasting FATHER there does not refer to the FATHER as opposed to the SON and the HOLY GHOST. This great coming One was to be an Everlasting FATHER in the sense of gathering in, as a father does, wandering souls. It was a prophecy, and was not meant to be a theological definition—a glorious though vague prophecy of the great Being who was to come.

## Answers to Questions

**7. I am troubled much sometimes with horrid, irreverent thoughts at sacred times; they are a great trouble to me. How can I overcome them?**

By praying to the HOLY TRINITY, by saying, "JESUS, help me"; and I venture to say to any single one of you who, either by day or by night, find some dark thoughts come into your mind, that they are the darts of the Evil One; we are to expect them; they come from the Devil. But if you say, "JESUS, help me; GOD, help me," and catch them on the shield of faith, you will be astonished how quite suddenly Divine strength will come into you, and those thoughts will vanish.

**8. If GOD knows from the beginning everything that is going to happen, do our prayers alter His will? I mean, if GOD has already arranged how and when our dear ones are to be taken from us. There is a dear uncle of mine, more than a father to me, who may die at any moment.**

I do not profess to explain all difficulties, but I do say that we are bound always to pray for anyone ill like this, adding "if it be Thy will"—because GOD must love that person more than we do, and it may be the right moment for that dear one to be taken away. We must pray as CHRIST did Himself, in submission to the will of God—I will speak about that presently—" If it be possible, let this cup pass from Me; nevertheless, not My will, but Thine be done." That is the perfect prayer, and I think the questioner cannot possibly go wrong if she prays for her uncle in the spirit in which our LORD prayed Himself.

**9. A father died some time ago without forgiving the writer for joining the Church of England. Should the writer be still miserable at the thought that her father does not forgive her now?**

I should say myself that she should not be miserable. She acted in accordance with her conscience. She was apparently

## *Answers to Questions*

of age, and the responsibility rested with her. Therefore, we may surely believe that her father in another world looks with other, broader, truer eyes upon events of which he may have taken a very narrow-minded view on earth. I should believe that in the clearer light her father saw things in a different way.

10. **How far may we believe that at the final resurrection we shall be reunited to those we love, supposing a relation to have lived and died in unrepented sin, while the other members of the family, by GOD'S grace, were saved?**

That is one of those absolutely insoluble problems—a question which cannot be answered. Personally, I believe that we must hope on and pray on for every one. It seems tr me that the great comfort is this: GOD created that soul. You do not know whether that soul did die in unrepented sin; in any case CHRIST died for him or her. Surely you can leave them to their merciful Creator and to the Redeemer Who died for them, and the HOLY GHOST, the Comforter. I believe the love of the TRINITY is infinitely comforting in these things; it is so strong, stable, and so faithful. To the questioner who sends that question I would say, I should not give anyone up in despair. You do not know anything about the state of that soul. Strive to enter in at the strait gate yourself, and there is nothing in the least wrong in remembering—in fact, it is only natural—that relative of yours before GOD in your prayers, as you did when he or she were alive on earth.

11. My last two questions come from an old man; he says he is eighty years old. He says:

**Will you point out where in the Scriptures it says, "I and My FATHER are one and the same," quoted by you, and reported in the papers?**

I do not think it was reported in the papers. If it was, it was wrongly reported, because it is not "one and the same." "I and My FATHER are one thing" is the Greek meaning.

## Answers to Questions

The Greek word is ἕν—"one thing"—and if the writer looks at the passage in St. John, if he knows Greek, he will see exactly what is said: "I and My FATHER are one thing." "He that hath seen Me hath seen the FATHER." "Before Abraham was, I am." That is to say, they are *so* closely united. That is one of the great assertions of CHRIST about His Godhead.

12. I answer the last question more fully, because it relates to the event we commemorate to-day.* This is the day on which in the Church we keep the wonderful day on which the angel announced to the Virgin Mary that she was to be the mother of the SON of GOD. The writer asks:

**Where is there proof, or even evidence, in the New Testament for the truth of the statement in the Apostles' Creed that JESUS CHRIST was conceived of the HOLY GHOST and born of the Virgin Mary?**

I want to answer that a little more fully. I have already answered it in writing very fully; but as there are no doubt some people who are vague and rather unbelieving about the Virgin birth, I should like to answer this last question more fully than the others. You will find the arguments of those who try to persuade us that there is no evidence for the Virgin birth of our LORD fall under four heads: (1) The so-called silence of St. John, St. Mark, and St. Paul; (2) The similarity of the story to other stories of other heroes; (3) insufficient evidence of the fact itself; (4) the assertion that it is "an unnecessary marvel."

Of course, I can only indicate in the briefest outline the answer to these four arguments; you will find them treated in considerable detail in Bishop Gore's first dissertation in his book called "Dissertations," Dr. Knowling's "Our LORD'S Virgin Birth and the Criticism of To-day," Professor Ramsay's "Was CHRIST born in Bethlehem?" and three excellent papers since published in a small book by the Dean of West-

* Feast of the Annunciation.

## Answers to Questions

minster, besides articles by Dr. Sanday in "Hastings' Bible Dictionary," bearing on the subject. But after weighing, to the best of my power, what has been said on the other side, I can find no strong argument in the so-called silence of the above-named writers.

1. St. John's main purpose was only to give a personal witness of what he had himself seen; his account is supplementary to the other Gospels; and just as the institution of the Holy Communion underlies his statements about "eating flesh and drinking blood," so the Virgin birth underlies his account of the Incarnation; in fact, as the Bishop of Birmingham so well says, St. John supplies the "justifying principle of that which was already believed." Again, how could he have been ignorant of that which Ignatius, a few years after the Fourth Gospel was written, called "a mystery of loud proclamation in the Church"? St. Mark's Gospel represents the preaching of St. Peter, and it is clear that, for obvious reasons, if the original function of the Apostles was to be "eyewitnesses," the first preaching of the Apostles would not, and did not, include the Virgin birth; St. Paul's Epistles are almost exclusively occupied in contending for Christian principles, not in recalling facts of our LORD's life. And yet St. Paul's whole conception of the "second Adam" postulates this miraculous birth. He says that CHRIST was "born of a woman," "born of the seed of David, according to the flesh," and yet was, according to St. Paul, "from Heaven," and, as the second Adam, was a new starting-point for humanity.

2. The argument from other birth stories is only plausible until it is examined. Anyone who has been misled by the poetical fancies of Sir Edwin Arnold's "Light of Asia" into believing in the close resemblance of the birth stories of CHRIST and Buddha should study the real evidence in that most truthful and careful account of Buddhism by Bishop Copleston, the present Metropolitan of India. The tendency to allege miracles with regard to the infancy of heroes can in

## Answers to Questions

itself be no argument against our having a real history of certain rare events attendant upon the birth and childhood of JESUS; it merely points to the truth that a hero or religious teacher is GOD-sent, and it should never be forgotten that the story of our LORD'S miraculous birth comes undoubtedly, not from the Gentile but from Jewish sources, in which quarter all such stories of the birth of heroes as were current in the Gentile world would have been specially abhorrent.

3. For the evidence itself I must refer you to the books which I have mentioned, and it is time now, not only for every clergyman, but for every layman, to be able to give a reason on this matter for the belief that is in him.

Every effort has been made to discredit the accounts in St. Matthew and St. Luke, and to show their inherent incredibility. All such attempts have entirely failed. But it is clear that the account of St. Luke is a document derived from the Virgin Mary herself, or, as Dr. Sanday thinks, from the women who surrounded her. St. Matthew's is an account which represents the point of view of St. Joseph.

That this belief was held at the end of the first century we have already seen, and Irenæus, in A.D. 190, says that the belief in the Virgin birth was a tradition and a belief of the whole Church throughout the world in his day; and we have similar testimony from Rome, Greece, Africa, Asia, Syria, Palestine, and Alexandria.

4. It remains, then, to ask, Is this doctrine of the Virgin birth an unnecessary marvel, which, after being believed by the Church from the beginning, may now be lightly discarded as unnecessary lumber at the beginning of the twentieth century? Far be it from any one of us to say that the great Incarnation of the SON of GOD could not have taken place in any other way. GOD can do anything in the processes of nature, which, made by GOD, are sacred in themselves; but it is at least remarkable that in the early days there were no believers in the Incarnation who were not also believers in the Virgin birth, and that there is a close connexion even to-day between

## Answers to Questions

the discrediting of the Virgin birth and the whittling away of the miraculous elements in the Resurrection. It is sometimes said that because we believe to-day in a spiritual body in which the redeemed will rise, rather than a resurrection of the actual atoms, therefore we may repeat the Creed without believing in an actual resurrection of our LORD and a real Virgin birth ; but how the redeemed shall rise was never an article of the Christian Faith so long as the spirits are clothed at last with bodies. St. Paul himself says : " There is a natural body and there is a spiritual body," whereas Christianity stands or falls with the fact of the Resurrection of our LORD.

Is it true for a moment that the story of the Virgin birth is an unnecessary marvel which has no bearing upon our spiritual lives ? Surely it is the one hope for us that we are able to cut the ropes which bind us to a bad past, and be new born in CHRIST JESUS; how could the old entail be better broken, how could the new start be better given, than by the birth of the Second Adam from a pure Virgin, which should send a shock of new life through the veins of a redeemed mankind ?

# St. James's, Clerkenwell

*SUNDAY EVENING*

## IV

## THE LOVE OF THE TRINITY IN CO-OPERATION WITH HUMAN PRAYER

" Ask, and it shall be given you ; seek, and ye shall find; knock, and it shall be opened unto you. For every one that asketh receiveth ; and he that seeketh findeth ; and to him that knocketh it shall be opened."—St. Luke xi. 9, 10.

THE message of this Mission is the love of the Trinity, and my subject now is the love of the Trinity as shown in co-operation with human prayer ; and the invitation which we hear coming from the heart of the Godhead, from the Holy Trinity, is this : " Ask, and it shall be given you ; seek, and ye shall find ; knock, and it shall be opened unto you. For every one that asketh receiveth ; and he that seeketh findeth ; and to him that knocketh it shall be opened."

We have listened in church after church to most marvellous voices coming from the heart of the Godhead, such as the thunderings and voices that St. John seemed to hear in the Book of Revelation. We have heard of " the grace of our Lord Jesus Christ, and the love of God, and the fellowship of the Holy Ghost " promised to us. We heard the Holy Trinity

## *Prayer*

before the Ordination crying : " Whom shall We send, and who will go for Us ?" We made the Ordination part of the Mission, and when twenty-one men came up and were ordained in St. Paul's Cathedral, we knew that to be one of the answers. " Here am I; send me," every one had said. And we saw what the cry of the TRINITY meant to us, whether we were ordained or not. There was not a living man or woman, boy or girl, who had the right to refuse to say, when the TRINITY cried for help, when they asked for human help—without which they cannot reach all the masses of the people and convert the poor—" Here we are; use us." And thank GOD that is the answer that some of you made.

But now we have a beautiful cry from the heart of the Godhead : " Ask, and ye shall have ; seek, and ye shall find ; knock, and it shall be opened to you." What we have to do now is to think over this very carefully, see what it means, and what it does not mean, and go home believing it in its true sense. There is no good unless we do that. There is no good in your going away and saying you were very tired of the service, or that it was very interesting. This is one of those crises in your lives when you either believe this, or definitely do not believe it.

I. In the first place, notice what makes such a promise possible. There are three things which people forget when they say such a promise is simply mocking us.

1. First of all there is the self-limitation of GOD. It is a very striking thing, as some one pointed out to me, what very similar lines many of the questions take in every Mission; and half the difficulties depend upon forgetfulness of this simple fact—that GOD has

## *Prayer*

chosen to limit Himself to certain ways and to certain methods in dealing with man. For instance, when we are asked time after time why, if GOD is loving, He does not make us all good at once; when we are asked why GOD allows suffering and sin in the world—and those questions are sent in constantly—the answer always is, and always has been: Because GOD is dealing with people of free will; because GOD has limited Himself to dealing with people of free will, and respects their free will. Therefore He cannot break their free will, therefore He cannot make them good, because the whole point of creation and redemption and sanctification is that there may be so many living people freely choosing, and, if GOD comes in with His omnipotent power and forces us to be good, our goodness is worth nothing. GOD can make room, and does make room, for human co-operation in His plan, because He has limited Himself to deal with man as a reasonable person with free will.

2. So, again, it is only intelligible if we understand the grandeur of man's position. Man is really a viceroy of GOD. I remember a useful little book by a Presbyterian called, "With CHRIST in the School of Prayer."* I dare say I read it twenty-five years ago, and I do not know any book that ever helped me more. I remember that he explains in that book that in one sense GOD rules the world through our prayers; that we are viceroys; that as kings we may say, "I will," as priests we run in between the living and the dead, and the plague is stayed; we hold up our hands, like Moses, above the battle; we say, like Abraham: "If there be fifty righteous, if there be forty, if there

* Andrew Murray.

## *Prayer*

be thirty, if there be twenty, if there be ten." You can only understand prayer at all, if you understand the position of mankind ; do realize that we are kings and queens, princes and princesses, under GOD ; and it is only when we understand this that we comprehend the place of prayer at all, or why prayer is encouraged.

3. And then, again, we only understand this if we realize that the HOLY TRINITY'S love is there before us. Let me explain what I mean. I believe that numbers of people imagine that they are going to try and change GOD'S will to their whim by their prayers. The man, for instance, whom I have quoted as praying for a rise in the price of shares on the Stock Exchange was just the man who really imagined that prayer was changing the will of GOD to suit his particular wish. Now, that is a total misunderstanding of prayer. The point that we must get into our minds is this—that the HOLY TRINITY'S love is there before us, that GOD wants us to be at our best, and is trying to do the best for us before we begin to pray at all. You remember how the great poet Tennyson, in looking forward to his death, prayed that there might be—

" Such a tide as moving seems asleep,
   Too full for sound or foam,
When that which drew from out the mighty deep
   Turns again home."

The great tide that had come out from the ocean was to bear him back on its bosom—that was his idea—and he would see his Pilot face to face when he had crossed the bar. This is the central idea of what I am going to say—that prayer is believing in a great tide of love which is coming out already from

## *Prayer*

the Godhead, and which is going to turn again home, if we will only let it, and bear us back on its great bosom —back home, back into the ocean of love from which it comes; and that is the great fundamental fact about all of us. Prayer is not trying to alter the will of GOD, but prayer is pulling up the sluices, undoing the locks, to let the tide get at us. The tide of GOD'S love is there, washing round us, trying to get the careless and the selfish and the slothful out of their miserable state, to bear them on the bosom of love to a life of love, and then back to the home. When once you have got that plain, it changes your whole idea of prayer; then you understand that prayer is only letting GOD have His will, allowing GOD to get at us. He has limited Himself not to use us unless we let Him. "Behold, I stand at the door and knock," says our Master. And therefore what we have to avoid doing is resisting the love of GOD. Our happiness depends on allowing the love of GOD, which is here in all its tremendous power, its unconquerable force, if we will only co-operate with it, to have us. And I want to know where is the man who, when he understands that, is going to say he will not have it; who really believes in the love of the TRINITY—GOD the FATHER, GOD the SON, and GOD the HOLY GHOST —which has brought him here to-night on purpose to get more hold of him, and then will go away and say that he will not have the love of the TRINITY, and will not pray, and will not co-operate, and will go on with his own selfish life—his cold, and, I venture to say, unhappy life—without it.

"When that which drew from out the mighty deep
    Turns again home."

## *Prayer*

It is at the turn of the tide that prayer comes in.

II. And then, secondly, notice how this conception of prayer absolutely sweeps away all those foolish things that are said about prayer. I have already shown how it sweeps away one foolish thing. To imagine that prayer is a sort of charm by which you can get rich is absurd. It is equally absurd for people to say : " Let us try testing prayer. We will have a ward in a hospital for which some one shall pray, and another ward for which no one shall pray, and we will see which set of patients get better the quicker." Some people, in their ignorance, once proposed such a test for prayer. Do not you see that the *spirit* of the prayer is the innermost part of the whole thing ? That would not be prayer at all. There must be trust and love before prayer begins at all; you must believe and trust and give yourself away to do the will of GOD, whatever it is, before true prayer is possible. I have often taken this illustration—and have already done so before in this Mission—when a man asks a friend to take his boy into his office and to bring him on, the father's friend says : " Yes, I will do my best with him." But if the boy comes down into the City, and gives no response to the efforts of his father's friend, arrives at the office half an hour or three-quarters late every morning, never takes the slightest trouble over his figures, does not observe the rules of the business, does not want to get on, how can the friend bring him on ? There must be co-operation on the part of the boy with the kind designs of his father's friend. Or take yourselves, you who are parents. Cannot you do more with the responsive

## Prayer

child, with the child who responds to you with open confidence, and asks you about everything, and comes and tells you his troubles and lets you help him—cannot you do more with that child than with the self-contained, self-centred, sullen child that will hardly speak to you about anything at all ? It is like that with GOD. GOD can bring on the man or woman who prays, the boy or girl who prays, who responds, who every morning asks to be made better ; but He cannot bring on the sullen, the selfish, the conceited child who thinks he can get on very well by himself, or thinks it too much trouble to make any response. Even CHRIST could do no mighty work in certain places because of the unbelief there. It is an awful thing to think that our LORD JESUS CHRIST might stand in this pulpit to-day and He might not be able, with all His love and power, to move some of us because of our unbelief. If we did not respond, even He could not do it. The second point, then, which I want you to realize is that this conception of prayer, the belief that the love is there beforehand, and that prayer is correspondence to love, sweeps away all those foolish ideas about prayer which pass from lip to lip among unthinking people.

III. And therefore I come to ask you these four questions :

1. First, do you pray yourself ? Perhaps a man says : " No, I do not ; I did not see that it was any good : if I had thought it was any good, I would have prayed." Think what that answer means in the light of the love of the TRINITY. Every morning each Person of the HOLY TRINITY is ready

## *Prayer*

to co-operate with you if you pray. There is GOD the FATHER, with His hand full of gifts—courage, wisdom, purity, strength, love—and He says : " Ask, and ye shall have ; seek, and ye shall find ; knock, and it shall be opened." All these gifts are for you. At the same time GOD the SON kneels by your side, and, using your Christian name, just as He used Simon's— " Simon, Simon, Satan desires to have you that he may sift you as wheat, but I have prayed for you that your faith fail not "—GOD the SON is praying by your side, ready to take your prayers, cold as they may be, poor and imperfect as they must be, and sweep them into His great intercession. But not only that : GOD the HOLY GHOST is trying to pray in you. " The HOLY SPIRIT," we are told, prays in us " with groanings that cannot be uttered." Therefore, every morning—GOD being infinite—we have the whole of GOD to attend to us, to each one of us, every time, not dividing His attention among so many millions of people, but the whole of GOD. You may say to the HOLY SPIRIT : " O HOLY SPIRIT, pray in me." And the beautiful thought is this—that we may be swept into the life of the HOLY TRINITY every morning; we may be made sharers of that life ourselves, and the HOLY SPIRIT will give us in that hour what we ought to say. You are offered a share in the daily life of the TRINITY. I dare say that you have never looked at it quite like that before. Resolve then to-night : " I will begin praying. I do want more strength against temptation where I work. I am constantly doing things of which I am ashamed afterwards. I want more love at home ; I want

*Prayer*

guidance to bring up my children." Ask for it. "Ask, and ye shall receive; seek, and ye shall find; knock, and it shall be opened." Or perhaps some one says: "Well, I did begin; I do remember that I prayed for a long time after I was confirmed; but I have given it up now, because I did not seem to get any answer." But now, if you look from this point of view upon prayer as being the response to the love of the TRINITY, are you quite sure you were not answered, but in a different way from what you expected? It is not at all promised that the answer will be in the exact shape which we expect. I have known people pray for things—I have prayed for them myself—and in the form expected they never came at all; but when I looked back, I saw that they came in a different way altogether. And therefore, if you look back to the time when you did pray, you may constantly find that your prayers are answered in a totally different form. They were answered, but according to love. I can think now of a thing I once asked for myself. I hope I asked in submission to the will of GOD, but, at any rate, I see now that it would have been the worst thing for me to have had what I asked. So I thank GOD for the manner in which He answered my prayer. Think over that, and begin again. If once you pray, so certain of the love of GOD that you will take the answer in any form it comes, all your prayers will be answered. Or, again, a man or a woman may say: "I pray sometimes, but I don't pray very regularly, I am afraid; I fear I often forget about it." But have you considered that the HOLY TRINITY never forgets about you? You must always remember that,

## *Prayer*

as morning by morning the sun of GOD's love rises on you, as regularly as the sun rises in the heavens, every morning the FATHER is waiting with all His gifts for you, every morning the SON is ready to pray for you, every morning the HOLY SPIRIT is ready to pray in you. Our response, then, ought to be as regular as the love of the TRINITY. We do not breathe once a week, we do not feed once a week. We breathe regularly and we feed regularly, because we have to correspond with the environment, as it is called, in which we live. The love of GOD is just as essential to the health of our souls as the environment of air and food is to our bodies. We are praying animals. One of the things which marks man out from all the other animals is that he is a praying animal. I ask, then, the question, Do you pray ? Resolve not only to pray, but pray as regularly as you breathe. "Pray without ceasing," says St. Paul. That does not mean that we are to be on our knees every moment, but that our whole life should be inhaling all the beautiful influences of the HOLY TRINITY, like a plant in the open air which grows stronger and stronger every day.

2. Then, my second question is, Do you intercede for others ? Do you pray for others as well as yourself ? You say : "But what good does that do ?" Well, I frankly say I should not know that it did any good at all unless I was told. I consider that intercession is a pure matter of revelation. Of course, it is attested by facts. You find that, when we all agree to pray for something, or when a man prays continuously for some one, there is a result. It is

## Prayer

one of those things which are verified by experiment, though, again, the answer does not always come in the same way in which we prayed for it. I venture to say that the experience of the last two thousand years has shown that GOD hears prayer and intercession. But we are not dependent on our own ideas about it; it is revealed to us that we are allowed a place in the plans of the HOLY TRINITY by intercession. You can see, if you read Henry Drummond's book on the "Ascent of Man," how even in Nature there is a place for intercession. The struggle for the life of others is innate in Nature. In Nature even the animal mother has the instinct which makes her fight for her cub. The struggle for the life of others is part of natural instinct; but when you come to the question, What is going to make you and me regularly intercede? the answer is, because we are told to do so. I find in the revelation that is given us that we do have this power: "If any man see his brother sin a sin which is not unto death, he shall ask, and GOD shall give him life." "O ye that are the LORD'S remembrancers, take ye no rest, and give Him no rest, till He establish and till He make Jerusalem a praise in the earth." "Pray ye the LORD of the harvest, that He will send labourers into His harvest." I ask you, as common-sense people, and I hope, believing people, what is the meaning of these passages unless there is power in intercession?

Or take those Old Testament stories about Abraham, Moses, and Aaron. They have no meaning unless the counsels of the HOLY TRINITY have left scope for our intercession for one another. Or take the most

*Prayer*

touching story of all—that of the man who was lowered down through the verandah at JESUS' feet. When they had let down the sick man, notice this : " JESUS, seeing their faith "—not *his* faith— " said to the sick of the palsy, Son, thy sins are forgiven thee ;" and then later on, " Arise and walk." What we do Wednesday by Wednesday in the Mission, or when we have a long list of intercessions at our prayer-desk, or by our bedside, is to let down our sick friends who are ill, or in trouble, or are far from GOD—we let them down at JESUS' feet, and JESUS, seeing our faith, says to the sick and the troubled : " Thy sins are forgiven thee," or, " Rise and walk." This, I say, is revealed to us. My second question, then, is, Do you intercede ? Do you run in between your sick friend and his trouble ? Do you run in between that boy going to the bad and the evil that threatens him ? Do you try and save him ? If not, you are not doing your duty. We are told that we are priests to GOD. We have to run in between. If you add to your Christian life, for however short a time each day, intercession for your friend, intercession for your wife and child and brother or sister, intercession for the parish, for the clergymen of your parish and diocese and the Bishops, intercession for the mission-field, you will find a new power in life, a new dignity in being a Christian, because you are exercising the priesthood of the laity.

3. Then, my third question is, Do you pray together ? " Where two or three are gathered together in My name, there am I in the midst of them." Some people say that there is no good in having daily service if only two or three come, but how can that

## *Prayer*

be, when it is clearly promised that where two or three are gathered together the LORD is there, and that if they agree touching what they ask, it shall be done for them ? It may be a prayer-meeting, or intercession service, or Morning and Evening Prayer. What I am asking you now is, Is this the first time you have been in church for a good many weeks or months, or perhaps years ? If so, why is it so ? Do you not believe in the power of united intercession ? Surely the HOLY TRINITY must know the secret of power. They must know the kind of response which we ought to make, and we are certainly told not to " forsake the assembling of ourselves together, as the manner of some is," but to meet and hearten one another in our spiritual lives. There are prayers in the Prayer Book which are hot with the breath of ten thousand saints who have prayed them in the past. There are additional prayers for certain special needs. It is easier to pray a prayer on which we have agreed, and therefore we pray over and over again for the King and the Church, for the sick and suffering. We ought, then, to make our third resolution : " I will not neglect church. If I am a communicant, I will come back to the great prayer service of the Church ; if I am not confirmed, I will come out and be a full member of the Church, and claim my priesthood of the laity ; I will pray together with my fellow Christians, and not live an isolated life."

4. Then, the last question which I want to ask you is, Do you thank GOD ? If I knew the history of your life, my brother and sister, I know I could tell you a great deal for which you ought to thank GOD. You

## *Prayer*

ought to thank GOD for being alive at all. You ought to thank GOD for having the home life and the loving friends you have. You ought to thank GOD for His care of you every day, for the food you eat and air you breathe. You ought to thank GOD for helping you and guarding you times out of number when you never thought of Him. You ought to thank GOD for answering prayers of yours which you offered and never stopped to look whether there was an answer or not. You ought to thank GOD for bringing you here. You ought to thank GOD for giving you one more chance of responding to the love of the TRINITY. And with our prayers every day there must be thanksgiving. The happy, bright, and powerful Christians are those who thank GOD every day.

And so it is I put the great invitation from the HOLY TRINITY before you. We can almost hear the cry from the Godhead: "Ask, and ye shall receive; seek, and ye shall find; knock, and it shall be opened to you." If we respond, then the tide of love will lift us, will sweep through us, and will bear us on to a life of usefulness, to a happier, stronger life than we have known before, for it is true to-day, as of old, that " they that wait on the LORD shall renew their strength; they shall mount up on wings as eagles, they shall run and not be weary, they shall walk and not faint."

# St. James's, Clerkenwell

*WEDNESDAY EVENING*

## V

### TRUE RESIGNATION

"And Mary said, 'Behold the handmaid of the Lord; be it unto me according to Thy word.'"—St. Luke i. 38.

I AM going to assume a great thing: I am going to assume that every man and woman of you have heard the call of this Mission, and mean now to resign yourselves wholly to the will of God. I am going to take as our subject the answer which Mary made when the great announcement was made to her: "Behold the handmaid of the Lord! Be it unto me according to Thy word." Here is the pattern of a perfect resignation. Notice five things about it:

First of all, that it is passively complete in its humility. Secondly, that she actively identified herself with the will of God—it was not only a passive thing; it was the active identification of herself with the will of God. Thirdly, it subjected her to the most terrible misrepresentation. Just think of the awful pain to a perfectly pure and holy maiden to have it said of her what that one single sentence means, that " Joseph willed to put her away privily ";

## True Resignation

think of the misrepresentation and the bitter contumely that she had to endure, in bearing and doing the Will of GOD. Fourthly, she endured it right through to the end. Fifthly, the result of her resignation and dedication was that the world was saved through her incarnate SON.

You and I—I told you I was going to assume it—are going to yield ourselves more utterly than ever to the love of GOD. You remember

> "The tide which moving seems asleep,
>   Too full for sound or foam,
> When that which drew from out the mighty deep
>   Turns again home."

The tide is at the turn; the tide of love has drawn from out the mighty deep; it has brought us here, and it turns again home. What we have to find out is, What are to be marks of the resignation with which we yield ourselves to the tide? It is everything to believe that we love Him because He first loved us. The cause of all morbid religion, of weak religion, of unhappy religion, is not believing that. We said that prayer was pulling up the sluices, opening the locks to the tide, that it might sweep us along.

Now, there have to be exactly the same characteristics of our resignation as those which characterised the resignation of the Virgin Mary.

1. First of all, a complete and passive acceptance of the call. Sometimes it is a call to a great and overwhelming honour—some work that seems far beyond our capabilities and our powers; and then sometimes there is a false humility which makes a man or woman step back from the call. If there are some here who say, " If I yield to-night, I

## *True Resignation*

must do a great deal more than I ever dreamed of : if I yield to-night, I must be a worker, and must go and preach the Gospel ; I must be a teacher in a Sunday-school, or do something perhaps far more responsible than even that—there is only one answer for you, if you are sure about it : " Behold the servant of the LORD ; be it unto me according to Thy word." Or perhaps it is that you are face to face with an operation for your life, as a poor woman was the other day whom I was called in to see quite suddenly ; or you are suddenly face to face with the danger of some one in your home whom you love very much ; or quite unexpected trials and disappointments come in your home and private life. The first thing you have to do is to look up, with the quiet humility of the Virgin Mary, and say : " Behold the servant of the LORD ! Be it unto me according to Thy word." That is the first characteristic of humble, gentle, complete acceptance. Now, are we showing that ? I do not suppose that there are many of us who have not got some trial, and there may be some at the very crisis of their lives. Do, to-night, as we kneel down before we part, have that first characteristic of humble, trustful, complete acceptance from the hand of love.

2. Then, secondly—and this is often forgotten—it is not enough passively to lay down, as it were, under the will of GOD. If we are really resigned, *the resignation is an active thing.* " Take up thy cross," the SAVIOUR said—" take it up." The old sacrifices, as I remember a great American preacher once showed, were offered with the sound of the trumpet. Therefore, in this Mission you may be shown by the HOLY

## *True Resignation*

SPIRIT what the will of GOD for you is. I can conceive some one being shown " The will of GOD for me is to be ordained; the will of GOD for me is for me to go somewhere where I can serve GOD better; the will of GOD for me is to give up that trade where my conscience is injured every day by my doing something which I know is wrong; the will of GOD for me is to face that." There must be, then, in our resignation to-night the active element. The Virgin Mary identified herself with the will of GOD actively as well as passively. I do put it to you who are hearing me for the last time, thinking over what your answer is to be; I want you to rise up and say: " I will take up that cross; I will take it up; I will not lie down under it." That is quite a different thing. The resignation of some people is simply lying down—rather, perhaps, in a grumbling mood—under the cross. But true resignation bravely and actively takes it up every day, happy and proud to be called to follow JESUS CHRIST with it. Therefore, activity must be an element in your resignation and mine.

3. Then, thirdly, the Virgin Mary took it up and accepted the call, although it meant the most terrible, galling misrepresentation. There may be some of us who, in doing what we think to be the will of GOD as it is revealed to us, are vilified and misrepresented for doing it, perhaps for years. We must be brave enough to face that; it does not in the least follow that you are wrong because you are misrepresented—not a bit. Most of the great reformers in the past have been entirely misrepresented. Lord Shaftesbury was vilified in a way we can hardly understand in our generation, though we all applaud him now as a saint and a

## *True Resignation*

hero. Because a thing is difficult, and because a thing brings us into unpopularity, we must not be afraid in the least to do it. We are not worthy of JESUS CHRIST if we are afraid. While the world hated Him, the FATHER said, " This is My beloved SON, in Whom I am well pleased." There are some people who think that, if they are put upon the cross, GOD has forsaken them, that GOD has ceased to love them. He had not ceased to love JESUS CHRIST when He was crucified. The third thing, then, to remember is that we have in our resignation actively to do the will of GOD at the cost of misrepresentation or unpopularity. And if any of you are hesitating, I say, think not only of the Virgin Mary, but think far more of that incarnate SON, the SAVIOUR of the world, Who bore His bitter Cross to the end.

4. Then, fourthly, the Virgin Mary went through perseveringly to the end. Just think what it was for her to see, first, her SON so popular and with all the crowds hanging on His lips ; and then to see everybody turn away from Him, as apparently a failure ; and then, at the end, see Him hung up between the earth and sky, on what we call a gallows. There was nothing more romantic then about a cross than about a gallows. " A sword shall go through thine own soul also "—that was the prophecy—and so it must have done ; and still, in spite of what we know of her failure in faith on one or two occasions—when she tried to interfere when she should not have done, and when, apparently, she misunderstood our LORD and sided with the brothers, through not understanding our LORD'S method and why He was waiting —yet she was faithful to the end. That must be the

## *True Resignation*

fourth mark of our resignation : we have to bear the work and worry, and perhaps the unpopularity and the battle, right on to the end—right on, year after year, year after year. As Mrs. Hamilton King says in the beautiful little poem called " The Sermon in the Hospital," which you can get for a shilling, and which all ought to get and give, if you can, after reading it, to any of your friends who have a lifelong sickness or trouble—this star of earth is the star of suffering. In other worlds we may be called to do something else. Only in this world shall we be called to suffer for Him. That puts us on our mettle. When He comes to us, pallid and loyal, saying, " Drink with me, drink with me," shall we refuse ? No, not for Paradise.

5. Then, lastly, there will be the same result of our resignation if we show those four characteristics in it. The Virgin Mary lived out her resignation to the end, and the result was that her SON redeemed the world. Many and many of the fruits of a faithful life come long after that life is gone. We have lately buried, amid a large mourning congregation, the wife of one of the clergy of this diocese, in a poor district, who toiled on day after day. Do you suppose that life was lived in vain ? As I said while I stood by the coffin in the church, crowded to the doors with people among whom she had worked, and the children, every one of whom she had known by name, and who had loved her—she gave at Christmas 800 presents to children, and knew the name of each one—her life will be remembered in that district, please GOD, for years to come, and there will be a harvest from the seed she sowed. The worker dies,

## True Resignation

but the work goes on. The blood of the martyrs is the seed of the Church. We bury the seed, but the harvest comes long after, as we read in the funeral lesson, " Thou fool ! that which thou sowest is not quickened except it die." We must never be disheartened ; a life may seem to be lived in vain, but so long as it is faithful, so long as it is resigned, though it may be unknown in the world, that life will bear a harvest in the next generation.

I ask you, then, to resign yourselves to the will of GOD ; I ask you to give yourselves to the love of the TRINITY. I do not know what your life has been, I do not know what has held you back up to now ; but this Mission has come to call you to the true resignation—active, positive, self-sacrificing, life-long—and if the whole of you resign yourselves, one and all, to the love of the TRINITY and the will of GOD, what a harvest there will be in the future !

# ST. GILES'S

*SUNDAY EVENING*

## ANSWERS TO QUESTIONS

Here is a question I have been asked, I should think, at every Mission, and have answered it two or three times, but still, I do not like to pass it by this time, because it may be a real difficulty to many souls, and I remember when I asked some working men to suggest a question—in 1889, the first week I went to Bethnal Green—they chose this very question, showing how much it was agitating the minds of working men.

### 1. Do you believe in everlasting punishment?

I have tried to explain again and again what I hold about punishment. We have to face this—that our LORD took the responsibility on Himself for all the stern sides of the Gospel. He it was, you find, not the Athanasian Creed, as some think, not the Church long afterwards—He Himself it was who said the strongest things about the punishment of sin: "where the worm dieth not, and the fire is not quenched."; "agonize to enter in at the strait gate." And yet it is impossible to believe that if a soul really turned to GOD it could remain in hell any longer. When self-will ceases, hell ceases, as a great writer said, because the sin is its own punishment, and the expression in the New Testament is very enlightening where the warning is given not so much against eternal punishment as against "eternal sin." While I freely say, and have said at every Mission, when self-will ceases, hell ceases, and while I repeat what Dr. Pusey said—perhaps the strictest and strongest man

## Answers to Questions

on the whole subject—" No soul will ever be lost that has not had the FATHER throw His arms around him, look in his face with looks of love, and has deliberately rejected Him "—yet we are bound to face what JESUS CHRIST meant by His tremendous language. I believe that what He meant was this: that, while if a soul could turn now or at the end of a million years, it could not remain in hell, the awful danger is that we may so bend our will the wrong way that we cannot turn. I was speaking in St. Anne's, Soho, of a terrible case which has very much disheartened me.* A man whom I had hoped, by trust and effort and influence, I had saved from drink, a man of high education and great gifts, was discovered drunk that afternoon. And when you see a man enslaved by a curse like drink, although I would never say in this world any soul is hopeless, one understands the possibility of not being able to turn. Then you understand what an awful danger there is in yielding to some sin from which we cannot turn ; and what our LORD pleaded with tears in His eyes was this : " For GOD's sake, beware of the danger of selling yourself to that sin so that in time and eternity you cannot turn." Who am I, to go and preach about the love of GOD, and leave out the other side ? To be out of the love of GOD is to be in the shadow. When people ask questions like this, I give them the answer, as I believe—and I preach no rose-water Gospel—that no soul can remain in hell after it has turned. But are you running the risk of never being able to turn at all ?

**2. I do my daily work to the best of my ability; it is a satisfaction to know it is well done, and I am paid for doing it, so I fear there is no merit in it. Yet I feel there is much to do for GOD. What can I do?**

That question often causes difficulty for people who come to the Mission services. They are stirred up to do something, but they are busy from morning to night. Take the case of

* See p. 291.

## Answers to Questions

a factory-girl who might be here, with her unduly long hours; well, what can that poor girl do? Is that work in the factory not done for GOD? Certainly it is.

> "Who sweeps a room as for Thy laws,
> Makes that and the action fine,"

George Herbert says. And therefore the work done in the factory, or the household, or the workshop, or the office, ought to be dedicated to CHRIST. The singer Jenny Lind said: "I sing for JESUS CHRIST." She used her splendid gift for Him. Although she was paid for her work as the questioner is paid for her work, she said: "I sing for JESUS CHRIST." It gives a lift up to our ordinary life in London if one feels it is consecrated. The man in the office or the workshop can consecrate his work. But when we have said all that, there still remains a certain time in which we can use our influence for others. On Sundays, at least, something can be done as a labour of love. St. Paul said that he had a right to take payment for preaching the Gospel; but he preached the Gospel free of charge to the Church. Therefore, you who ask this question and the others who hear it should say to yourselves: "My common life can be dedicated, but is there not something I can do over and above?" Cannot I influence the factory-girl who works next to me to come to the service? Cannot I do something for the Church Lads' Brigade? Cannot I join it? Cannot I teach in a Sunday School, or help to start a branch of the Church of England Men's Society? Your ordinary work, as well as your work done for love, can all be dedicated.

> "Take my life, and let it be
> Consecrated, LORD, to Thee."

3. Then comes the last question, which is a touching one:

**I have recently lost a most dearly-loved sister, after a very short illness, with cancer. She was universally loved, and led a most useful life, always doing good whenever she had an opportunity. She was full of life**

## Answers to Questions

and health and brightness, and thoroughly enjoyed life. It seems so strange to me that a life like this, or one like Mr. Holden's, of All Saints', Margaret Street, should be taken, while so many who seem to do so little good live on. I am sure this must often perplex other people as well as myself.

Now, of course, there is absolutely no explanation if this life is all; I mean if this little tiny day of life, even if we live up to seventy years, is all, there is no explanation whatever. It is a most cruel business. Affection and friendship all will be blasted, and I should decline altogether to answer such a question if I was not a believing Christian. But what is the answer if I am a believing Christian? In the first place, the life of the dear sister, and of Mr. Holden too, goes on; this little life we see is like the crest of the wave on the Atlantic which is caught in the sunshine for a moment, but the great wave sweeps on. And, therefore, if you believe in the continuity of life, and in other service and other worship in the life of the Church—the majority are on the other side of the veil—then it becomes more intelligible. That sister of yours—you do not know what beautiful service she has been asked to do. She has been promoted. It is like General French in the campaign in South Africa. He was the only Cavalry General, and it seemed a dead loss to Ladysmith for him to be ordered away. The inhabitants could not look beyond Ladysmith, but the Commander-in-Chief thought out the whole campaign, and saw the whole of South Africa spread out before him. He intended that General to be the man who should relieve Kimberley. Now, do you not see, if you apply that parable, how it explains many things? We see Ladysmith, that is all—this little earth —but the great General in Whom we believe, Who commands the whole campaign over great spaces of which we know nothing, of which we can conceive nothing, has the universe before Him; He can order this soul to this part, this to another; it seems dead loss to us, but it is not to the whole

## Answers to Questions

work of the Church throughout the universe. And, therefore, if we can only remember what a small part of the battle-field our little earth is, then we can understand more how these noble souls are called away from service here to service there. They are promoted. We talk about eternal rest, but the truest rest is beautiful work. You cannot imagine energetic, earnest souls doing nothing. Imagine the great energetic soul of Archbishop Temple doing nothing for ever and ever! Impossible. It would not be satisfying to an earnest, loving soul like that, or to Mr. Holden, or to that sister who was so useful to the world. Therefore, when we take the full revelation of the Christian religion, while we must weep when we lose our dear ones—it would be unnatural if we did not—we must not mourn for them as those without hope, but as they that sleep in Him.

# St. Giles's

*SUNDAY EVENING*

## VI

### THE LOVE OF THE TRINTIY IN THE INCARNATION.

"GOD so loved the world, that He gave His only-begotten SON, that whosoever believeth in Him should not perish, but have everlasting life."—ST. JOHN iii. 16.

AS we go on in the Mission we get deeper and deeper into the love of the TRINITY, and we have now reached the love of the TRINITY as shown in the Incarnation.

"GOD so loved the world, that He gave His only-begotten SON, that whosoever believeth in Him should not perish, but have everlasting life."

I say the words slowly, because we are so Gospel-hardened, we are so accustomed to these tremendous things and these tremendous phrases, that they are just like coins that have lost their edge through being used so much. There is no prayer that Christians want more than "O GOD, save us from being Gospel-hardened." We sit in our pews and listen to what we have heard a thousand times before—the old, old story, until it loses its meaning, though the words are strong. Therefore, I want to repeat over to you again, as if you had never heard it in

## The Incarnation

your lives before, "GOD so loved the world, *so loved the world*, that He gave His only-begotten SON, that whosoever believeth in Him should not perish, but have everlasting life."

I want you first to think of where we should be without the Incarnation. (1) I gave that answer to a poor sister who had just lost her dear one; I gave it as a Christian, but I could not have given that answer if I had not believed in the Incarnation. If GOD had done nothing, and I was asked to go and see a sister dying of cancer before my eyes, or spend the night in the Cancer Hospital—I was once up all night there with a man dying with cancer, until five o'clock in the morning—do you suppose I could easily love GOD? I could not, because I could not feel that He had done anything or suffered anything. When some man says to me, "Come, let us fight this difficult battle together. I will bear the worst with you; I will go and suffer with you, fight with you, bear the unpopularity with you, and all that is brought against you: I will fight side by side with you," I honour that man, and I would go and follow him, stand by him, and I should feel that he had done something to show his sympathy. And when GOD, as I believe, comes down among all the cancer and the consumption and the misery, and says, " I will come and bear it with you; I cannot explain to you now why it has to be borne, but I will bear the worst with you. I suffered more than I ask you to suffer," I can understand that; and when I am dying, or when I am with some one dying, it is everything to know that GOD knows of the suffering and death, and has borne it Himself. And, therefore,

## *The Incarnation*

I say without the Incarnation I could not answer one of these questions that are put to me about the pain and misery and sickness we have in the world.

2. So, again, I should have no idea what GOD was like. Sometimes, perhaps, you have asked yourself, " What is GOD like ?" I should not be able to tell you. I might prove to you that there was a GOD, and my reason might be convinced by arguments; I might be convinced that there must be a power behind the veil, because the world would be unintelligible without a GOD; but I could not love GOD, because I could not love a mere abstract essence; I could not love a mere power. The Mohammedans cannot love Allah; they are afraid of Allah, as they call their deity. I can love JESUS CHRIST, because He is lovable. He lives before me in a way I can understand; He lives among men in a way that is intelligible to my mind; He appeals to my heart—His strength, His love of children, His tenderness to the weak and the sick. " See how we prevail nothing; the whole world has gone after Him "—they said that even in those days, and how much more can we say it now, when thousands and tens of thousands are being converted every year to One whom, having not seen, they love ! Thus we understand more clearly what we have in the Incarnation, and what we should have lost without it. The second thing I should have lost without the Incarnation is that when I knelt down I should have no idea what GOD was like, and should find it difficult to feel any love for Him.

3. Then, thirdly, I should not know, you would not know, what you were to be like in your life. Imagine

## The Incarnation

yourself sitting down and not believing in the Incarnation, and asking yourself what you ought to be like. You might have the Commandments, but they would not be anything like enough to give you an intelligible idea. What the boy in the office brought up as a Christian now says is, " What would JESUS do ?" What the statesman asks, if he is a Christian, when he is dealing with a difficult problem, is, " What would JESUS do ?" You who have tried to do what is right in your life, that is the sort of question you would ask. What would He do about this question or that if He was Bishop of London ? It is the only standard I have to guide me in my life. I have an intelligent idea now of what I ought to be like, and you have an intelligent idea of what you ought to be like. But if it was not for the Incarnation we should have none at all. We should not understand what GOD was like ; we should not know what we were to be like.

4. Then, again, how far off GOD would be ! I was asked a question earlier in the Mission as to how it was possible for prayer to go so many million miles. When a boy is praying in London, how can his prayer go so many millions of miles till it reaches God ? It is very natural to ask the question ; but the answer is very clear—that GOD is not millions of miles away at all. " He is about our path and our bed, and He knoweth all our ways,"

> " Nearer He is than breathing,
> Closer than hands and feet."

How do we know that ? I should not know it unless in some way GOD had revealed Himself ; unless the SON

## The Incarnation

of GOD had come and said, "He that hath seen Me hath seen the FATHER"; unless some one had bridged over the great gulf between GOD and man, and made us one again. I might have imagined that my prayers really had to go a great distance, and might have conceived the idea that they had to go millions of miles. As I said last week, GOD is listening to you, the whole of GOD; He knows you by name. GOD the FATHER calls to you, GOD the SON calls to you, GOD the HOLY GHOST calls to you; He will pray in us with groanings that cannot be uttered. But you do not know this except through the Incarnation.

5. And then, fifthly, there is no possibility of Atonement without the Incarnation. I shall in due course take the love of the TRINITY in the Atonement, but I only mention it now to show that no Atonement is possible without the Incarnation. First, because the SON of GOD had to come and make Himself one with us before anything He did could possibly affect our standing at all. He made Himself one with us first—our elder Brother—or else He could not have made any propitiation for our fallen race. But my point now is that if we had no Incarnation, we should have had no Atonement for sin. It would have been impossible.

And, therefore, if you will consider all this, and see that without the Incarnation we should be left with no answer to suffering, no knowledge of what GOD is like, no knowledge what we are to be like, no certainty that GOD was near, no Atonement, then you will understand a little better what it means when I say again as my message now, "GOD so loved the world, that He gave His only-begotten SON." No

## The Incarnation

wonder we have it in St. Paul's Cathedral in Latin, so that anyone who comes in there from any part of the world may, from this almost universally understood language, understand it, or have a chance of understanding it—" GOD so loved " speaks in stone down St. Paul's Cathedral.

II. My second point is that this has always been the Christian religion. Let us not spend time on that, because I was a very long time speaking to the students at University College* on this point. There has never been any other Christian religion except this—never. St. Paul believed this. This was his religion. " GOD sent forth His SON made of a woman, made under the law." " GOD sent forth His SON." How can you reconcile that with JESUS CHRIST being only a very good man ? " Declared to be the SON of GOD with power." Does that sound like a very good man ? " Through Whom are all things." Is that the sort of thing you would say about a man ? " Who, though He was rich, yet for our sakes became poor." When was He ever rich as man ? Never. From those four undisputed Epistles of St. Paul—the two to the Corinthians, Romans and Galatians—I have already proved to demonstration that St. Paul believed that the Incarnation was the centre of the Christian religion. Take St. Peter and read what he says about " the Shepherd and Bishop of our souls," to see what he believed. Take St. John. This is St. John : " GOD so loved the world, that He gave His only-begotten SON." Take the old Christian liturgies—take a hymn like the *Gloria in Excelsis*, that has

\* See page 268.

## The Incarnation

come down to us from the beginning; you find the same thing: "Thou art the Everlasting SON." Take the Nicene Creed, which the early Church fought about with those who did not believe, and its final shape states that the SON was of the very substance with the FATHER, the same, identically the same substance with the FATHER. And I could prove to you—only I shall not go further into that now—that what I preach now was at the beginning, has been up to now, and always must be, the Christian religion. The Incarnation practically is the Christian religion.

III. Then, thirdly, notice how the love of the TRINITY, of each Person of the TRINITY, comes into the Incarnation. One of the most beautiful things which we are seeing in our religion is the way in which the Persons of the HOLY TRINITY work together in all that is done. I have showed you how They work together in answer to prayer. In the Incarnation GOD the FATHER gives His SON. We used to hear years ago about the Sacrifice on the Cross being made to pacify an angry FATHER. It is GOD the FATHER'S idea; it springs from Him, the source of action. He *gave* His only SON. GOD the SON freely comes forth from the Godhead: "Lo, I come to do Thy will, O GOD!" And men say this is immoral! I have heard it said that the doctrine of the Atonement is an immoral doctrine. He freely came forth of mere goodwill. GOD the HOLY GHOST is the agent of the Incarnation. "The HOLY GHOST shall come upon thee, and the power of the Highest shall overshadow thee; therefore, the holy Thing that shall be born of thee shall be called the SON of GOD." That is the announcement on the

## The Incarnation

Feast of the Annunciation. The Incarnation, then, is a marvellous thing. We are so accustomed to it that we forget what it means—the awful and Divine plan of the HOLY TRINITY, the three Persons, GOD the FATHER, GOD the SON, and GOD the HOLY GHOST, Who reveal at last Their great idea—the secret which had been kept from the foundation of the world. This was Their great plan from the beginning.

IV. And, if we believe it, what effect ought it to have upon our lives ? I will ask anyone who follows me, and so far, perhaps, has not realised up to now what an astounding thing the Incarnation is, to ask himself, " If I believe that astounding event, what ought I to be ?" The careless person who comes into church when he happens to feel inclined, and when he has nothing much else to do, and who rather patronises religion ? Do you really think that can be the right attitude of one who believes in the Incarnation ? Perhaps it is possible that some of us may have been like that once ; is it possible that some of us are like that now ? But anyone must see that if this astounding thing is true there is something almost horrible in an attitude like that—patronising GOD, patronising the HOLY TRINITY—regarding it as rather a favour to come and look in at church. There must be something wrong in that. Therefore, go down upon your knees, if there be anyone who has been patronising the HOLY TRINITY, and say, " GOD the FATHER, GOD the SON, and GOD the HOLY GHOST, have mercy upon me for my presumption."

No ! the answer of those who believe in the Incarnation must be clearly something different from

## The Incarnation

that. It must mean, must it not ?—I want to carry you with me, and in preaching to you I speak to each one of you—it must mean, if I believe that, a life of growing purity. If I may have the SON of GOD within me; if He loves me, and gave Himself for me like that; if He has come like a good shepherd over the hills to find me, and has found me, then I must live a life, in His strength, of something like correspondence to His; I must confess the sins that I have done; I must be perfectly plain about what my life has been, and how careless and unworthy it has been, if I feel it has been so. Then I must not be content with that. Having got myself straight with GOD, I must ask Him to come to my heart.

> "Come to my heart, LORD JESUS:
> There is room in my heart for Thee."

And nothing short of that will do at all. That is what He has come for. He has come down from Heaven to earth to make Himself one with us, to come inside every one of us and live His life over again in us, that we may be CHRISTS in the home, in the diocese, in the business place, in the warehouse. That is what He has come for. The Christian religion is not saying "I am saved." There has been a great deal too much unreality in Christians. It is not a legal quibble by which we can be saved, whatever happens. We have to be changed, inside and out, by having the power of JESUS CHRIST in us—nothing less. That is what the Incarnation is for. And I want to ask you, very lovingly and very earnestly, is that the case with you ? Have you taken JESUS into your heart ? Do you want Him ? There was a certain place where they did not want Him at all;

## *The Incarnation*

they asked Him to depart out of their coasts. They found that if He stayed among them they would lose money. At another place, we are told, there was no room in the inn; they were so busy with other people. I wonder whether that is the case with any of you here. Some people think they would lose money if they were Christians; they would have to live a rather more strictly honest life, and would lose a good deal of custom. Or there may be others who have really no room, and do not like to say so. It does not sound quite the right thing to say that they have no room for Him in the inn of their soul; but they are so busy with other things, they have so many social engagements, so many friendships to keep up, there is no room for JESUS in their house. Well, He comes again, He comes again now, to make the great offer which He came down from Heaven to earth to make to each one, as though there was not another one, and says: " Behold, I stand at the door and knock; I cannot come in unless I am asked." The great question is whether you will ask Him in or not. Is it worth while keeping Him out for all those other things? Why not turn them out and have JESUS CHRIST within? It does not mean turn out your work. You will go back to your work nurses, factory girls, business men, workmen, but you will go back changed people if you take CHRIST back with you. And it will be far better to say at once to some one, "I am a changed man, with different ideals." There is nothing better than committing yourself at once to the new life. The man who drank should say at once: " That is all over now." The man who has never been inside a church

## The Incarnation

for six months should say, " I will go regularly now to show my gratitude." The man who has never said a prayer, pray to-night ; you may never have another chance ; it may be the last knock this very evening. But, if you let Him in, if you say in your heart,

> " Thou didst leave Thy throne and Thy kingly crown
> When Thou camest to earth for me,
> But in Bethlehem's home was there found no room
> For Thy holy Nativity ;
> O, come to my heart, LORD JESUS !
> There is room in my heart for Thee !"

then He will come in, and, though His coming in may mean sacrifice, and may mean trouble, and may mean the hatred of the world, may mean being unpopular, never mind : you will have found the treasure of the earth, and when He comes in He will bring joy that no man can take from you.

# St. Giles's

*WEDNESDAY EVENING*

## ANSWERS TO QUESTIONS

**1. Is it wrong to have a great fear of death? Ever since I have been a child I have been afraid of death, and I cannot get over it, although I am now eighteen.**

The answer certainly is that the fear of death in itself, the not wishing to die, is not sin. It would be unnatural for a young person of eighteen, or in the prime of life for the matter of that, to wish to die. Love of life is natural to us all, and is satisfied by the promise, " He asked life of Thee, and Thou gavest him a long life, even for ever and ever." But there is no doubt that this morbid fear of death must be conquered. I might tell again a story I have often told before, for the comfort of that young soul. A girl said to me when she was very near death : " I feel the great shadow coming down, down, down upon me, every moment nearer, and I am terrified." I said to her, praying in my heart what answer I should give her, that she might not be terrified of death : " Well, you would not mind my picking you up, and taking you into the next room, would you ?" " Oh no, Bishop," she said ; " I should trust you." " Well," I said, " think of Some One ten thousand times stronger and kinder than I am just coming and picking you up, and taking you into the next room." " I will think of that," she said. And when I next saw her she was lying dead with a smile upon her face. In other words, we must believe in the tenderness and

## Answers to Questions

strength of JESUS CHRIST. " Though thou goest into the valley of the shadow of death, thou needest fear no evil, for I am with thee." Just as we receive grace to live by, we shall receive grace to die by when the time comes. Try, therefore, to banish that terror of death.

2. "**My GOD, My GOD, why hast Thou forsaken Me? If it be possible, let this cup pass from Me." To me, says the writer, it is one of the strongest assurances we have of Divine understanding and sympathy; but a friend of mine, who has been recently influenced by a Unitarian, has asked me how I reconcile that first utterance with the Divine personality of CHRIST, and why an omniscient Deity should shrink from a self-appointed sacrifice.**

The answer is that our LORD JESUS CHRIST was perfect man as well as perfect GOD, and that when He uttered that cry, He was tasting, so far as it was possible for Him, the sense of being deserted by GOD the FATHER. As Mrs. Browning said:

" It went up from the Holy's lips, amid His lost creation,
  That of the lost, no son should use those words of desolation."

It was far worse than death to taste that sense of darkness and desolation. When, therefore, that cry rings out on Good Friday, it is the SAVIOUR of the world tasting the worst for us. Yet was He forsaken ? Listen to what He says: " My GOD, my GOD !" all the time showing that, when we are feeling a sense of desolation, we are to say during the darkness, " My GOD, my GOD !" And what will happen ? The peace will come back to us as to Him; as we always remember, on Good Friday, the darkness rolled away, and He says, " FATHER, into Thy hands I commend My spirit." The darkness was past, and the light shone again.

Then as to the other saying, " Let this cup pass from Me."

## Answers to Questions

There we see the real struggle to bring the human will into perfect conformity with the Divine will. Our LORD was really tempted; He was really tried. The whole thing is a drama, a mockery, and no help to us, if He did not feel the temptation. He was really tempted, and He never fell. He did perfectly conform His human will to the Divine will, but it was a real struggle to do so. With the human will again and again He had to pray: " If it be possible, let this cup pass from Me; nevertheless, not My will, but Thine be done." Then, after the prayer, He went forth strengthened. The Divine will bound the human will to bear what He had to bear next day. That is exactly what we have to pray for. Some of you may be facing some terrible sorrow now—the death of some friend, or you may have been told by the doctor you have got some disease that may take away your life. You are quite right to pray, " If it be possible, let this cup pass from me," so long as you add, " nevertheless, not my will, but Thine be done."

3. Then comes a simple, but a very touching question about evil thoughts:

**I cannot get rid of evil thoughts, although I have tried my hardest. I do not want to think them—I hate and loathe them—but they will come; they do not seem to come from my own mind. What shall I do?**

Do you not remember that excellent chapter in Dr. Dale's book on the Ephesians, in which he argues the certainty of the existence of an evil spirit, and that these temptations are " the fiery darts of the wicked one," and adds that the very fact of your feeling that they are not your own ought to be a comfort to you? He says that it is one of the comforts of his life to know that the dark, dreadful things which occur to his mind were not from himself, but were temptations of the evil spirit. And what you will find is this: that if you put up the shield of faith you will catch the fiery darts of the wicked on it. And if you

## Answers to Questions

say when those darts come, "GOD, help me; JESUS, help me; HOLY SPIRIT, help me," you will find, as thousands have often found before, that the dark thought goes, that the passionate impulse cools down, some power of self-control comes from Some One--we know it comes from GOD—and you must not mind, you must not think GOD has deserted you because perhaps for a long time this struggle goes on. St. Paul himself said: "I must keep under my body and bring it into subjection: lest that by any means, when I have preached to others, I myself should be a castaway." These evil thoughts are not a sign that you are wicked, but a sign that you must go on holding fast by GOD and resisting them, and little by little you will find self-control become easier.

### 4. Should I go to the Presbyterian Church, or to other places of worship, Roman Catholic or otherwise?

It is perfectly clear that we ought, all of us, to make up our minds as to what we believe about the Church and stick to it. If we make up our minds that we are Presbyterians, after real study of the question, we had better go to our Presbyterian place of worship. If we are Churchpeople, we ought to come to our Church; of course, that is a quite sound and clear thing to do. As I should say to a Presbyterian, "Go to your place of worship," so I should say to a Churchman, "Come to your place of worship." It is a question of principle when it becomes a habit of life. I cannot imagine any persons growing up strong determined people who had no principle as regards the place of worship to which they went.

### 5. Why does GOD allow some people so little chance in the world, and let their life be cut short in the midst of their sin?

This arises from an answer I gave before to the question why it was that good people were cut off and the useless ones—as the questioner said –left. I answered that by saying

## Answers to Questions

that I believed they were promoted to higher service. But now this questioner asks: "No, my difficulty is not that. It is why people are cut off in their sins and their carelessness." It is impossible for me to answer that question, because, unless I had the knowledge of every human soul which GOD has, I could not say why one soul is summoned from this world or not at any particular time. I answered what underlies the question before. When self-will ceases, hell ceases, but the stiffening of any will in sin, until it is unable to turn, is what CHRIST warns us against. But it would be impossible, except for GOD Himself, to say why one soul is called away at any given time from this world rather than at another time.

6. Next is evidently a perfectly honest question by a business girl as to whether it is wrong ever to go to the theatre.

**I find the theatre a means of recreation occasionally; but I am in doubt as to whether I am doing right.**

Personally, I believe that, if the play to which that girl goes is a thoroughly good, sound, moral play, with nothing whatever to warp her character or degrade her mind, it occasionally is a perfectly legitimate recreation for her. I believe myself that the line which some have taken about theatres and plays is altogether wrong. On the other hand, I cannot shut my eyes to the possibility of bad plays, and as Chairman of the Public Morality Council it has been my constant aim that we must move the whole of the moral opinion of London not to tolerate either shows or plays in our midst which will lead away the young.

**7. Should I read books on Sunday other than good books?**

Of course, Sunday is a day which is given us for the purpose of uplifting our souls to GOD. It is the one rest day, and, although every one must exercise their own discretion about

## Answers to Questions

the particular book, the thing to do is to have a principle. Does what you do on Sunday leave you more ready for working for GOD in the week ? If you take that principle, and put GOD first on Sunday all through, I think, if you ask the guidance of the HOLY SPIRIT, you will not have very much difficulty in deciding what are the books to read on Sunday during your leisure time.

**8. Will you tell me if a friend whom we have lost can see us down here and knows what we are doing, and if we shall know each other by-and-by ?**

Of course, that question occurs over and over again every Mission, and I can only say that I believe that it is so. I believe that five minutes after death we are the same as five minutes before ; that our fathers, mothers, friends, sisters, brothers are still our fathers, mothers, friends, sisters, and brothers. CHRIST respects human ties. When He restored the young man, He gave him back to his mother. I believe that He is always reuniting mothers to their sons in Paradise, far more than we are apt to think. " We are seven in family although two may lie beneath the yew-tree in the graveyard." The sentence in the creed, "I believe in the Communion of Saints," ought to be a very much greater reality than it often is.

**9. We read in the Scriptures that at the last day we shall be judged, and the sheep will be separated from the goats, yet one hears so often from the pulpit that judgment is going on all the time—" Whatsoever a man soweth, that shall he also reap." Is not this a contradiction ?**

I do not think myself that there is any contradiction really in that. The judgment is going on every day. Take, for instance, all the little decisions we have made—the word you said at business, the temptations that you have either conquered or yielded to—they are all an irrevocable record and you are either a better man or a worse man than you were

## Answers to Questions

twelve hours ago. But in another sense the judgment is in the future. All this comes out at the end. What is the result of it all? What does the character turn out to be after all the discipline and probation of life? It is, therefore, quite true to say judgment is going on every day. It is also true to say everything will come out clear at the judgment day.

10. **Although I have been a Christian for over twenty years, I do not understand the doctrine of the TRINITY. Will you explain it a little?**

I could not do more in answer to that question than point to a book which has come out lately by Mr. Illingworth on the TRINITY: you can get it at any library now. It is a very beautiful book, and as clear a one as could possibly be written on such a deep subject. What I have been trying to show all this Mission—which is on the love of the TRINITY—is how practical, how comforting it is, and how much it goes right to the very core of all our lives, to believe in GOD the FATHER, GOD the SON, and GOD the HOLY GHOST. The Great Truth is revealed to us, it is told us; otherwise we could never have known it. I have tried to show you the practical bearing of it. People look on the doctrine of the TRINITY as a sort of far-away doctrine, but it is the one thing that makes our hearts warm towards GOD; it is the one thing which makes the love of GOD possible. Without the existence of the HOLY TRINITY how could GOD have been Love before Heaven and earth were made? He must have loved someone. If GOD the FATHER loved the Holy SON, and GOD the HOLY GHOST sounded the depth of the love of each, then GOD is Love Himself. As a matter of fact, then, those who think the doctrine of the TRINITY has put GOD far off make a most curious mistake. It is because we believe in GOD the FATHER, GOD the SON, and GOD the HOLY GHOST that GOD is so near us.

11. **Is it right, being very ill, to have the Holy Communion at home? The writer feels the consecration**

## Answers to Questions

ought to take place in a consecrated building, or at least at a consecrated table.

I do not think that our Prayer Book holds that view at all. If you cannot come to church, you are perfectly justified and encouraged to have the service of the Holy Communion in the place in which you live, as long as there can be a reverent service held there. The questioner should not hesitate to ask her parish priest to bring her the Holy Communion, and he is bound to do so.

**12. "The smoke of their torment ascendeth for ever and ever." This has always been a stumbling-block to my husband.**

We must not take these visions in the Revelation as a literal description of what is actually taking place. People are sometimes so prosaic in their interpretation of the Bible. We are given a series of visions, often in the Old Testament and often in the New. I know that they have a perfectly real meaning, yet to imagine that this passage implies physical torment which is to last for ever would be, in my opinion, giving a false interpretation to Holy Scripture.

**13. I looked upon Confirmation as only an admission to the Holy Communion, and did not expect the gift of the HOLY GHOST. May I believe that I did receive the gift in spite of my ignorance?**

Surely that is the very thing we mean when we say that GOD hears our prayers "above what we ask or think." You probably were not taught what Confirmation was, but GOD gave you the gift, and what you have to do is to "stir up the gift of GOD now which is in you through the laying on of hands." It is still in you, but you have to stir up, as St. Paul says, into a flame* "the gift of GOD which still is in you through the laying on of hands."

**14. Are war and Christianity consistent? The complacent attitude of really good men towards this awful system of settling national differences is surprising.**

* ἀναζωπυρεῖν.

## Answers to Questions

Of course, war can only exist in an undeveloped, a not fully developed, Christian world. What our LORD did with regard to slavery is very instructive. He did not denounce slavery, but He put a principle of brotherhood in the world which finally abolished slavery. Our LORD did not lead a slave revolt—some people may think that He ought to have done so; no, He planted a principle in the world which finally made slavery impossible. So He has planted a principle in the world which finally will make war impossible. But while it took centuries to abolish slavery, it may take many more centuries to abolish war. What we have to do is, by our prayers and by our influence, more and more to get arbitration substituted for war; to encourage anything like the Hague Conference; to use every means to get that spirit into the world which finally will make war impossible. It is not, then, at all inconsistent to pray for the abolition of war, and yet be prepared as a nation for war. GOD can only get out of each age the morality of which each age is capable. The terrible wars of Joshua—why did such things occur ? Why did Abraham think for a moment that it was right to sacrifice his son ? Because GOD can only train each age gradually, and get out of each age the morality of which that age is capable. We have not yet grown to the measure of the stature of the fullness of CHRIST. All nations throughout the world should try to make war impossible, as, please GOD, it will be some day.

**15. Is it fair to say we know a thing if we only believe it ?**

I can only answer that this is St. John's own language: " We *know* that our fellowship is with the FATHER and with His SON JESUS CHRIST." We know it. There is such a thing as intuitive knowledge, and I venture to say that many of you who began as young men or young women to pray in faith, testing the great experiment, testing the great promise, now *know* that your prayers are answered—know it by intuitive

## Answers to Questions

knowledge, by experience. I have said in the passage criticised\* that it was not mathematical knowledge, but that the knowledge which came from faith was true knowledge. What I say to you now is, that if you begin during this Mission (if you have not yet started) serving GOD and praying to GOD, and taking these great promises as true, you will *know* they are true before many years have passed.

16. Next comes an old question often asked in days gone by in Bethnal Green, but evidently asked now in genuine difficulty:

**In Gen. iv. 17 it is written concerning Cain and his wife. We take it that Adam and Eve were the first man and woman, and their children were Cain and Abel; how is it possible for Cain to have taken a wife? I have never heard it explained.**

In a little book which I wrote fifteen years ago in Bethnal Green, called "Old Testament Difficulties,"† I wrote on this difficulty: There is no one, it is said, for him to have married except his own mother, Eve. But this is one of those gratuitous assumptions which are so freely made by those who make use of the argument from silence. According to this school of interpreters, whatever is not mentioned in the Bible is therefore asserted not to have happened. In the New Testament this argument is pressed in the face of the assertion of St. John that if everything had been written, "The world itself would not have contained the books which should be written." In the case of these dim events in the far-off ages, of which a short and hasty summary is given in the Bible, it is still more absurd to press such an argument. One hundred and thirty years had elapsed before the birth of Seth, who apparently was born very soon after the murder of Abel; this would have allowed ample time for one or even two

\* In the "Mission of the Spirit" (Gardner, Darton, and Co., Ltd.).
† Published by the S.P.C.K.

## Answers to Questions

generations to have grown up of whom no mention is made, except incidentally. Incidentally, however, others are mentioned. Cain was afraid that " whosoever found him would slay him " ; he is able to " begin building " a city which, though probably only at first a collection of rude huts, must have involved some sort of a community, so that it is evident that there was no difficulty in Cain finding a wife, though doubtless, if the Adamite race was only one, she must have been a blood-relation. In the same connexion, it may be mentioned that the puzzling expression, " The sons of GOD saw the daughters of men that they were fair," is best explained by an intermarriage between the descendants of the godlike race of Seth with the descendants of Cain—a mistake which helped to produce the state of depravity that preceded the Flood.

# St. Giles's

*WEDNESDAY EVENING*

## VII

## THE GROWTH OF THE CHRIST-LIFE WITHIN US

" My little children, for whom I travail in birth again until CHRIST be formed in you."—GAL. iv. 19.

I AM going to take a very tender and a very touching passage. When the tender, loving heart of St. Paul is yearning over his people, this is what he says:

" My little children, for whom I travail in birth again until CHRIST be formed in you."

I take that passage for this reason. We ended up on Sunday by all saying together:

" Come to my heart, LORD JESUS:
There is room in my heart for Thee."

That was our answer to the love of the TRINITY as shown in the Incarnation. Now, the question is, What does that really mean? What I think is such a danger in Missions is being content with vague language. You hear people say, " Come to JESUS," or, as we said:

" Come to my heart, LORD JESUS:
There is room in my heart for Thee."

## The Christ-Life

What, then, do we really mean by that, and what does St. Paul mean when he says, " I travail in birth until CHRIST be formed in you "? He means five things.

1. First, a living faith in the Incarnation; it means that we believe it to be true that " GOD so loved the world, that He gave His only-begotten SON," and that all that we see happen before our eyes in the New Testament was the revelation of GOD, and that this was the bringing down the love of GOD to us.

2. Then, secondly, he means trust in a Person. If all this is true, JESUS is as much alive now, He is as much here with us as He ever was; He is the same yesterday, to-day, and for ever. As I have said, it makes all the difference to one's idea of the Church; if people imagine that the Church is a kind of ecclesiastical organisation, no wonder they do not care about it, and no wonder it seems to stand between them and CHRIST. But if you picture the living CHRIST moving up and down every day with us, now picking up the little children at the font, and saying, " Suffer the little children to come unto Me, and forbid them not ;" if you picture Him breathing on us at Confirmation, and saying, " Receive ye the HOLY GHOST," standing with us by the altar-rail when we kneel, and saying, " Here is the bread of life and the wine of love ; take, eat, drink ;" and that it is a living CHRIST doing this all the time—then the Church is a different thing. It is the hands and feet of CHRIST as He goes after the lost sheep. It binds us to CHRIST. The second thing then (if this is true) which St. Paul means is that there is a living Person, alive now, to Whom we are to give ourselves and Whom we are to trust. He stands

## The Christ-Life

at the door of our hearts and knocks, and, therefore, we really are to say to that Divine Person :

"Come to my heart, LORD JESUS."

3. Then, thirdly—and this is where we so often go wrong in our ideas—having received JESUS into our hearts, having let what a great writer has called the "expulsive power of a new affection" come in to drive out the bad, we imagine that nothing more is to happen. But, on the contrary, when CHRIST has come in He has to grow in us. That is the point. St. Paul's picture is of a child growing gradually in the womb until it be fully formed. In another Epistle the child is to grow on until it becomes a full-grown man. That is the image which St. Paul often uses. CHRIST has to come into us and live His life over again in us ; to possess our minds so that we may have the mind of CHRIST. I was reading lately in a book on St. Paul : " We are to have the *mind* of CHRIST, we are to have the *heart* of CHRIST, we are to have the *spirit* of CHRIST. And even our bodies are to be members of CHRIST, and all the Christian life is a gradual growth of CHRIST in us until He possesses the whole man and the whole woman." But it is a gradual thing. People say, "Oh, I cannot be a Christian ; I feel this difficulty, I feel this temptation. I feel this weakness." But you must expect to do so even after you have accepted CHRIST. CHRIST has to grow in you until He has possession of every power, and every fault in you, but the conquest is a gradual thing.

4. Fourthly, it is often done with the mother's

## The Christ-Life

pangs: "I travail in pain, I travail in birth, for you till CHRIST be formed in you." It is not only that the pastor, St. Paul, who is loving his children, has to bear the pains and travail himself, but it often means sacrifice and discipline and pain and struggle while the CHRIST is growing in a man or woman. It is not easy at all, the growth of the CHRIST-life. As it grows it has to kill the old Adam, and the old Adam dies hard in every man and woman. What so often distresses people is the pain of the Christian life, the discipline of it, and the struggle of it, but the travail of it is just what we should expect.

5. Fifthly—and this is the most comforting thing of all—if the process means the mother's pangs, the end is the mother's joy—"For joy that a man is born into the world." "For joy!" That is what we have to aim at: to have the joy of having CHRIST formed in us at last, and having that formed CHRIST growing on into the measure of the stature of the fullness of CHRIST.

Now, that is the plan of the Christian life according to the metaphor which St. Paul puts before us. How does it apply to you and to me? We have to answer that. (*a*) First—and it sounds an awful question—do we *want* to have JESUS CHRIST formed in us? You might say, "Oh, of course I do, Bishop—of course I want to!" But it is not enough to say that. If we want to, it must be absolutely the one desire of our life; everything must be sacrificed to it. Why I ask the question "Do we want to?" is because people say vaguely, feebly, that they do want to, without counting the cost at all. If we want to have CHRIST formed in us, and if we really mean "Come to my

## The Christ-Life

heart, LORD JESUS," everything must be turned out to make room. It does not mean that we are not to have innocent joys, pleasures, recreation, or half-holidays, our happy home-life, if we have it; but it means that everything which conflicts with the CHRIST-life growing in us must be put aside. We must not say "Come to my heart, LORD JESUS," if we do not mean to put aside everything which is incompatible with the growth within us of the life of JESUS CHRIST. Now, are we ready to do that? The Mission has done us no good if we are not ready. If you want to keep that quarrelsome temper, if you want to keep up that quarrel with your neighbour, if you want to keep that little sin—which you thought, perhaps, too small to be noticed—or keep on that pleasant habit which you know is wrong, or that false friendship—you cannot have JESUS CHRIST formed in you; none of us can. Therefore, I do hope we shall try and answer the first question together: " I want, I am going to try, and I am going to make it my great prayer that CHRIST may be formed in me, and that is going to be the aim of my life. It will mean work for others; it will mean unselfishness; it will mean a less self-centred life; but I do want it."

(b) Secondly, do we believe enough to have it? Is our faith clear in this mighty thing of which we have been speaking? Do we believe in the love of the TRINITY as revealed in the Incarnation? If not, why not? There is no reason against it at all. I defy anyone to show a single reason against it. What fails is the imagination in taking in so great a thing. Therefore, what I want to-night is an exercise of our imagination—that is, of our power of picturing a really great

## The Christ-Life

incident, so that with wonder, love, and praise we shall feel a trustful belief in the glorious Incarnation. Put aside your doubt; try and expand your mind to take in the great and glorious plan of the HOLY TRINITY.

(c) Thirdly, are we completely trusting?

> " Take my life, and let it be
> Consecrated, LORD, to Thee."

Now, is there a single one here who has not said that? Are you conscious that you have not said it? CHRIST cannot be formed in us until we have made the great personal surrender.

> " Take my life and let it be
> Consecrated, LORD, to Thee "—

the whole of my life—and you will find, instead of being an unhappy man or an unhappy woman, you have never been happy before, because such consecration lights up the most monotonous life, and makes every life into a romance; every day becomes worth living—and you have not too many days to live; every day becomes a treasure which you are to make use of for CHRIST.

(d) Fourthly, are we ready to use the means of grace by which the CHRIST-life becomes strong in us? A child, even before it is born, has to be fed and strengthened, and afterwards to be fed and strengthened to grow to a full man. Are we strengthening and fostering the CHRIST-life in us, to use St. Paul's own metaphor? Do we pray every day regularly and earnestly? Are you confirmed? If not, why not? Do you not want all the strength that you can get, in

## The Christ-Life

what the Bible calls "the falling of the HOLY GHOST"? Do you read your Bible, keep the example of CHRIST before you, and pray over your Bible? If you are confirmed, do you come to the Communion, and become partakers of the Divine nature, that CHRIST may foster His life in you Himself? If not, why not? Are not these things what you may call the A B C of Christianity? Are they not the simple things which have come down from the beginning, and which, because they are so simple and so deep, therefore are the very things that every earnest Christian ought to feel bound to use, if he wants the CHRIST-life fostered and fed within him?

(e) Fifthly, are we ready for the travail, and are we looking for the joy? What has Lent been to you? Have you killed out everything which is hindering the CHRIST-life? Or are you sparing yourself the necessary pain? Are you cutting away what is wrong? You must not mind the pain, because of the joy that is coming. "A woman, when she is in travail, has sorrow because her hour is come, but when she is delivered of the child she remembereth no more the anguish, for joy that a man is born into the world." And if you only realise the joy in store for you when the CHRIST-life within you has grown, and your thoughts and mind and body are at the disposal of CHRIST, then you will not mind the pain.

(f) Lastly, are you travailing in pain, as St. Paul was, over anyone else? Is there anything in your life like this tender, motherly love: "My little children, for whom I travail in birth again until CHRIST be formed in you"? What about your own children? Are you watching over them with tender love till

## *The Christ-Life*

CHRIST be formed in them ? What about your Sunday-school children ? Are you teaching any ? Are you doing anything for anybody else ? What about your friend ? Are you trying to help that friend to have the CHRIST-life formed in her or in him ? Do you not see that when we say,

> " Come to my heart, LORD JESUS:
> There is room in my heart for Thee,"

this ought to mean the development within us of a love which travails in pain to bring out the CHRIST-life in others ? There ought to be a pastoral instinct developed in every one, because in that way we are led to help one another. Do you not see, then, that " Come to my heart, LORD JESUS," has a very deep meaning in it ; that we have first to picture to our minds the living CHRIST Who came down to bring home the love of the TRINITY to us, and then have to ask Him to come in knowing what it means ? Oh, my people, I pray over you. I dare not use St. Paul's words, " I travail in pain until CHRIST be formed in you," but I pray for you all, and long over you that CHRIST will live and grow in you, and that every one of you may go out as a CHRIST to the world.

# ALL SOULS', LANGHAM PLACE

*SUNDAY EVENING*

## ANSWERS TO QUESTIONS

1. **A poor soul, who has been in great anxiety about a brother who died, apparently, in sin and unforgiven—we cannot say whether forgiven or not—and who has been converted during the Mission, wants to know whether GOD is displeased when we are unhappy.**

It is quite clear that we were meant to be in a happy state of having "joy and peace in believing." Christians were meant to be the happiest people in the world. But, on the other hand, it is quite true that sometimes for a time a cloud comes, but when that cloud came over our SAVIOUR, and He said, "My GOD, my GOD, why hast Thou forsaken Me?" He was not really forsaken by GOD. He had no sin. Therefore it is quite clear that sometimes a cloud of depression is allowed to come over us, and we must just bear it. "My GOD, my GOD!" said the SAVIOUR all through the cloud. Therefore let no one despair; GOD is still their GOD, and if we hold on through the darkness, that darkness will pass away.

2. **A difficult question is asked by one in great poverty whose husband thinks that he deceived the Income Tax authorities in the past, and she wishes to know whether in their poverty he must pay back any sum of which he may have defrauded the revenue.**

## Answers to Questions

Certainly, I should say that at all costs we must stand by our conscience. When we see the mention of "conscience-money" in the papers, it is a sign of the reality of conscience in the world. But I think the writer should make herself quite sure that her husband—who seems to be suffering mentally—is not under some delusion. If not, the duty must be done at any cost.

3. One who was at St. Anne's, Soho, writes: "Being a foreigner, I could not grasp one point in your sermon." It was about the story I told of a boy on London Bridge in the rain, poor and lame, who was heard saying to himself, "I could not bear it but for thinking of the golden gates."

### Does the doctrine of reincarnation explain much of the misery of this life?

The writer is evidently rather taken with the theory of Theosophy, that reincarnation is the explanation of the inequalities and sufferings of this life. It certainly would be some explanation, if it was true. Many people in East London were caught by the idea that when you saw the inequalities and troubles of life, it was a help to believe that the people concerned had sinned in a previous state of existence. I never saw what gospel of comfort it was to poor East London, because the argument was that East London had sinned in a previous state of existence, and that the West End had not. But, as a matter of fact, whether it would be an explanation or not, there is no evidence whatever that we have inhabited some other body previously or lived in some previous state of existence. The more you look at it the more you see that reincarnation is destructive of the idea of the message of the Mission which we have discussed—the Love of the TRINITY in the Incarnation. I am going to preach to you the message of the Mission again now, and I say that Christianity is inconsistent with the theory of reincarnation. John the Baptist was said to be a reincarnation of Elijah, but some one answered in East London, in free and open discussion: "Why did he, then,

## Answers to Questions

appear as Elijah on the Mount of Transfiguration?" According to the usual doctrine of reincarnation, you cannot have a reincarnation back into the form previously inhabited. I spoke about the subject yesterday to a young man who was giving up his religion for Theosophy. I told him that he was giving up the treasure of the world for something for which there is no evidence whatever.

# ALL SOULS', LANGHAM PLACE

*SUNDAY EVENING*

## VIII

## THE LOVE OF THE TRINITY IN THE ATONEMENT

" For if the blood of bulls and of goats, and the ashes of an heifer sprinkling the unclean, sanctifieth to the purifying of the flesh, how much more shall the blood of CHRIST, Who through the eternal SPIRIT offered Himself without spot to GOD, purge your conscience from dead works to serve the living GOD ?"—HEB. ix. 13, 14.

WE come now to one of the most beautiful parts of the Mission message. We have seen the love of the TRINITY in answer to prayer : how GOD the FATHER bends down and hearkens with His hands full of gifts, and GOD the SON kneels by our side and prays for us, and GOD the HOLY GHOST comes within us, and prays in us " with groanings that cannot be uttered," and stirs us up to pray, and makes us live according to the will of GOD ; and how every time we pray we are swept into the life of love of the HOLY TRINITY. We have seen the love of the HOLY TRINITY in the Incarnation ; how They planned it out, because man would be so far off without an Incarnation, because we should have no idea what GOD was like, because we should not know what we had to be like at all, because we should not be certain that GOD

## *The Atonement*

was not thousands and millions of miles away. We saw that, we have thought of that; and some of you will remember how that prophet, Bishop Westcott, pointed out in one of his writings, "The Gospel of the Creation," that it was possible that the Eternal SON of GOD might have come down and taken on Him our human nature, and lived here among His people in joy and happiness, have been worshipped and adored and loved, have told us about GOD, and gone back with the adoration and love of the children of men, with no pain, and no death, and no Crucifixion. We can hardly believe that we owe our greatest gift—" thanks be to GOD for His unspeakable gift!"—simply to our sin. As Bishop Westcott said in substance, From the eternal ages it was probably the design of the HOLY TRINITY that this should happen, that GOD should come and dwell among men, for this would in any case have been the crown of creation; but when man, necessarily given free will if he was to be a reasonable and loving companion of GOD afterwards — for what is the worth of the obedience of a slave ?—given free will that he might learn to love the good and be at last in eternity with GOD, because he had chosen the good—when that man whom GOD loved fell away, turned his powers against GOD, when he used the very powers of his body, which is such a holy thing, and such a sacred thing—there being no sin in the body at all; CHRIST wore the body without sin—when that body and its powers were used to degrade the soul; when the soul that was meant to be so trustful, so loving and humble, was exalted in pride towards GOD Who made it; when,

## The Atonement

instead of caring for one another, the strong defending the weak, the man chivalrous towards every woman because she was his sister in the sight of GOD, men preyed on one another, and satisfied their brutal passions ; when, instead of helping one another that all might have a chance of life, in a mere lust for gold, they trampled the weak under foot—then the HOLY TRINITY had to plan out something else for fallen man. Incarnation was not enough ; there must be something which will satisfy the broken law. If you think of it, a king cannot decree that there shall be no prosecutions for crime throughout his dominions. The moral standard of the empire would go down in six weeks. A judge cannot let off a prisoner the moment he says he is sorry. If he did, imagine the state of England in a year. No. As the HOLY TRINITY in their disappointed love thought over what could be done for the fallen race, the erring, wandering child, the first thing which had to be safeguarded was this : the moral law of the empire of GOD must not be trifled with ; Some One must obey it ; it must be satisfied ; the moral standard of GOD's universe must be sustained ; there must be some offering made for sin, spotless and without blemish ; there must be some life lived out, if necessary, to the death, as a perfect oblation and a perfect example of a perfectly fulfilled law.

That was the first thing that must be done. Secondly, one of Them must go down among the guilty race—guilty, but still loved—and must unite Himself so closely to that guilty race that what He did they did, that what He did in human nature might cover His brethren and His sisters ; that, just as in a

## *The Atonement*

regiment the man in cells would be let out at the inspection for the good name of the regiment, because the good name of the regiment covered him, and he was part of the regiment, so one of the HOLY TRINITY must go down and be so closely united to that human race that His good name would cover them all because they were in Him, and that when His name, His peerless name, was mentioned it might cover all the human race. He must be, as Tennyson said :

> " Nearer than breathing,
> Closer than hands and feet."

That is the second thing.

Thirdly, it must be done for all ; it must cover the 150 drunkards, for instance, in a meeting held lately in Westminster, and the even more guilty men who are responsible for the state of our streets in other ways. It must cover the worst criminal if he is penitent, the most abandoned man, the poor hunted girl, and the poor boy who has never had a chance in the slums, as much as it covers the rich or the well-known or the distinguished. An Atonement, to be made at all, must be an Atonement for all, that not one must be left out, if the great plan of the HOLY TRINITY was to be carried out. That was the third essential thing.

Fourthly, this forgiveness must be no mock thing. It must not be enough for people to go about and say " I am saved," and imagine that saying " I am saved " meant they were. It must be something which meant a moral change in the man or the woman, that while the initial confession, the spontaneous repentance, would be accepted at the moment, it

## *The Atonement*

would be so on the understanding that it developed into a change of life. The penitent thief could be forgiven at once on the cross, but only on the understanding that if he lived he would be a reformed thief; if anyone turned in a church on Sunday evening from their sin, he would be accepted, but on the understanding that he left the church determined, by the grace of GOD, by every motive of gratitude, having seen whither he had been tending, to change his whole life, or the whole thing would be a mockery. There has been too much mockery, too much hypocrisy connected with the Christian religion.

But fifthly—and this is often forgotten—while there would be free and instantaneous forgiveness, followed by moral reformation, we must be content to bear, perhaps for life, the punishment of our sin; the paralysed man to whom was said, "Son, thy sins be forgiven thee," would have a blessed relief, but might have to lie upon a couch as a penalty and as amends for the sins that brought him there; the drunkard or the fallen, while forgiven, might have that weak and shattered constitution to bear to the end, and he must bear it bravely, thankful for his salvation, for his forgiveness, for his moral reformation—bear it patiently and bravely to the end of his life.

And so They decided it should be done, and the great heavens opened, and the miracle ensued which we get so much accustomed to, but which the angels never get accustomed to : down came the SON of GOD from Heaven to earth, and the great pageant was enacted before the eyes of the world. GOD the FATHER gave the SON ; GOD the SON said : " Lo ! I

## *The Atonement*

come to do Thy will, O GOD "; GOD the HOLY SPIRIT was the agent of the Incarnation—for it is expressly said that JESUS CHRIST was " conceived by the HOLY GHOST." When the holy SON laid aside His glory and omnipotent power to put Himself by our side, GOD the HOLY SPIRIT, as we read the story, helped to work the miracles—took part in raising Him from the dead—and according to this majestic verse in the Hebrews had a share in the Atonement: " How much more shall the blood of CHRIST, who through the eternal SPIRIT offered Himself without spot to GOD, purge your conscience from dead works to serve the living GOD ?" And yet this is said to be an immoral doctrine ! This glorious plan of love is non-moral ! We have discovered that after two thousand years, or some people have. This is something which does not affect character ! Well, it is our fault for the way we have preached it, if that is so. I will venture to say that a more glorious story, a more splendid manifestation of Divine love. anything more beautifully planned or more divinely carried out, has never been recorded in the history of our race. In Heaven they never forget it for a moment. " Worthy is the Lamb that was slain to receive glory, and honour, and power ; for Thou wast slain. and hast redeemed us to GOD by Thy blood."

Now, the question is, What effect has this plan of the TRINITY, so nobly executed, had upon your life ? That is the question which I come to ask you, as I ask myself. What is the first effect which it was meant to have ?

The first effect was that there should be no men or women who have not faced their sins without hiding

## The Atonement

one back, who have not without self-deception, without making excuses, confessed them all to GOD, and have received, as the primary beginning of Christian life, a full pardon for all their sins. " I saw the ocean of light and love," as John Wesley says, " flow over the ocean of darkness and death, and in that I saw the infinite love of GOD." And the first question I want to ask you is, Has it yet flowed over you ? Have you tried to find out what your sins are ? We say in a light way, " We know we are sinners." That is practically no good at all. Many a man has repeated the General Confession all his life, and all the time, perhaps, he has got a secret sin in his life which he has never faced at all. And therefore I do hope now that the Mission has reached its crisis—because afterwards it has to issue in praise and thanksgiving—now that it has reached its most critical moment, there shall not be a man who is going on in self-delusion, without having cleansed his conscience or discovered whether he has anything on it or not. Take such questions as these: " Have I obeyed GOD's law of perfect purity in thought and word and deed, and am I doing it now ?" " Have I obeyed GOD's law of love ?" Am I in charity now with everyone, or am I nursing some quarrel which I mean to carry on the moment I leave the church ? Am I obeying the law of love in my relations with others, especially those with whom I work every day ? " If we love not our brother Whom we have seen, how can we love GOD whom we have not seen ?" Am I obeying the law of witness ? " To this end was I born, and for this cause came I into the world, to bear witness to the truth." " Am I a witness to

## *The Atonement*

the truth ? Does everyone know that I am a Christian ? Or do I hide it ? Am I afraid of it being known ? Then I am not bearing witness as the stars and moon witness to the sun." Am I, as a matter of fact, exercising an influence where I work on the other side ? Have I sneered at religion before now ? Am I obeying the law of day by day, one of the great laws of the kingdom—taking one day at a time, trusting day by day ? Or am I worrying ? Am I irritable, fussy about everything ?

Those are only suggested questions on the laws of GOD. Take the Commandments as explained by JESUS CHRIST Himself, and ask yourself quietly such questions, so that we may have a real clearing of the consciences of everybody connected with the Mission. And, as the Prayer Book says, if you cannot do this yourself, go and see your Vicar, or some one else whom you trust, and get him to help you to make your conscience clear. What are we ministers here for but to help our brothers and sisters to peace through JESUS CHRIST our LORD ? The first thing is to find out where we are wrong, and then confess it. The second thing is to lift up the hand of faith and take salvation. There may be some of you who have been really penitent, but who are in a morbidly scrupulous state, who do not have joy in CHRIST, joy in GOD, because they do not believe they are forgiven, who have confessed but have never taken with the hand of faith the great salvation. Let them take it now ; we are meant to have—" joy and peace in believing." We are meant to sing the *Magnificat* at every evensong as forgiven people in the daily service. The whole Prayer Book speaks to us

## The Atonement

of forgiveness. " He that is once cleansed needeth not save to wash his feet, but is clean every whit."

And, thirdly, are we reformed ? are we changed ? are we better tempered ? are we more loving ? are we growing into the righteousness of CHRIST ? Christianity is not some forensic system, which does not touch the character. Our forgiveness was meant to have a moral effect, and there is something wrong with a man who goes on being forgiven and does not get any better. If the blood of CHRIST is to cleanse your conscience from dead works, you ought to be getting more hold over your passions and your temper ; you ought to have more influence in the world, and you ought to be growing in grace, if you are forgiven. Are you doing that ? Ask yourself that. Let us have no unreality about this Mission. If you are simply saying " I am saved," and are going no further than that ; if you imagine there is some way in which the righteousness of CHRIST is to cover you and you are to remain unchanged, you are mistaken. That is not the plan of the TRINITY at all. You were to be changed ; a new heart and a new spirit were to be put within you. Pray to have a new heart and a new spirit, and the mind of CHRIST, because you are forgiven.

And then, lastly, what effect has it upon your life of service ? " How much more shall the blood of CHRIST, Who through the eternal SPIRIT offered Himself without spot to GOD, purge your conscience from dead works "—to do what ?—" to serve the living GOD." That was the whole object. Heaven is not full of pardoned felons. That was not the idea. Heaven was to be full of ransomed saints, faithful

## *The Atonement*

servants, all those who serve GOD in their generation and pass on to their eternal rest. That was the plan of the TRINITY in the Atonement. What are you doing for GOD? I have spoken to men to-day elsewhere\* on "Work," and of the opportunities in this great city. Is there anything more you can do than you are doing? The HOLY TRINITY cries, "Whom shall We send, and who will go for Us in this great city? Who will save the boys? Who will teach the children? Who will bring in the girls who are going wrong?" Cannot you say, because you are forgiven, "Here am I; send me." The Atonement has failed in its great effect unless we offer ourselves back in answer to the love of the TRINITY in loving service for ever. That is the message of the Mission; what is our answer?

\* See p. 303.

# ALL SOULS', LANGHAM PLACE

*WEDNESDAY EVENING*

## ANSWERS TO QUESTIONS

**1. Ought one who sinned years ago against the eighth commandment, and who has confessed her sin, to make restoration?**

It is quite clear confession means restitution, and, although in the case of a sin committed many years ago against some one who perhaps may be dead by this time, it is impossible for restitution literally to be made, I have often myself made those who have confessed some sin against the Seventh Commandment subscribe to some rescue agency as a restitution for what they have done, so that they may be helping to undo in others the work which they themselves have done, the mischief they helped to do years ago. But the writer of this, who, apparently, cannot now make restitution to the people concerned, or does not know those from whom the money, or whatever it was, was taken, must make some form of restitution as best she can. If she cannot find the people, she cannot restore it to them.

**2. If in order to reach Heaven it is necessary for an individual, as far as he prayerfully can, to lead a blameless life, why did CHRIST die, seeing that if the individual had lived this life before CHRIST he would have reached Heaven just the same?**

This is a great misunderstanding. The death of CHRIST is retrospective. CHRIST's death is an eternal event. In the Book of Revelation He is said to be " the Lamb that was

## Answers to Questions

slain from the foundation of the world." Therefore the death of CHRIST, and all that the Atonement meant, affects all, both those who lived before and after, and in all probability, when our LORD went into hell—which means, of course, the place of departed spirits—He went to see what is literally in the Greek the "souls in safe keeping;" He went to teach them, to tell them the glorious news of what He had accomplished for them all. The writer, then, is under a great mistake in imagining that people who lived before CHRIST were really in a different position from those who lived after.

**3. A governess is not allowed to teach the children Christianity, but only allowed to give ethical instruction. Is it her duty to supplement this by Christian instruction unknown to the parents?**

No; certainly not. We must take our stand upon some one principle, and the principle upon which we take our stand in education is the right of the parent, and, however lamentably mistaken they are in imagining that they can bring up their children ethically with no foundation of Christian doctrine, still, a governess employed by them must, if she stays on at her work, act according to what the parents wish, and it would not be right to do evil that good might come.

**4. Was our LORD tempted in all points as we are? He never knew what remorse was, and therefore He was not tempted like as we are.**

It is certainly true that our LORD did not feel remorse, but I should not have said myself that remorse was a temptation. I should have thought remorse was different from temptation; of course, it is perfectly true that our LORD, although tempted in all points, did not have remorse, because He had no sin.

**5. I am puzzled by what has been said regarding Confirmation. Is not the HOLY SPIRIT received in Baptism?**

## Answers to Questions

Quite so. In the Confirmation service we thank GOD for what He has already granted, that the child has been baptized with water and the HOLY GHOST. But, then, we pray that he may receive the HOLY GHOST, the Comforter. The difference is this: in the Bible Confirmation is called "the falling of the HOLY GHOST;" there is the gift of life, given in Baptism, and the HOLY SPIRIT is helping a soul all through the boyish and girlish days in answer to prayer. But of Confirmation, you find this description in the Bible: "Then laid they their hands on them, and they received the HOLY GHOST, for as yet He was fallen upon none of them." What the Bible calls "the falling of the HOLY GHOST" in strength comes in Confirmation. We sing in the hymn

> "And every virtue we possess,
> And every victory won,
> And every thought of holiness,
> Are His alone."

If you look at the Confirmation service you will find that the gift of the SPIRIT in Baptism is acknowledged.

### 6. Can a man be a good man who never attends church?

Certainly; we must never for a single moment say that good is not good wherever we find it. That man who does not attend church is losing a glorious chance; he is unawakened to his privilege, but, if he is living up to his lights, we have no right to say goodness is not goodness. In fact, in our day, numbers of people who imagine that they do not believe in Christianity are breathing the air of Christianity. There are thousands of unconscious Christians. It has been a difficulty to many to find how good many an agnostic is. But they forget that most agnostics whom we know live in Christian countries. They live in a country in which Christianity has been believed and practised for nearly two thousand years. The whole place is full of an atmosphere of

## Answers to Questions

CHRIST, and a man breathes it, whether he knows it or not; and therefore you see in him Christian virtues. It does not mean that he would not be a better man, and receive much more help and strength by coming to church and using to the full means of grace. But it seems to me that we sin against the HOLY GHOST if we do not say that goodness is goodness wherever it is. It can only come from one source, and that is GOD.

### 7. Shall we always remember with shame our sins against GOD?

The answer to that question is that we are to remember our sins, but we are to remember them as sins forgiven. "She to whom much is forgiven, the same loveth much." We cannot forget some sin in the past, but we must remember it as sin forgiven; and the thought of it being forgiven ought to make us more loving, zealous, and forbearing with others.

### 8. A poor girl of seventeen, who has lost her mother, and whose father after eight years of melancholia is not restored to his mind, wants to know whether she ought to protest against the way in which he constantly abuses those who have been most kind to him.

I should say she ought to treat him as an invalid; I should not cross him; I should not think it necessary to contradict him, because I should say certainly from the letter that he was not really altogether in his right mind now.

9. Then comes a thing which has puzzled and distressed a good many lately, judging by the letters which I have received.

### Is there not the risk of infection in the Holy Communion?

After a most careful colloquy with the best doctors, we find that the danger of infection is regarded by them as absolutely infinitesimal, and that therefore no one should, in an ordinary

## Answers to Questions

way, be in the least afraid of coming to the Holy Communion from any such fear as this. On the other hand, where there is any known disease in any person of an infectious nature, at Davos Platz, and in other places and hospitals where consumption is largely treated, I allow the Holy Communion to be administered in a special way; that is, the bread is soaked in the wine, and they are placed together in the mouth of the consumptive patient, so as to avoid infection to anyone who might afterward use the same chalice. The answer, then, is that we are taking every possible precaution now so that no one need have any fear in coming to the Holy Communion for that reason.

**10. Is it a contradiction that Judas is stated to have hanged himself in one place, and that in another place to have purchased a field, and falling headlong, burst asunder?**

There is no real contradiction. It is only two descriptions of a very awful scene which we can hardly describe in detail, where no doubt the hanging was accompanied by dreadful results.

**11. One who on the eve of marriage lost his beloved, has continued to address her as though in her presence, and, further, to pray for her and to her, as is usual in the Russian Church. Is this right?**

Personally, I think that the poor afflicted lover cannot cherish too much the thought that in the Communion of Saints that dear one is close to him and is with him.

> " They sin who tell us love can die ;
> With love all other passions fly ;
> All others are but vanity."

And certainly he can, in that guarded way in which the early Christians did, pray for her in his private prayers. She, no doubt, is praying for him too. But pray to her ? I doubt very much in my own mind whether the Russian Church—

with members of whom I had many conversations when I was in Russia—pray *to* the Saints. They have a very keen belief in the Communion of Saints, and they certainly do ask the saints for their prayers for them; but I should myself, if I were the writer, content myself with the thought of the close communion of that dear soul with him still, with the belief that she is praying for him, and that he may ask for her light and refreshment and rest.

### 12. How can anyone be happy who finds some loved one missing in Heaven?

That, of course, is a terrible difficulty. I can only believe that we look on things in that other world with the eyes of GOD. It is impossible that GOD will give up loving any soul, and punishment may be the best for that soul—punishment given in love. Therefore I cannot help believing, although I do not pretend to explain the great mystery, that we in that world will look on things from GOD's point of view, and that if some loved one is not with us, but suffering punishment, we shall feel that that punishment is the best for that soul. When self-will ceases hell ceases, and whatever is best for that soul GOD is giving it. I often fear there is a great danger now in our setting up to be more kind than GOD, and more loving and pitiful than JESUS CHRIST. After all, we have not died for their souls, and JESUS CHRIST has. So I leave the condition of any soul, my own included, with great confidence to JESUS CHRIST, Who has died for us all.

### 13. Do you think that GOD, Who loves His little ones so tenderly, will punish a little brother—an invalid brother—who is allowed to die at sixteen unbaptized?

We are bound by the sacraments, but GOD is not bound by His own sacraments. We are bound. It is at our great responsibility we neglect them, and there has been a great lack of duty on the part of the family from whom this question comes. That boy should have been baptized; he was

## Answers to Questions

sixteen when he died. But, on the other hand, I should myself, if I was a member of that family, leave the lad with confidence to the tender mercies of GOD Himself.

**14. What does it mean by delivering such an one unto Satan for the destruction of the flesh, that the soul may be saved in the day of the LORD JESUS?**

You will find in the New Testament a belief which is unfamiliar to us, and that is that an excommunication or a curse led to physical consequences. For instance, you will find as to the irreverent treatment of the Holy Communion, St. Paul says, " from which cause many are weak and sickly among you, and many sleep." Ananias died under the curse of the Apostle. And it is quite clear that in the early Church the belief was that the excommunication or the curse had a physical result upon the person who was cursed, but that he was to bear such result patiently for the good of his soul. We see the same thing happen in another way ; we see men who perhaps are suffering the awful result of some sin, and yet that suffering is blessed to their soul. I have seen a man in the hospital with a broken leg, who has learned to bless that broken leg, because for the first time when he was there he heard the news which saved his soul. There are some men to-day who are bearing and will carry to their grave the result of their early sins ; they thank GOD for the painful result, because that is the thing which has brought them the salvation of their soul. I admit that the whole question about this physical result of excommunication is very mysterious in the New Testament ; we do not know whether this man suffered in his body throughout the rest of his life ; we are not told ; but what we are told is not to mind what physical suffering we have, so long as our soul is saved in the day of the LORD JESUS.

# ALL SOULS', LANGHAM PLACE

*WEDNESDAY EVENING*

## IX

## HOW CAN WE BE FORGIVEN?

"If we confess our sins, He is faithful and just to forgive us our sins."—1 ST. JOHN i. 9.

THE Mission has now reached its crisis. We must not be content, any of us, to-night, unless no soul leaves this church at least on the way to be forgiven. I shall explain what I mean by "on the way to be forgiven" in a minute. There is no reason whatever why every soul among you should not be able to sing at Easter—

> "Redeemed, restored, forgiven,
>   Through JESUS' precious blood!
> Heirs of His home in Heaven,
> O praise our pardoning GOD!
> Praise Him in tuneful measures,
>   Who gave His SON to die,
> Praise Him Whose sevenfold treasures
>   Enrich and sanctify."

—not one. In order to convince you of that, I would remind you of what I have said already: that the love of the TRINITY has had five things to do—five problems, as it were, to solve. The broken law which we had broken must be perfectly obeyed by

## How can We be Forgiven?

Some One ; one of the HOLY TRINITY must come down and make Himself absolutely one with the human race—with you and me, that is. It must be done for all, so that not one could be left out ; for " GOD would have all men be saved and come to the knowledge of the truth." Forgiveness must mean restoration. There must be no mock forgiveness, no people who imagine that they are going to be covered with the robe of somebody else's righteousness, and remain unrighteous beneath : that would clearly be absolutely unreal. Those who are forgiven must be content to carry the results of their past sins, and suffer, if necessary, for the rest of their lives, so long as they are forgiven. We know that this is just what happened, that Good Friday—which every Christian must keep up as a very holy day ; I never can think how any Christian who believes in what really happened on Good Friday can spend the day in mere amusement or recreation— reminds us that that is just what happens, that the broken law was perfectly kept by JESUS CHRIST to the death ; He came down and knit Himself to us. It was done for all, so that no one is left out, not one ; so that forgiveness can mean for all perfect restoration. If we are, then, crippled, maimed, one hand cut off, one eye plucked out, it does not matter ; we shall have grace to bear that, to bear the thorn in the flesh right on to the end, and the patient bearing of that physical limitation will give us grace to help others, as it did St. Paul.

So we face now this tremendous question, How can we be forgiven ? That is what we want. If " The love of the TRINITY in the Atonement " was

## *How can We be Forgiven?*

our message on Sunday,* " How can we be forgiven ?" must be the question for to-night.

1. First of all, we have got to find out what our sins are. People are in such very different phases of their spiritual life. I may be speaking to some who at the very beginning of Lent, or years ago, looked into their past life most thoroughly, repented of every boyish and girlish sin, dragged it to light, and asked the Heavenly FATHER to forgive it for CHRIST'S sake, and have long ago been forgiven for it. Do not go back upon that—for Heaven's sake do not go back upon that; remember it as sin forgiven; let it stir you up to Christian works, stir you up to love, stir you up to contrition—contrition is sorrow for sin that is already forgiven. But there may be among you a number, and perhaps a great number, of souls who are not in that state at all. They are those to whom I must now speak.

You have come to the Mission service, you have been caught in the spirit of the Mission, and you do not want this Mission to pass on and leave you untouched; you want to be forgiven; you want to accept the great Atonement. What are you to do ? First of all, find out what those sins are. It takes some time; if you have not begun at all, you cannot do it now in a moment. You must take your life and divide it into parts—your boyhood, your girlhood, since you were grown up, since you were married (if you are married), dividing your life into portions. And then, with regard to those portions of your life, take the Commandments of GOD, which you ought to have kept as explained by JESUS CHRIST,

* See p. 145.

## How can We be Forgiven?

and test your life by them. You will find in a book of questions on the Commandments help to bring the Commandments home. Sometimes we do not quite realise what the Commandments mean to us in our life. Take, for instance, such questions as these : I imagine you by yourself, and you are asking yourself, Has GOD been first in my life—quite first ? Has that been the rule of my life ? Have I made some graven image of GOD in my mind which makes GOD appear cruel and harsh and hard-hearted ? Is that the GOD I have pictured to myself ? Then I have broken the second Commandment. Am I a hypocrite ? Do I come here, kneel down and say my prayers, when all the time I am taking GOD'S name in vain, and my life outside is not corresponding to it at all ? Am I honest in my business ? Am I charitable to my neighbour ? If not, I am acting a lie; I am breaking the third Commandment. What about my Sundays ? Am I keeping GOD'S holy day ? Is GOD first ? Does His worship come first on my Sundays, and are all the other days of the week consecrated to GOD ? That comes into the Fourth Commandment as much as the Sunday—to serve GOD the rest of the week. What is my home-life like ? Am I a good brother or son ? Am I a good daughter or sister ? I put the questions so that anyone may ask what fits their case. Am I a good influence at home to help all the brothers and sisters ? or is my temper the curse of the home ? You must ask that, or you may be breaking the Fifth Commandment. What has my influence been upon those with whom I work in the City or in the business house ? Have I ever said something which has left a stain upon a boy's or girl's soul, or have I

## How can We be Forgiven?

sneered at them when they have wanted to be religious, or read their Bibles, and go to Church ? Then I may have murdered that soul, or helped to murder it. Thou shalt not kill souls any more than bodies. Have I done that ? I remember once a sister came to me who had been a doubter and sceptic, and by her doubts and scepticism she had destroyed all the faith in her sister, and when she came back to the faith she could not undo the harm she had done to her younger sister, who remained an agnostic. Have we done anything like that ? Then we must confess it, and find it out. Have we been honest ? If we are boys in shops, or messenger-boys, are we strictly honest in our work? If not, we must not shirk the question that not to be strictly honest is stealing. Can anyone run through our accounts, if we are in business ? are we stealing the reputation of other people ? A person's character is worth more to him than money, very often, and yet people who would be very careful about money will try and steal the character of some one else, and think nothing of it. Are we bearing false witness against our neighbour ? What about the stories we tell about others ? Do we spread ill-natured gossip ? Have we done that ? Is there some one unhappy because of what we have said about them ? We cannot pass over that when we want to be forgiven. Are we coveting something on which our heart is set ? What is our object in life ? Is our object in life to be rich or popular ? Then we must be careful about the Tenth Commandment.

I only suggest the sort of questions to use, to show that self-examination is not a thing that can be

## How can We be Forgiven?

lightly passed over. When you have found out what you have done, find out what you are doing. What is your besetting sin to-day ? What is your besetting habit ? I am not mentioning things like drink or gambling. There may be some one here who drinks— one never knows ; drink comes out in the most unexpected quarters. We have had many petitions for men and even mothers taking to drink and gambling and betting. You must find out what all those things are. And having found out what they are, what is the next thing to do ?

2. Confess them. And, mark you, confess them to GOD before waiting to see how sorry you are for them. I will tell you why I say that. I was very much struck by the "Instructions of Bishop Wilkinson," who did such a wonderful work some twenty-five years ago in St. Peter's, Eaton Square, among the rich. In his book he says in substance: If any man will confess his sins, GOD is faithful and just to forgive him his sins. Do not wait to see how sorry you are. Confess them first. There is many a person who finds out a sin, and the HOLY SPIRIT has not yet softened that heart really to see how bad it is. Sometimes people do not see how bad the sin is till long afterwards, when they get their consciences more sensitive ; and they look at a sight about which I am going to speak in a moment, and then they begin to see it. But the next step is, before you feel, even if you do not feel, adequate contrition or repentance, confess the sin : " I have done this—it was I who did it," and confess it without excusing yourself, without trying to soften it down, without trying to say that other people

## *How can We be Forgiven?*

have done just as bad—not confessing it merely in a general way, and saying, "I know I am a sinner;" that is no good, but "I am *the* sinner; I am the man who did that; I am the woman who did that; I said that." That is why religion is so unreal, because we say glibly we are "miserable sinners," and we hardly ever take the trouble to find out in what, and we hardly believe it ourselves. But when we have gone into the question of what we have done, and seen it in black and white, then we can say with real sorrow and penitence, or, at any rate, quite definitely, "GOD forgive me, the sinner who did that."

3. Then, thirdly, there comes a question, How are we to confess these sins with penitence? How are we to be sorry for our sins? Now, let me answer that by an illustration. Cannot you imagine a little child who comes to its mother to say that he has told a story, and he may not feel very sorry about it, but still he is sorry enough to come and confess it; but when he comes up to the mother, and he looks into her eyes, and sees that mother's eyes full of tears at the thought that he could have been untruthful, does not he feel much more sorrow than he felt before, because it comes home to him what he has done when he sees the tears in his mother's eyes? That is exactly the difference the Cross makes to a Christian when he confesses his sin. The Cross is, as it were, the tears of GOD. The Cross shows what sin is to GOD; it shows what the lie or the dishonesty, what the years spent without prayer, what the malice, what the unclean thought or act has meant to GOD. It has disappointed GOD, and in the Cross we see the measure of the sin of man. It was my pride, my sin, that caused

## How can We be Forgiven?

that. Behold the Lamb of GOD, and what it cost Him to take away the sin of the world! That is why the Cross brings penitence when nothing else does. "They shall look on Him Whom they pierced, and they shall mourn for Him, as a man mourneth for his only son." They shall look on Him whom they pierced. And as we examine ourselves this Mission we shall not feel true sorrow unless we examine ourselves at the foot of the Cross; and as we see, as it were, the tears in our mother's eyes, and when we realise what love we have sinned against, then there will be sorrow and contrition; our hearts will be soft, and we shall say: "O GOD, I see now what I have done, how bad it was; I see the open wound; I see my sin there; I nailed Him to the Cross." Before the Cross it is a hard heart that does not feel sorrow.

4. And, besides sorrow, we must face restitution. If you have told a lie, you must untell it; and if you have stolen something, you must give it back; if you have taken away some one's character, you must do something to restore it. There must be no unreality in our repentance, and you must do it with a strong determination never to commit that sin again. I think there is something terribly depraving to the character in a person coming to confess and confess and confess the same thing (as if the confessing it was quite enough) over and over again to GOD, but confessing it without making any real effort to get rid of it. Forgiveness means restoration. We are forgiven when we confess honestly, but on the understanding that we will do our very best to get rid of the sin, and be really restored. If, then, we are to be forgiven this Mission, it must be not only that we

## How can We be Forgiven?

confess with sorrow, and not only make what restitution is possible, but make a firm and determined effort to get rid of the sin. "He is then faithful and just to forgive us our sins, and to cleanse us from all unrighteousness."

Now, do you want to be forgiven? Are you ready to take this trouble, to undertake this painful task of repentance and confession? If you say, "I cannot undertake it by myself," then go to your Rector, or to any other man you trust belonging to your own church, and let him help you—let him help you to free yourself from your sin. It is exactly what the Prayer Book tells you to do; if you cannot by this means get comfort, go to some discreet minister of the Word and open your grief. That is what ministers are sent for, to help the poor sin-stricken soul. Either by yourself or with help, for GOD's sake have forgiveness before Easter. And when you have confessed, either by yourself or with the help of another, then lift up the hand of faith and take the absolution. Our whole service is ringing with absolution. There is no more beautiful absolution than there is in the Communion Service — a solemn, beautiful absolution in GOD's name. Some people think that is not an absolution at all. Of course it is an absolution. And what we want is to take that declared absolution from GOD, and to believe in it. There are some people who confess and repent, but they have not faith enough to believe they are forgiven. We are meant to live a forgiven life. We ought to have joy and peace in believing, that we may have hope. A forgiven life is a bright and happy life, meant for the Christian. Therefore it is that I beg you, as you

## *How can We be Forgiven?*

value the peace of your soul, as you value your future usefulness in the world, as you value your eternal salvation, find out, confess, and be forgiven for those sins that are on your conscience ; and then, with your feet on the 'Rock of Ages,' go forward to a life lived for GOD.

> " Finish then Thy new creation,
> Pure and spotless let us be ;
> Let us see Thy great salvation
> Perfectly restored in Thee."

# St. Marylebone

*SUNDAY EVENING*

## ANSWERS TO QUESTIONS

**1. How do we know that we are forgiven, especially when we go on committing the same sin again and again ?**

In one sense this is an easy question, and in one sense a very difficult one. The reason that GOD has entrusted to those whom He has ordained the blessed task of pronouncing, either in public or in private, His absolution is that penitent souls may be sure that they are forgiven. You will find a beautiful Absolution in the daily service, and the still more powerful and beautiful one in the Holy Communion; and that is a real Absolution, if we lift up the hand and take it. It is the pronouncing by GOD'S ambassador GOD'S absolution. Or you will find in the service for the sick another even more definite Absolution, which may be pronounced in private to those who cannot by themselves reconcile their own consciences with GOD. And, therefore, the answer to the first half of the question is that GOD has done His very best to make us sure we are forgiven. He has given His promise and sent His ambassadors with pardon signed and sealed, and what more can He do ?

But you say, "When we go on committing the same sin again and again." That makes me ask the question, Are you sure you are in the condition which makes forgiveness possible ? The ambassador when he pronounces forgiveness does so only on behalf of GOD, and it only avails for the soul that

## Answers to Questions

is really penitent, and you must ask yourself, if you are falling again and again into the sin for which you ask forgiveness, are you really trying to conquer it, and are you really sorry for it ? We have to watch as well as pray against our sins.

**2. Is it wrong to go to Holy Communion when the preparation is a mere form ?**

It should not be a mere form. This Mission is for earnest souls, and I pray the writer of this question not to leave the Mission without resolving to make his or her preparation not a mere form. Religion is a great reality. I could not help thinking of this as I heard the terrible end of the lesson tonight for Palm Sunday, " Thou hast spoken truth, thou shalt see my face no more." Pharaoh's chance was over. On Palm Sunday also we read that JESUS wept over Jerusalem, saying : " If thou hadst known, even thou at least in this thy day, the things that belong unto thy peace; but now they are hid from thine eyes." GOD grant that that awful sentence may not be spoken over any soul among you. " Now is the accepted time, now is the day of salvation."

**3. I cannot remember the sins of my past life to confess them. What shall I do ?**

I have said already what we were to do in such a case. We were to break up our past lives—our boyhood, our manhood, our later years—if it be so. Take the Commandments ; pray for the light of GOD'S SPIRIT, and the HOLY SPIRIT will find out and reveal to us what is our sin. I believe that it is because people have not undertaken that elementary task of examining their consciences, and really asking for forgiveness, and being forgiven, that there are so many morbid, unhappy Christians. The really happy people are those who have looked their past lives in the face, confessed their sins and made peace with GOD, and the rest of their life is a life of thanksgiving. Therefore, find out your sins, and confess them. "If we confess our sins, He is faithful and just to forgive us our sins, and to cleanse us from all unrighteousness." But you cannot have forgiveness without self-examination and confession.

**4. What are we to say to one who turns to a life of comparative goodness from a life stained with frightful sin, and yet feels no shame or sorrow for the past?**

I have said that we were not to wait to confess our sins until we were sorry, but to confess them at once, however hard we may feel; and that if we took those sins to the Cross, looked up in our SAVIOUR'S face, and saw the marks of what our sins had cost Him—the wound in His side and the marks of the Cross—we should feel real contrition. A child may confess a sin to his mother in a half-hearted way, but, if he sees the tears in his mother's eyes, that child is ten times as sorry, and confesses his sin with real sorrow. What brings real contrition and penitence is confessing our sins at the foot of the Cross. The Cross represents the tears in GOD'S eyes; it shows us what our sins have cost Him. I say, then, to this questioner, use Holy Week up to Good Friday in confessing those sins, and looking at Him—" They shall look on Him Whom they have pierced, and they shall mourn for Him as one mourneth for his only son "—and by Good Friday you will be really sorry for those sins. Contrition is sorrow for sins already forgiven. "She to whom much is forgiven, the same loveth much."

**5. Will a person be among GOD'S blessed children in Heaven whose faith completely fails, and who becomes an atheist; who still prays, reads the Bible, and does all he can to gain light, and dies in this condition?**

It is quite impossible for me, I need hardly say, to answer a question about the eternal fate of any soul. I am not the judge of the world; GOD is the judge, and therefore we can never do anything but repeat the conditions of salvation.

## *Answers to Questions*

My own belief is this: that " he that wills to do the will of GOD shall know of the doctrine whether it be of GOD." That is the promise, and any man struggling on through doubts and difficulties to-day, who tries to follow the Crucified in his life, will get the clear light if he is really living up to what he has got ; he will some day see his ideal realized in our SAVIOUR. I would say to this poor struggling doubter, Live up to what light you have got ; do the will of GOD, and some day I believe the promise will be fulfilled that he that willeth to do the will of GOD shall know of the doctrine, whether it be of GOD."

# St. Marylebone

*SUNDAY EVENING*

## X

## THE LOVE OF THE TRINITY IN CHURCH AND SACRAMENTS

" And he arose, and came to his father. But when he was yet a great way off, his father saw him, and had compassion, and ran, and fell on his neck, and kissed him. And the son said unto him, Father, I have sinned against heaven, and in thy sight, and am no more worthy to be called thy son. But the father said to his servants, Bring forth the best robe, and put it on him ; and put a ring on his hand, and shoes on his feet ; and bring hither the fatted calf, and kill it ; and let us eat, and be merry ; for this my son was dead, and is alive again ; he was lost, and is found."—St. Luke xv. 20-24.

I HAVE a special reason in asking you to notice every word of this verse, because it is just the parts of it that perhaps you would not notice which form my special message now.

The father kissed him, and he said, " Bring the robe, and the ring, and the shoes, and make a feast." We have, on this last night of the Mission message, to ask ourselves, Is there any further manifestation of the love of the Trinity which has to be preached if the full message is to be given ? We have seen the love of the Trinity in answer to our prayers; we have seen the love of the Trinity in the Incarnation ;

## Church and Sacraments

we have seen the love of the TRINITY in planning out how the human race could be saved; we saw that, as They counselled together in the eternal counsels, They had to find some way by which the broken law could be perfectly kept, that one of Them must come down and make Himself one with the guilty race; that what was done for one must be done for all, and that forgiveness must mean restoration; and we saw, and we adored as we saw, the love of the TRINITY manifested in the Atonement.

But what other problem had the HOLY TRINITY to face as They looked down in love upon this fallen race? I can imagine the holy Persons saying, as it were, to one another, "How are We to make them sure about it? How are We to bring the salvation near enough? How are We to make them believe they are forgiven? How are We to make them sure of the love? Here is the prodigal coming back: We must have a ring for him to put on his hand; We must have a robe for him; We must have a visible home for him to come back to; We must have shoes to put on his feet; We must have a feast to welcome him"— in other words, We must have a Church and sacraments. And therefore the last message of the Mission is the love of the TRINITY in giving us a Church and Sacraments.

And nothing is more beautiful than the way They worked it out. Cannot you see JESUS CHRIST in the valley and on the mountains? Leaving the crowd, and taking the disciples by themselves, and teaching them—He is set upon one glorious thing. You ask, "Why does He not go and heal the sick, and preach to the multitude?" He is doing something

## Church and Sacraments

even more important for the human race. When at last they understood who He was, and He had said to Peter, " But whom say ye that I am ?" Peter, representing the Apostles, and speaking clearly on their behalf, said, " Thou art the CHRIST, the SON of the living GOD." Then came the answer : " Blessed art thou, Simon Barjona ; now on this rock I can build My Church, and the gates of hell shall not prevail against it." Here was the home for the prodigal being prepared by the SON of GOD. When He went back to Heaven visibly, though still present in the spirit, with the sound of rushing mighty wind and tongues of fire, down came the HOLY GHOST into that home. It became a living home, a living society, a living people. The perplexed disciples became the world's Apostles ; the timid people became brave, and the Divine society started on its glorious progress round the world to be the home of thousands and millions of souls, warmed with the love of Heaven. As Dean Church, in his paper on the Christian Church,* in substance, says : " Just as the Gulf Stream—that warm Gulf Stream—passes through the cold ocean, so the warm and loving Church of the living GOD has passed on its way through the cold world." This loving society was to be the home of the soul, something that the world could see and something which would bring the love of the TRINITY home to every nation and every tongue, and the poorest man and the poorest woman in the worst slum in London—a Divine society which should carry with it in its hand the ring, the robe, the shoes for the feet, and the feast. There have always been these from

* Oxford House Papers (Rivingtons).

## Church and Sacraments

the beginning. There has been Baptism. "For as many of you as have been baptized into CHRIST have put on CHRIST." The Apostle uses in another place the expression "the seal." For Confirmation the same word is used—"the seal." "Grieve not the HOLY SPIRIT of GOD, whereby ye have been sealed unto the day of redemption." Sealing appears to describe the joint effect of Baptism and Confirmation. Always the same, from the very beginning, the outward and visible sign of the falling of the HOLY GHOST in strength has been the laying on of hands; afterwards there has always been the feast, the visible feast, to which the returning prodigal could come as a sign and a pledge of love; something which could be seen, and yet only the sign of that which could not be seen.

So for centuries, without any variation, the love of the TRINITY has been manifested to the human race in Church and Sacraments. And I am bound to ask—for we must approach the full message of the Mission—what response have you made—speaking to you one by one—to the love of the TRINITY, so tenderly shown in Church and Sacraments? But you say, "The Church is so divided." Whose fault is that? Not CHRIST's fault. CHRIST prayed with His last breath, "That they may all be one, as Thou, FATHER, art in Me, and I in Thee; that they also may be one in Us, that the world may believe that Thou hast sent Me." The world was to be convinced that the FATHER had sent the SON through the visible unity of CHRIST's Church. Is there no pride, is there no self-will to be confessed on the part of all of those of us who have broken up the unity of the Church? If there is one prayer we must pray, it is for the unity

## Church and Sacraments

of the Church, the unity of the home once again. We are much more united than people think. If you take the Anglican Church and the Roman Catholic Church, you will see that the things which we believe in common are much more numerous than those on which we differ. When I was over in Russia, speaking to the members of the Greek Church at the oldest monastery in Russia, the Archimandrite gave me at the end of my visit an ikon, or image of our Blessed SAVIOUR. and said : " Take this, Bishop, back to England, the image of the one Master of us all." And there it stands in my chapel above the altar. And as to the orthodox nonconforming bodies of England, why, what does Mr. Gladstone say himself ? " I bow my head," he said, " before the doctrine of the Incarnation, the Atonement, and the HOLY TRINITY, believed in in England to-day by all orthodox Christians ; I bow my head before those three mighty verities which are common to them all." And therefore the peace of the Church, the harmony of the home, must be the first prayer of every earnest Christian.

Then we come to the Sacraments. I dare say I am speaking to many so-called Nonconformists who honestly believe, or have been brought up to believe, that an outward and visible sign, like Baptism or Confirmation or Holy Communion, gets between the soul and GOD. Yes, it does, if a mother's kiss gets between the mother and the child—if the mother's kiss gets between the love of the mother and the child, so as to stop it ; it does if the rope on the ice-slope which connects me with my guide gets between me and my guide. And therefore I do ask those honest, earnest people who have been divorced

*Church and Sacraments*

and driven from the old home to which they all once belonged—for it is within the last three hundred years that all the nonconforming bodies in England have taken their rise—to ask themselves this question : " Has there not been misunderstanding ? Is it really JESUS Who said, ' Go into all the world, and baptize them in the name of the FATHER, and of the SON, and of the HOLY GHOST ' ? Then Baptism cannot be only a form, because JESUS was no formalist. Is it really true that in the New Testament, in the Acts of the Apostles, it is said, ' Then laid they their hands upon them, and they received the HOLY GHOST, for as yet He had fallen upon none of them ' ? Then it cannot be wrong to think that the laying on of hands is the outward and visible sign of the falling of the HOLY GHOST, because it is in the Bible. Have I been misunderstanding the Holy Communion ? If JESUS CHRIST took bread and said, ' This is My Body,' and took wine and said, ' This is My Blood,' then it is not the Church that founded the doctrine of the Holy Communion. JESUS CHRIST would never have used that language unless He meant that in some very special way we became in the Holy Communion partakers of the Divine Nature. He must have meant in some special way to convince me of His love and give me of His SPIRIT." Therefore, I ask those who have, perhaps, been kept for years from the old home and the old Sacraments, to think over why they should not have the ring put upon their fingers as the prodigal did ; why they should not have the robe ; why they should not have the feast which has been prepared, and accept the love of the TRINITY in the ordained way.

## *Church and Sacraments*

Or, again, some are kept back, I know, by what is called " sacerdotalism." It is imagined that in this manifestation of the love of the TRINITY man has too much of a place, and that the man who pronounces the absolution is getting between them and GOD. But this is a misunderstanding altogether. Man is nothing in himself : an ambassador is absolutely nothing—he only brings the message ; but, if he is sent as the messenger, and if he is given his message, and if the words actually said to him are, " Whosesoever sins ye remit, they are remitted, and whosesoever sins ye retain, they are retained," he has to deliver his message, but he cannot himself forgive the sin ; and when he pronounces the absolution, unless the soul is penitent, the soul is not absolved. He only, as an ambassador for CHRIST's sake, brings the pardon signed and sealed to convince the doubting soul that he or she is forgiven. And what is there in that to get between GOD and the soul ? The teaching of the Church of England is perfectly plain that, if any soul by itself is penitent and confesses, it can by itself accept the voice, if it has faith enough—the outspoken voice of absolution from the Church—and may be at peace. And yet, with infinite tenderness, and reflecting the careful consideration of the love of the TRINITY, the Prayer Book lays down that if a man cannot do this by himself, he may open his grief to GOD in the presence of another, and receive the word of absolution by himself, addressed to himself.

And so I do, at the bottom of my soul, believe that half these things which divide us are pure misunderstandings of the doctrines of the Church. and that many and many a soul is kept from a living faith and

## *Church and Sacraments*

a certainty about the love of GOD by refusing the ring and the robe and the feast. And so with a full heart I look you in the face, and I say :

" O come to the merciful SAVIOUR, Who calls you;
   O come to the LORD, Who forgives and forgets ;
  Though dark be the fortune on earth that befalls you,
   There's a bright home above, where the sun never sets."

And, as a pledge of that, as a token of that, and that you may be quite certain of that, there is a bright home here on earth, with tokens of love brought down by the HOLY TRINITY themselves. Will you refuse the kiss of GOD ? Will you put back the hand that would place the ring on your finger ? Will you disdain the blessed feast ? If you receive the love of the TRINITY as the love of the TRINITY has planned it for you, you shall be folded here and in Heaven into the peace of an eternal home.

# St. Marylebone

*WEDNESDAY EVENING*

## ANSWERS TO QUESTIONS

**1. What arguments can a daughter use to her father who, while he is quite content that his children should go to church, and takes a general interest in their so doing, never goes near the church himself?**

A daughter, of course, has to argue very respectfully with her father, very lovingly; but surely she can say, and make him believe, that GOD the FATHER loves him, that GOD the SON died for him, and that GOD the HOLY SPIRIT wants to sanctify him, as well as the children, and that he must not be left out. Why should he be left out? And the boys, if there are any, when they grow up, will do what their father does, and not what he says. If the father says, "Go round, children, to the Sunday-school, go to church," but never goes near them himself, what the boy says in his mind is this: "Religion is all very well for boys, but it is not a manly thing." And when he grows up, he will send his children, if he has any, to church, but he will not go himself. And therefore any father or mother who thinks a little good advice to children is all that is required must remember that as a rule children grow up to do what their parents do, and not what they say.

**2. What is the "sin unto death"? Not knowing what "the sin unto death" is, I feel a difficulty myself in interceding for everybody and everybody's sin.**

## Answers to Questions

It is quite true that there must be something which is called in the Bible " the sin unto death," and I believe it is what is described in another place as " the sin against the HOLY GHOST." People sometimes imagine they have committed the sin against the HOLY GHOST, and are in a state of despair. But the sin against the HOLY GHOST and the sin unto death is saying, " Evil, be thou my good." While a soul says that, GOD cannot turn it. So long as you are in a state of really loving evil and choosing it, and lying down in it, you are in a state of living death. If any one of you is afraid that he has sinned against the HOLY GHOST, and is in an anxious state about it, that very state of anxiety shows he has not committed it ; if he had, he would not mind.

**3. Can it be truly said that our LORD was subject to the same temptations as others, taking into consideration the fact that He knew He was GOD ? Knowing this seems to put a very heavy handicap in His favour.**

The mystery of the Incarnation is this, that JESUS CHRIST was perfect man as well as perfect GOD, and therefore He was really tempted. What we see in Gethsemane was a real temptation ; it was a real temptation to go back with the angels and escape the bitter trial of the Cross. But He had to bring His human will into conformity with the Divine will. He put Himself on our level and fought with our weapons. It is a very difficult thing to translate this into words. The revealed truth is that our LORD was perfect man as well as perfect GOD.

**4. How can I be sure that my sins are forgiven, and that I shall inherit eternal life ?**

This is from a long letter, evidently written in a state of depression. To my mind this is just the case contemplated by the Prayer Book. The Prayer Book teaches that, if a man or woman can by themselves confess their sins to GOD, and hold the hand of faith up and receive the forgiveness, they can do so ; but you will find in the Holy Communion Service that

## Answers to Questions

you are encouraged, if you cannot by this means quiet your conscience, to " go to some discreet and learned minister of GOD's word and open your grief." This soul ought to go to the priest of GOD whom he most trusts and open his grief, and be helped by him to peace and happiness. How did the father convince the prodigal that he was really forgiven ? He gave him the kiss, and the ring, and the robe, and the shoes for service, and the feast. He gave him something visible. He did this to confirm his faith. So the Church and ministers and Sacraments are for the same purpose.

**5. Why is the GOD we speak to a silent GOD, Who does not let us know one way or the other whether He is actively concerned with human affairs ?**

I understand the difficulty, but it all depends whether we believe that GOD has revealed Himself or not. If He has revealed Himself, He is not a silent GOD ; He has broken the silence ; Almighty GOD has spoken. It really comes to that : either the Christian religion is true or not true. If the Christian religion is true, GOD has spoken. And it is that message of love and salvation which we have preached in this Mission, and meditated on, which is GOD's voice.

**6. A girl married a young man in a good position, who turns out to be dishonest and is now in prison. Her father, now dead, was an upright man, and if he knew in the other world the condition of his daughter, would not his agony be unthinkable ?**

I always frankly admit the difficulty of such questions. It is a difficult thing to understand how souls could be happy when those they love go wrong, whether in this world or the other ; but what I feel is that in the other world we shall look at things from the point of view of GOD. If we see the sin, we see, perhaps, the repentance which will come afterwards, and restoration. If that soul has to be punished, we see the good of the punishment. From the other world I believe

## Answers to Questions

we look at things with larger, other eyes—more with the eyes of GOD. Our love cannot be as great as GOD'S. If GOD allows punishment, it must be good.

**7. "Is not this the carpenter's son? Is not His mother called Mary, and His brethren James and Joses, and Simon and Judas?" How do you explain this?**

That is what the inhabitants of Nazareth said, and it shows how naturally our LORD did live as a man, how He identified Himself with the place where He lived. He was a real man, and really lived the ordinary life of a man, so really that people said He had no honour in His own country, although He was honoured for His character and His goodness. Yet they could not tell that He was more than man, and that is the answer to the question. It only shows that He was real man as well as real GOD.

**8. Why did CHRIST spend so many years of His short life preparing, and only three years in the ministry?**

That is one of the surprises in GOD'S working, the long time required for preparation, and very often the short time for activity. Think of St. Paul, who went into Arabia for a long time. In the case of our LORD the time of His ministry, short as it was, availed for the salvation of the world and the establishment of the Church for all time. GOD knew what was best.

**9. I cannot realise the Divine presence in my prayers. What shall I do?**

We walk by faith and not by feeling. Thank GOD, the reality of our prayers does not depend upon what we feel at the time. The less we have of feeling, the more we have to pray in faith. These things are perfectly true— GOD the FATHER comes with hands full of gifts, GOD the SON is praying by you, GOD the HOLY GHOST is praying in you. Go on, and the feeling will come.

This is also very much the answer to one who writes

that he feels no faith, but sees that it is a reality, for he knows other people with warm and loving faith. "He that willeth to do the will of GOD shall know of the doctrine, whether it be of GOD."

10. Then comes a question about an answer which I gave,* which has been much misunderstood, about attending other places of worship:

### May we attend other places of worship?

I tried to make it plain that I thought, whatever body or denomination you belong to, you should attend the place of worship connected with it; to change about from one to the other was really a breach of principle. But the questioner in the original letter seemed to think that he or she was committing a mortal sin because he went on one occasion to a place of worship that was not his. That was exaggerating the importance of the act. That soul did not commit a mortal sin in doing so. But that answer has been interpreted into meaning that I thought it a good thing to go about to any place of worship your friend might be attending. As a rule, stay in your own church as a matter of principle.

### 11. If the example of our wrongdoing influences other lives for evil, even though we have received pardon for those sins, are we to see the consequences of our sins?

There is no sorrow more poignant than repenting of sin, and yet not being able to undo the harm we have done. That leads to lifelong contrition. We must do all we can to undo the harm; but the fact of having done something the results of which you cannot undo does not, by the mercy of GOD, prevent you from being forgiven, though it should make you a humble and contrite person for the rest of your life. I do not want that soul to think he or she is not forgiven, but they must not underrate the mischief that has been done.

* See page 126.

## Answers to Questions

12. I have several long questions about Sunday and the Sabbath.

### How should Sunday be kept?

I cannot answer these fully, but I would only say this: that, of course, Sunday is not the same as the Jewish Sabbath. The old Jewish regulations do not apply to Sunday, but at the same time Sunday is a day of rest and worship, and we carry on the idea of rest and worship from the old Sabbath into the Sunday. It is meant to be a day of joy and spiritual rest. GOD has to come first. It should not be a miserable day; it ought to be the best day in the week. "This is the day the LORD hath made; rejoice and be glad in it." Therefore, in keeping Sunday, keep to the principle of GOD first. We should not only ourselves worship GOD, but give others, especially our servants, opportunities for doing so; we should also give rest to other people as well as ourselves.

# St. Marylebone

*WEDNESDAY EVENING*

## XI

### GLORY TO GOD

"Glory be to the FATHER, and to the SON, and to the
HOLY GHOST."—BOOK OF COMMON PRAYER.

I DO not think that there can be very much doubt as to what the last message of the Mission before Easter Day must be. I should almost like, if it had been possible, to have asked those who have followed this Mission throughout what they would themselves say the last message of the Mission must be. I have only been myself a kind of mouthpiece of the Mission; it has not been my Mission at all. Just think for a moment what has happened in these six weeks. We began on the day after Ash Wednesday. For myself I only knew one thing about the Mission on that day, and this was that it was to be on the " Love of the TRINITY." That was all that I knew about it; and yet think how gradually the whole of that simple message has been expanded before our eyes, how we have been led on to see what the love of the TRINITY really means: that GOD the FATHER knows every one by name, without one being left out; that GOD the SON died for every one, as if there was not a single one to die for

*Glory to God*

except that one—most of us have been baptized, and if so we have still the mark of the Cross of our SAVIOUR individually to show that we were redeemed one by one; and that GOD the HOLY SPIRIT, who has never gone back after He came down at Pentecost with the mighty rushing wind and tongues of fire, is trying by every means to sanctify and make holy every one; that—

> " Every virtue we possess,
>   And every conquest won,
>   And every thought of holiness,
>   Are His alone."

And then we were led on to see what that meant with regard to prayer. I have already said that every one who prays is swept into the life of the HOLY TRINITY, is part of the life of the HOLY TRINITY—the HOLY FATHER with the gifts, the HOLY SON interceding, the HOLY GHOST praying in us. Then we were led on to see the great manifestation, the great plan, the wonderful idea, which the HOLY TRINITY had in the Incarnation; how without it GOD would have been so far off; without it we should have no idea what GOD was like; without it we should have no idea what we were to be like; there would be nothing warm about our religion—it would be all cold, abstract, far away; our prayer might have to go up millions of miles, as some one suggested at one of the services, and we should not know whether it would do so or not. And so the HOLY TRINITY planned this great ladder between earth and Heaven which we call the Incarnation. And then we were led on to see the further plan : how were the wandering children to be brought back ? how was the sinner to be forgiven

## *Glory to God*

without impinging on the justice of GOD, without lowering the moral tone of the universe ?—how was it to be done ? Then we saw the glorious plan of the Atonement, that One was to come down and to become one with the human race. We saw it all carried out in every detail, the great plan of the HOLY TRINITY. I think that service in which we spoke of the Atonement* was the one that brought more souls to the foot of the Cross, and more souls to repentance, and more souls to be forgiven than on any other night of the Mission. And then, you remember, in very love the HOLY TRINITY thought further : " How can We make them certain ? how can We assure not only the souls now alive, but the souls who shall be alive two thousand years on ? how shall We make every returning prodigal quite sure he is forgiven ? how shall We prevent those who have not fallen away into gross sins from becoming self-complacent ? how shall We, as it were, lay our hands upon every one in every generation as Our own ?" And the glorious idea was conceived that they must have a kiss and a ring and a robe, the shoes and the feast—in other words, must have the Church and Sacraments for all time. And then we have been guided to see what kind of response is expected to all this, and have considered, especially with the men : Wonder, Faith, Hope, Work, Praise. And still as part of the Mission there were those reverent congregations in Westminster Abbey, where we asked : " What am I ? What am I here for ?" " What does GOD think of me ?" " Where am I going ?" And GOD spoke to us in the silence of that great Abbey, as letter after

* See p. 145.

## Glory to God

letter shows. And then there are all the letters of thanksgiving which I have received. And all this has come to pass in six weeks out of the single idea of the Love of the TRINITY, which was all we had on the day after Ash Wednesday.

And that being so, there is only one note for to-night : " Glory be to the FATHER, and to the SON, and to the HOLY GHOST ; as it was in the beginning, is now, and ever shall be, world without end." There could not be another, because the whole thing has been of GOD from beginning to end ; there has been nothing whatever of man in it—" Not unto us, O LORD, but unto Thy name be the praise." And when we sing " Restored, redeemed, forgiven," to the tune of " Home, sweet home," let the souls who know they have been restored, redeemed, forgiven, and have been brought home, utter their thanksgiving and their glory in that old hymn.

But, of course, this message is far more than a thanksgiving for a particular mission. " Glory be to the FATHER, and to the SON, and to the HOLY GHOST " is the motto of a life ; and I want to try and explain why it is that the glory of GOD is the end of man. I believe some people at the bottom of their mind have this sort of idea, as I have said elsewhere,* " Why does GOD want so much praise ?" A good man does not like much praise, he dislikes it. Why is the glory of GOD to be the end of everything ?" And in order to answer that, which I am sure is often at the bottom of many minds, I want to take three illustrations which give different sides of the answer to the question.

* See p. 320.

## Glory to God

1. First of all, take the sun, the glorious sun in the morning; and, if you have ever watched from a mountain-top the sun rising, as I have often seen it—the sun coming up like a great giant, and the snow-peaks tinted one by one as the sun rises, and then passing into a glorious light—you would have seen how every peak reflects the glory of the sun; and still more wonderful, as the sun gathers strength, and shines down upon the valleys and upon the dewdrops, and upon every blade of grass, every dewdrop in the meadow shines with the glory of the sun, every dewdrop reflects the sun, and every dewdrop reflects the sun differently. Now, let us apply that illustration. "The heavens declare the glory of GOD, and the firmament showeth His handiwork." But much more than that. Every living soul, like a dewdrop in the morning, may reflect the sun of GOD's love, and reflect it differently. Every one is wanted. Every nation, as it is converted, will reflect the Gospel differently; it will bring its own particular colouring to the Gospel; and the Church of the Japanese, the Holy Catholic Church of Japan, will be different from, though the same Church as, the Holy Catholic Church of England. But the point to-night, before the Mission is over, is that every living soul can reflect the glory of GOD in a different way. Not a single one of us is the same as another; we are all different; there never has been anyone the same as you since the world began, never. And therefore the first way in which you are to reflect the glory of GOD, and in which you can make your own "Glory be to the FATHER, and to the SON, and to the HOLY GHOST," is by living

*Glory to God*

in the sunshine and the love of the TRINITY, by living in communion with GOD the FATHER through JESUS CHRIST by the SPIRIT. Now, are you prepared to try and do that ? Are you prepared after this to go back, after the Easter holidays are over, into the house of business in Marylebone and be a witness to the love of GOD ? Are you prepared to go back to your home from this Mission, and, like the dewdrop reflecting the sun, reflect the love of which you have heard ? If not, it will all be in vain. It is not a question of GOD glorifying Himself; it is a question of your attaining the object of your being, by being a witness. " To this end was I born, and to this end came I into the world : to be a witness to the truth." To this end am I here, for this cause came I into the world, to reflect the glory and the love of GOD. And everybody can do this ; it does not matter how poor you are, how insignificant, it does not matter in the slightest degree whether you are known to the world or not. If you are one of the dewdrops reflecting the light, you are fulfilling the object of your being.

2. Now, take another illustration. Sometimes in going about England you go to a place which is the estate of a great and good man. You find everybody speaks well of this man. You see all the cottages well looked after, repaired, and in good condition ; you see the children playing about, all evidently well cared for, and living a healthy life. And you find a good name for this Christian, unselfish landlord through miles and miles of the country. Everybody gives him a good name, as we say ; they glorify him—every one, to use the word for to-night, glorifies his name   Now,

## Glory to God

does not that illustration show us how we may glorify the name of GOD ? The world in which we live is His property, His kingdom. We want people to speak well of GOD ; we want to put an end to those who blaspheme GOD and distrust GOD, and create a false image to themselves about Him, and think Him a cruel tyrant ; we want people to give our GOD a good name for love and power and strength. Do you realise that GOD has trusted Himself very much to His servants, that we are fellow-workers with GOD ? We are partly in charge of the estate ourselves ; we are His viceroys. He rules the world through our prayers ; His good name depends upon the conduct of those who profess His name. If a steward is harsh at the door, the master gets a bad name. The good name of the master depends upon the steward. If we want to glorify His name, and make people speak well of our GOD, we have to spread His kingdom and keep His laws, and show that keeping them makes us happy. No one can live in London without knowing that the laws of GOD are justified ; that those who keep the laws of morality, of love and unselfishness are the happy people in London. I have seen home after home among the poorest in London as happy as any in the world. Why ? Because GOD's laws have been obeyed ; there has been self-control. The children brought up in this way, we find, are happy. Therefore, one of the first ways in which you can make people speak well of GOD is by obeying His laws, and showing that obedience to those laws makes you happy. I often think of the East-End father who once said to me : " I don't go to church, Mr. Ingram, myself, but I will say this, that my boy who does is

## *Glory to God*

the best boy I have got." The boy made his father speak well of GOD and think well of GOD's house. Therefore, as you try and translate your feelings and aspirations in the Mission into something practical, and run your sentiment into the mould of permanent resolutions without which a Mission is no good, ask yourself : " Am I glorifying the name of GOD ? Am I increasing the honour of His name ? What am I doing to make His estate, His property, better ? Am I teaching in the Sunday-school ? Am I visiting the sick, sitting up with my sick neighbours, and making people say, " Well, she is a Christian ; she was good to me in my time of trouble "? Are we trying to be friends of the poor, and, perhaps, helping the Friends of the Poor in the Church Army ? Are we, if we are young men, acting as officers in the Church Lads' Brigade, or helping at a boys' club ? What are we doing ? Are we doing anything at all ? We can hardly be considered to be glorifying the name of GOD if we are not making somebody speak better of GOD, and believe more in GOD than before ; it would be difficult honestly to say, " Glory be to the FATHER, and to the SON, and to the HOLY GHOST," if it is not the motto of our lives.

The second way, then, is to think of some practical course in which we may glorify the name of GOD for the rest of our lives, and make our life a " daily psalm of glory to His name," as we sing in the hymn on New Year's Day.

3, Thirdly, one of the most touching things is to hear a grown-up man or woman say, " I owe everything to my father," or " I owe everything to my mother," or, better still, " I owe everything to my

## Glory to God

father and mother. I had such parents! Do not praise me, Bishop, for doing this or that; it is nothing to do with me; I owe everything to my father and mother." It is a beautiful thing to hear that, and I have heard it very often. And do you not see that that gives us a third way of ascribing glory? It is not a question of anyone wanting to have self-glory; self-glory is the last thing to be mentioned in this connexion at all; but what is wanted is the grateful love of children. " I owe everything to my FATHER in Heaven; I owe everything to GOD the SON, Who died for me; I owe everything to GOD the HOLY SPIRIT, Who has sanctified me." That is what is wanted, and we have to give it with our lips as well as our lives. That is why at the end of every Psalm we say, " Glory be to the FATHER, and to the SON, and to the HOLY GHOST; as it was in the beginning, is now, and ever shall be." We often say it so carelessly that it becomes a form; but if we said it with meaning, with the same sort of tone as a man says, " I owe everything to my father," we should understand much more what glorifying GOD was. And, mind you, you have to give this glory quite as much if you are like the elder brother who did not wander very far from his father's home. I think there is danger in a Mission of people, who cannot think of any great outstanding sin which they have committed, imagining that the Mission has had very little message for them. But are you at all like that elder brother who had not wandered? He was not a very attractive person, was he, in the story? He had not wandered like the Prodigal Son, but he had wandered very much in soul and mind. He had allowed self-sufficiency and conceit and pride to come

## Glory to God

into his heart, and he had not been softened by the home, but had been hardened by it. And what I want to ask you is this : Do you not see that if, by GOD'S mercy, you have lived a sheltered life, and have not been like that drunkard or that poor girl in the streets, you have to ascribe your safety and your preservation to your FATHER'S care—your FATHER in Heaven ? You remember the story of the saint who said, when he saw a criminal being taken to the gallows : " There, but for the grace of GOD, goes John Bradford." And we must be very honest in ascribing to GOD the FATHER, GOD the SON, and GOD the HOLY GHOST the grace and the help which may have preserved us from the grosser sins. Those who are in the home must give the same loving ascription of the glory to GOD for it : " Glory be to GOD that He gave me the grace ; glory be to GOD that He protected me when I was so tempted ; glory be to the FATHER, and to the SON, and to the HOLY GHOST." They must welcome back the returning prodigal, knowing that, but for the grace of GOD, they would very likely have been worse than he was. And then, those who know they have been prodigals, let them ascribe glory to the Power which has brought them back. It may be some friend who brought them to the Mission ; it may be the word of some priest who helped them ; it may be the prayers of the great congregation in answer to which they have been restored ; but, behind all these things, what has brought them back; what is ready to put, still further, the ring on them ; to bring them to their baptism, if they are not baptized ; to confirm them, if they are not confirmed ; to bring them to the Communion, if

## *Glory to God*

they are not communicants, is the love of GOD the FATHER, GOD the SON, and GOD the HOLY GHOST. And they ought, especially now, as their last ascription of glory and thanksgiving, to say, " Glory be to the FATHER, and to the SON, and to the HOLY GHOST !"

And therefore if we take our last Mission message as the motto and inspiration of our lives, how happy our lives will be ! Think over what we have been taught about GOD Himself—that GOD'S love surrounds us every day ; that what we have to do—and this, I find, has touched many a soul—is to lift up the sluices and let the love and power come in. We have not to wait for GOD to hear us ; GOD is ready to hear our prayer before we ask. Let the tide come in and get hold of us—the great tide

> "Which moving seems asleep,
> Too full for sound or foam,"

in Tennyson's glorious words ; that tide is all round us—it " moving seems asleep." Lift up the sluices now ; let every soul that has kept them down lift them up ; let the tide of love and power come in—come in and sweep you to repentance and forgiveness, if you have not repented and been forgiven, and sweep you on to loving service, and, if you will, it shall sweep you on to the Eternal Home.

# ST. PAUL'S CATHEDRAL

*EASTER SUNDAY*

## XII

### THE LOVE OF THE TRINITY IN THE RESURRECTION

"He must be raised again the third day."—ST. MATT. xvi. 21.

WE have been meditating on the love of the TRINITY in itself, the love of the TRINITY in answer to prayer, the love of the TRINITY in the Incarnation, the love of the TRINITY in the Atonement; there only remains to consider the love of the TRINITY in the Resurrection.

Now, the words used by our LORD in the text clearly seem the solemn rehearsal of a previous plan made long before by the HOLY TRINITY; "The SON of man must go unto Jerusalem, and suffer many things of the elders and chief priests and scribes, and be killed, and be raised again the third day." There are several other expressions in the Bible which seem to let us into the counsels of the HOLY TRINITY: "Let *Us* make man in Our image, after *Our* likeness"; "Whom shall I send, and who will go for *Us?*" In the first of these utterances the HOLY TRINITY seem to reveal Their plan of creation of man, and in the second—most marvellous of all—to call for the help of the man whom They had made.

The Atonement, again, was clearly another wonderful conception of the Holy THREE in ONE; how the broken law could be perfectly kept, and yet the keeping of it be made of avail to the very people who had broken it; how the sinner could be forgiven at once, and yet not in such a way as to interfere with the necessity for his final restoration; how the mercy of GOD could be reconciled with His justice—all this formed a problem which was incapable of solution, unless one Person of the HOLY TRINITY knit Himself to the fallen human race, and yet in His human nature kept perfectly the broken law. And therefore we can see in some degree the force of the first part of the verse: "He must be put to death and be killed"—the world being what it was, perfect obedience meant death—and on Good Friday we kneel in adoring love before the love of the TRINITY in the Atonement.

But what we have to face on Easter morning is what would have been the position of the human race if the love of the TRINITY had stopped at the Atonement; for to do so will enable us to appreciate more fully the joy of Easter Day.

In the first place, we should have had no certainty that death was not the end. We might have guessed that it was not; we should no doubt have made the best of the instinct of immortality which we all possess; we should have got what comfort we could from the teachings of Science about the persistence of force; but how should we have looked the dying or the mourner in the face, unless JESUS had said, "I

## The Love of the Trinity in the Resurrection

am the Resurrection and the Life; though he were dead, yet shall he live, and he that believeth in Me shall never die," and unless He had proved the truth of that promise by being raised Himself on the third day? With misty aspirations and vague hopes and stumbling guesses, we should have followed our dead ones to the grave, and it was because the TRINITY, in their love, knew this, that they planned to themselves, " not only must the SON of man be knit to the human race, not only must He suffer many things of the elders, the chief priests and scribes, but He *must* be raised up the third day."

In the first place, then, without the Resurrection, the mourner would have been left disconsolate by the open grave; but, more than this, the sinner would have been left "unhouseled, disappointed, unanealed." The Atonement must not only be made, but it must be ministered; the blood must not only be shed, but it must be sprinkled on the sinner; the sacrifice must not only be offered, it must be pleaded; and for this the death must not only be endured, but be transfigured. And how completely and certainly it was transfigured on Easter Day the cross on St. Paul's Cathedral stands to witness. Think for a moment why the cross is brandished in triumph on the top of the Cathedral; since standing in this pulpit last Easter Day, I have asked that question of the business men in New York, the farmers of Canada, and our fellow-countrymen in St. Petersburg and Moscow, and there is only one answer: Because what was the " gallows " of two thousand years ago has been transfigured by what happened afterwards to Him Who hung upon it; because the death of

## The Love of the Trinity in the Resurrection

shame has passed into the life of triumph; because the badge of disgrace has become a mark of glory. But it could only be so if Resurrection followed Death, and so it was essential that " He must be raised up the third day "!

Again, we can scarcely realise the blow to every effort for the uplifting of the human race, if the love of the TRINITY had stopped short of the Resurrection. GOD knows it is hard enough now sometimes to struggle on; the forces of evil are so well organised and so strong; the world is so mixed up with the Church that sometimes even the Church of the Risen CHRIST itself hesitates when some great moral issue comes before it, and, as is so well described in one of Macaulay's poems :

> "Those behind cry ' Forward !'
> And those in front cry ' Back !'"

But picture for a moment what would happen if there was no Risen CHRIST at all ; if the entombment was the last seen of Him, and the stone rolled across the sepulchre was the end of the story, and we were left to face the problems of London gazing blankly at a cold and silent tomb. " Another good man who found the world too much for him ! Another foolish enthusiast who was before his time ! Another credulous person who trusted that GOD would stand by him in the crisis, and found Him fail him !" So the man of the world would have commented as he passed on his cynical way ; and what could any of us have said in reply ?

But *now*—but *now* how different is the story ! Forth from the silent heavens " the LORD hath

*The Love of the Trinity in the Resurrection*

made bare His Holy Arm in the eyes of all the nations, and all the ends of the earth have seen the salvation of our GOD." It makes no difference whether we say, " GOD raised Him from the dead," or " the SPIRIT raised Him from the dead," or " He rose Himself from the dead "—all expressions are used ; the fact was that the HOLY TRINITY were at work ; and when the HOLY TRINITY are at work, nothing can stop that work.

" Put the watch, by all means, if you like to do so ;" " Make it as sure as you can "—as Pilate said with unconscious irony—" roll the great stone across, and choose a heavy one." Certainly, if you are foolish enough to think that it will have any effect. But you might as well try and stop the rush of the Falls above Niagara with a pebble as interfere with the plans of the HOLY TRINITY when they are really launched. The decree had gone forth, " He must be raised again the third day," and without an effort, without a stir, in Divine silence, with the unconquerable and yet gentle strength of the Dawn, with the ease of the original creation, watch, stone, enemies brushed aside, He was raised again the third day ; again the voice from Heaven sounded, " Let there be light, and there *was* light."

Do you ask, What difference does this make to the Christian worker ? All the difference in the world. It is true that, what the love of the TRINITY could do so easily, when there was no question of working through hampering and sluggish and rebellious human wills, cannot be so quickly done when, one by one, the will of each living man and woman must be won first to voluntary co-operation ; it is true that

## The Love of the Trinity in the Resurrection

the " self-limitation of GOD " to working out His plans of love by persuasion and moral attraction, and never by coercion, necessitates a slowness of progress and a laboriousness of resurrection very different from the flash of life on Easter Day.

But the power is manifested—that is the splendid revelation of Easter ; the ultimate victory is assured ; GOD is shown to be a million times stronger than the Devil ; light is seen to be the great reality, and must therefore finally conquer the darkness. He Who was raised up the third day leads a slowly but surely conquering army, and one day the banner of the Cross will float triumphant over a redeemed world.

Lift up, then, the hands that hang down, and the feeble knees : if GOD be for us, who can be against us ? He that spared not His own SON, but delivered Him up for us all, how shall He also with Him freely give us all things ?

This is the great truth of Easter : The love of the TRINITY which planned creation ; the love of the TRINITY which answers prayer ; the love of the TRINITY which conceived the idea of the Incarnation ; the love of the TRINITY which designed the Atonement ; the love of the TRINITY which raised JESUS from the dead on the third day—that same love sweeps on like a resistless tide. We may dash ourselves against it to our own utter and perhaps endless loss ; we may stand aside, and so lose the opportunity of our lives ; we may erect every kind of barrier between it and our souls, so that, cold, unhappy, and useless, we may let the tide surge by ; but let all the humble here open up the sluices, tear down the

## The Love of the Trinity in the Resurrection

barriers, fling themselves into the service of it, lose themselves to find themselves, and with a completeness and a happiness and a strength which will be a surprise to the world, they will dry their tears, claim their pardon, and hasten the coming of the glorious Kingdom.

# ADDRESSES IN WESTMINSTER ABBEY

# WESTMINSTER ABBEY*

*MONDAY MORNING*

## I

## WHAT AM I ?

IF it had not been for the very kind and loving letter written by the Dean of this Abbey, begging that in the Central London Mission the Abbey might take some part, and if it had not been that I wish to respond to his kind invitation, and redress in our generation the old misunderstanding that existed so long between the Abbot of Westminster and the Bishop of London, I should scarcely have dared to add even four short addresses to the work which I had already undertaken this Lent. You must take my addresses, then, and my visit in the spirit in which I come. I come in a spirit of love, and I ask you to take what I say to you— I shall speak as straight as I can to your souls— as words simply spoken out of love to brothers and sisters whom I desire to help. And I propose to answer four questions : (1) What am I ? (2) Why am I here ? (3) What does GOD think of me ? (4) Where am I going ? And I ask and answer those questions

* These addresses were given at the special request of the Dean during the dinner-hour at one o'clock, special places being reserved for men under the pulpit.

## *What Am I?*

as a man among men, one of yourselves, preaching the answers to myself as I try to bring them home to you.

We will ask and answer this question first, " What am I ? " What am I, this person who is here ?

1. The first thing we certainly know is that I am a dying man. That is one thing, however sceptical we are, we know for certain : the living know that they shall die. Somebody dies in this great city every eight minutes, day and night. Four or five of my clergy have died in the last four or five weeks. And, although we all know it theoretically, I think that you men of the world will agree with me when I say it is astonishing what a surprise it often is to us when death does come. Those who have read them will remember the words of the " Northern Farmer," in Tennyson. There is a grim humour about them, yet they are wonderfully true to human nature. He suddenly found that he had to die, and this is what the great poet puts in his mouth as what he said :

" Do godämoighty knaw what a's doing a-taäkin' o' meä ?
I beänt wonn as saws 'ere a beän an' yonder a peä ;
An' Squoire 'ull be sa mad an' all—a' dear a' dear !
And I 'a managed for Squoire coom Michaelmas thutty year.

" A mowt 'a taäen owd Joänes, as 'ant nor a 'aäpoth o' sense,
Or a mowt 'a taäen young Robins—a niver mended a fence ;
But godamoighty a moost taäke meä an' taäke ma now
Wi' aäf the cows to cauve an' Thurnaby hoälms to plow !"

It wants a poet to put himself in the mind of a man like that, and, although we smile at it, there is many a man who is saying to himself unconsciously, " Does Almighty GOD know what He is doing in taking

## *What Am I?*

*me ?* Take me, the financier of this great corporation, the man on whom all the other clerks depend so much, with all these operations under my control ! Almighty GOD to take me, the father of a family ; Almighty GOD to take me, whom all the younger ones look up to ! Almighty GOD to take me, the Bishop of the diocese !" Yes, and we have got to face it, the world will go on just the same the day after we are dead ; there will be just the same crowded streets, and the same people pouring over London Bridge. There will be some, no doubt, who will weep for us—it would be hard if there were none to do that—but soon they too will join the great majority, and the world will go on the same, and the grass will grow over our graves, and when the men have carried us, stumbling downstairs, from the house where we died, it will be *our* body which they will be carrying, and we shall be, so far as this world is concerned, absolutely forgotten. Although I think I am the last man to ask anyone to take a morbid view of life, I do say that the man is a fool who forgets this. The man who, when he asks himself the question, " Who am I ?" does not answer, " First, a dying man," has left out a very essential part of life. You will find men planning out the future, with death left out, the one thing apparently not worth consideration. You will find men who know perfectly well, if they think of it, that when they die their family affairs will be in confusion, who make no will ; you will find people who have got their accounts so mixed up with other people's accounts that if they died to-day there would be great confusion and perhaps misunderstanding about their honesty. And, above all, you will find men whose spiritual affairs are in an inextricable confusion, who are themselves clear-headed business men in the City or in the offices round here, but who are thoughtless about the affairs of their soul, forgetting and ignoring the fact that the end may come at any moment. And therefore, from this point of view, before we ask and answer the question from another I would press upon you this question, and I will try and press it upon myself: Am I ready to die any day? Am I ready when the Master calls to answer that call?

> "The door must be on the latch in your room;
> For it may be in the dawning,
> Between the night and morning,
> CHRIST will come."

2. Then comes the second answer. After all, to say that I am a dying man, although it is a stern fact, is nothing like the most serious answer to the question, "What am I?" The second answer is, "One who cannot die." If death was the end, as Aristotle said and thought, after all, it would be hard to answer the sensualist or the suicide or the worldling when he says: "Death is the end; let us eat and drink, for to-morrow we die." It would be difficult to dissuade the man oppressed with business worries, who wants to get out of it all and put an end to himself, and says: "Well, it may be cowardly, but I am sick of life;" or to convert the man who is immersed in the affairs of the world, and says: "Well, this is the only world I know; it is very interesting; I will get the best out of the world: I have fifty or sixty or seventy years, and I will make the best of them." But if it is true that I cannot die, that five minutes

## *What Am I?*

after death I am the same as five minutes before, the whole complexion of things is altered. Then the sensualist, five minutes after death, and in the next world, finds himself alive with all the victims whom he has betrayed to accuse him in the other world. The suicide wakes up to find he is alive with a murder on his soul. The worldling who has dulled his thoughts and conscience in the noise of the world finds himself in a silence in which he must hear.

" How still it is !"

says the spirit in " The Dream of Gerontius."

> " I hear no more the busy beat of time,
> No, nor my beating pulse, nor fluttering breath;
> Nor does one moment differ from the next."

And if you say, " Yes. but how are you sure that you are a man who cannot die ?" we have an answer. It is not a thing which is mathematically certain like death ; it is not a thing that a man cannot disbelieve : a man may disbelieve it. But I believe it, first, because my body has changed many times, and yet I am the same person as the boy who went to school. I have survived all these changes ; why should I not survive the next ? The candle does not go out when I seem to blow it out ; the flame passes into another force. Force persists even in this world. There is an instinct in me, and in millions of other people who have lived—an instinct of immortality which lives in every heart. The one thing you will find it hardest to realise to yourselves is the very conception of ceasing to exist. The Bible is, I venture to say, a meaningless book with-

## What Am I?

out this belief in Immortality. Its promises are vain, its warnings are nothing, if a man does not live beyond the grave. And what I must cherish beyond everything else as a Christian is that JESUS CHRIST taught it. When a boy looks up in my face, and says, " Are you sure, Bishop, there is a life beyond the grave ?" if I could not look back in his face and say, " JESUS said, ' In My FATHER'S house are many mansions; if it were not so, I would have told you ' "—if I could not give that answer, I could not look him in the face. And therefore the second thing which is, I believe, absolutely certain is that I am a man who cannot die; that I shall pass out of this busy, toiling, moiling world into a quieter world; that, even if I have forgotten GOD here, I shall be bound to remember Him there; that five minutes after death it will matter not so much to me what I think of GOD, but it will matter everything what GOD thinks of me. And here in the silence, because you have come out for half an hour from the toil of life, and because it will be too late five minutes after death to ask yourself the question, and it will be too late for the sensualist, the lover of pleasure, the lover of the world and the careless man who never gives a thought to GOD or his neighbour, to change then, I do pray of you to ask yourself, Where do I stand with GOD ? Where does this immortal being stand, whom GOD loves still, and whom He has created ? " The love of the TRINITY " is the message of the Central London Mission; I, then, on whom the love of the TRINITY is still bent, and who still have a chance left to love GOD, shall I not take this chance before that silence comes after death ?

## What Am I?

3. And that brings me once again to ask the question in a different way. This dying man, this undying man, what is he besides the body ? We talk about a soul, but " soul " conveys very little to anybody's mind really. A man once asked me whether his soul would come out of his mouth when he died. When we talk about the soul, what we really mean is a living personality. It is not that our body has a soul, but we are immortal spirits living in bodies. And when I speak of myself I speak of you. What does this immortal being consist of ? I have a free will, I have a mind, I have a heart, I have a conscience, and I have the instinct to pray. In other words, I can choose, I can think, I can love, I can judge, and I can pray. Those five things, if you think over them, are exactly the things which make you up. You are all those five things. I can choose. It is one of the answers to the difficulties that pour in upon me all through this Mission. The answer to half the difficulties is the self-limitation of GOD in dealing with free will. GOD has limited Himself in dealing with us. When He made men and women such as you and I are He gave us free will, in order that we might freely choose the good, and therefore become worthy to be companions with Him through all eternity. What is the good of a man who is made to be good ? None at all. Therefore, when GOD made men and women in His image, after His likeness, one of the great characteristics of man was free will, power to choose, power to choose or not to choose. We must never be blinded to the facts of the case by the self-limitation of GOD in dealing with people of free will. We may either choose or we can

## *What Am I?*

refuse, and we are bound to ask which we are doing. Am I choosing the good ? Am I choosing the hard moral path of a straight life which leads finally to happiness, although the temptations are strong ? Am I choosing GOD or the devil ? Am I choosing the life of the SPIRIT or the life of the flesh ? Which ? Besides free will, I have a mind, and my mind is given me to think on the noble things of life, to think of GOD. I have a heart to love.

"I needs must love the highest when I see it."

What am I loving ? what am I giving my heart to ? That is the sign of my character. I have a conscience; it can be kept either sensitive or dull. The conscience may be seared with a red-hot iron, to use the forcible language of Scripture. Is my conscience sensitive, or is it growing more callous every day ? I am a praying animal; that is where I differ from the other animals. Am I up in the morning praying and getting into communion with GOD, or has that power become atrophied from want of use every day ? GOD save us from allowing atrophy to deaden the best part about us! As a dying and an undying man, then, with all these powers given me by GOD, have I dedicated them to GOD, or have I listened for perhaps the first time for weeks to-day to His voice ? It is not too late, and the true answer from our hearts should be this, "Speak, LORD, for Thy servant heareth."

# WESTMINSTER ABBEY

*TUESDAY MORNING*

## II

### WHY AM I HERE?

" For what end was I born, and for what cause came I into the world ?"

THAT is the question I propose to face with you now, and we must put aside all obviously futile answers, when we have so short a time. It is pure waste of time to discuss the futility of the answers, " To get rich," " To get on," or " To be popular." All those things, it is quite clear, if we were right yesterday, must not only be wrong answers, but must be stupid answers. So we put them aside. It is too ridiculous to suppose that an undying spirit, here for a few passing years, could possibly be right to devote himself to amassing wealth or riches which he cannot carry away when he dies. Let us, then, take much deeper answers, and answers for which a great deal is to be said.

First, " I am here that I may be happy." There is a great truth in that. When we ask why GOD ever made anything; why, when He was perfect in Himself, He ever said, " Let there be light, let there be life," it is quite true that the answer must be, To spread

## Why Am I Here?

happiness, that there might be so many more millions of people sunning themselves in the sunshine of His own happiness; and the poet Stevenson has spoken quite truly of " my great task of happiness." And therefore, perhaps, rightly understood, that might be a true answer. But it is too vague, and not definite enough for our purpose. Then an answer might be that life is given to love and to be loved, and we have a great authority in Browning; if I remember rightly, the exact quotation is—

" Life is but the chance of gaining love."

And if we were to expand that and explain it, I think we might almost make it the answer, if we understood thoroughly what it meant. Or, again, a very obvious answer, and in its sense beautifully true, is that we are here to please GOD; and certainly, if you understand that, and if you expand it sufficiently, we might make that the answer, but not if we use it in the sense in which it is often used—pleasing GOD individually in ourselves, without any regard to other people.

I. But what, then, if these, on various grounds, seem unsatisfactory, is the true answer ? " Why was I born, and for what cause came I into the world ?" I believe there is only one complete answer, and that is the answer which CHRIST gave Himself as representative of the human race : " For this end was I born, and for this cause came I into the world, to *bear witness to the truth*." And I believe there is only one answer which anyone, man or woman, has any right to give, and that is : " To this end was I born,

## Why Am I Here?

and for this cause came I into the world, to bear witness to the truth."

To some this may seem an astonishing answer. It may astonish some who in their modesty say, " Is it possible the truth can be entrusted to me ? Cannot the truth witness for itself ? Can I, a humble clerk in a great office, be entrusted with the task of witnessing for the truth ? Is it possible that the spread of the Kingdom can depend upon me, and that I have been sent from Heaven down to earth to bear witness to the truth ?" And, in order to see that the answer is not so incredible or startling as it at first sight appears, we must remember three things.

1. First, we must remember the wonderful position which is given to man in creation. We have spoken of the self-limitation of GOD, which explains so many difficulties—the self-limitation of GOD in dealing with man. He limits Himself because man is so noble, because He has given such authority, such power, such responsibility, to man that He has to deal with him as a responsible person—just, for instance, as a father, if I may take a simple illustration, when the son grows up to twenty-one twenty-three, or twenty-five, will deal with him differently from the way in which he dealt with him when he was a child. When you take the various things said about mankind in the Bible, they are tremendous in their import. Not only are we made in GOD's image, after His likeness, but we are said to be kings, priests, a kingdom of priests—not the clergy only, but everyone—the whole Church a kingdom of priests. We are told that we may be fellow-workers with GOD, that we are to join in the

## *Why Am I Here?*

plans of the HOLY TRINITY, and we are to carry them out. When we think what that means, we realise the folly of trying to fill our lives with some little futile object ; when we were born to co-operate with the HOLY TRINITY in the most majestic designs for the redemption of the human race—how pitiably small our present lives appear !

2. Then, secondly, we must remember what Mr. Holden, in his book " The HOLY GHOST, the Comforter," calls " the indirect approach of the HOLY GHOST." I have pointed out elsewhere how GOD, all through His dealings with mankind, has used outward and visible signs—the pillar of cloud by day, and the pillar of fire by night, the outward and visible sign of His protecting care. Naaman must go and wash in the Jordan—the outward and visible sign of the inward and invisible healing he was to have. Our LORD put clay round the eyes of the blind man, and said to him, " Go and wash in the pool of Siloam " —the outward and visible sign of inward and invisible healing. And therefore, when we use in the Church outward and visible signs, such as water in Baptism, the laying-on of hands in Confirmation, the bread and the wine in the Holy Communion, we shew our belief that GOD is continuing to act towards the human race in the way in which He has always acted in all His revealed dealings with man in the Bible. But if this is true of the indirect approach of the HOLY GHOST with regard to material things, it is equally true—even more startlingly true—with regard to His indirect approach through men. The prophets are called out in the Old Testament that He may speak through them. Ananias is sent to tell St. Paul,

## Why Am I Here?

formerly Saul, what he is to do. There is no flaming sign in the sky for every generation, but a pleading ministry is instituted through which the HOLY SPIRIT is to speak generation after generation. The indirect approach of the HOLY GHOST is even more startling when we see how men are used than when He uses material things. Before, then, we dismiss the idea that we were sent into the world to bear witness to the truth, we must remember GOD'S invariable method of indirect approach.

3. Thirdly, we must remember and note the infinite importance which is attached to the witnesses in the New Testament in every age. In the apostolic age the chief witnesses were the Apostles, who were able to describe what they saw; and we can imagine what an impression it would have made upon us to have heard St. Peter and St. John describe what they saw in the tomb which made them so certain. As Mr. Latham says, they probably saw the clothes left in a particular way, and the head-cloth folded turban-like, indicating that no man's hand had been at work there, but only the Hand of GOD. It would have been a great thing to have heard St. Thomas say what he had seen; how he had been told to put his hand into the wound in the Master's side, and to touch the marks of the Cross, but had not dared to do so. But do we realise that the conversion of the world was being carried out by other witnesses of whom we do not know the names—the five hundred who saw JESUS in broad daylight on the mountain, not one of whose names we know? They were witnesses[*]—

[*] This is more fully developed in the second introductory sermon (at Holy Trinity, Marylebone). See page 13.

## *Why Am I Here?*

" the unknown good who rest in GOD's still memory folded deep "—through whom the world has been converted. And there were some in the next age, martyrs who were witnesses to the death. And if you ask me what I am trusting to to convert East London and North London, it is not the clergy—the five hundred clergy who work with such beautiful devotion year after year—but I am trusting to the fifty thousand communicants who like stars are shining in every street, in every workshop and warehouse. These are the witnesses to whom I trust, and to whom JESUS CHRIST trusts. Therefore, when you take into consideration those three things—the great standing of mankind, the indirect approach of the HOLY GHOST, and the position assigned in the conversion of the world to the witnesses—it becomes much more probable, and, in fact, absolutely certain, that the true answer to the question, " Why am I here ? for what cause came I into the world, as a man ?"—I am not speaking as an ordained man—is simply this : " To bear witness to the truth." And if I fail, or if you fail, as a witness, we fail altogether. It does not matter in the least if we have a reputation of being the best business man in Westminster ; it does not matter in the slightest whether we have used our opportunities to get great popularity in our set ; if we are failures as witnesses, we are failures altogether. If there is not some one who believes more because of us, if there is not some one who shines more because of us, our life up to to-day has been a failure in the sight of GOD.

II. To what, then—and that brings me to the next branch of the question—are we to witness ?

## *Why Am I Here?*

1. First, we are to witness to GOD the FATHER'S love as revealed in CHRIST. We should not be certain of it unless it was so revealed. When you see a man very much worried at every moment of his life and irritable at home; if you see a man or woman constantly depressed, with no hope, no joy, it is very hard for you to believe that they have faith in a good and loving GOD. Surely there ought to be a joy and peace in believing, and hope. " May GOD fill you "—that is one of the most beautiful prayers in the New Testament—" the GOD of Hope fill you with joy and peace in believing, that ye may abound in hope through the power of the HOLY GHOST." And therefore I do think that we are failing as witnesses if there is not a calmness and a joy and a hopefulness in our lives which convinces people that we believe in GOD's love. Is that the case with your life ? I ask myself the same question that I ask you. Am I a faithful witness to the love of GOD ?

2. Take another thing to which we have to bear witness. We profess to believe in a very awful, although a very blessed thing: we profess to believe that the SON of GOD came down from Heaven and died upon the Cross. It is an awful thing to believe. The faith of some staggers at it until they have faced it and believe it. When St. Paul believed it he knelt at the foot of the Cross, and said over and over again, " He loved me, and gave Himself for me." But if we believe that, I ask you—I want to carry every one with me—has not the world a right to expect that it will have some effect on our lives ? If we believe so tremendous a thing, we shall be witnesses to it, and the clerk who

works next to us in the office will see, if he stays by us long enough, that we believe in a crucified SAVIOUR; there is a mark of self-denial, a mark of unselfishness about us. At first, perhaps, he is not in sympathy—he may not understand what it is; but gradually it will dawn upon him that the man he works with, the man who sits next him every day, believes in the Cross. Is that the case with us? If not, we are failures as witnesses.

3. And we have to bear witness to the power of the HOLY GHOST. We profess to believe that the great gates of Heaven opened when the SON returned at the Ascension, and down through those gates came the HOLY GHOST to be a power to lead us, even to drive us according to the will of GOD. To be driven by the SPIRIT down the track of the will of GOD is the destiny of every Christian. Is that the case with us? Is it possible for a man to believe we are thus driven, if every gust of public opinion sways us this way and that, if we are blown about by every wind of doctrine? It is impossible; they cannot believe there is that power within us—a Divine power to drive us against the tide of human opinion. When we see a ship sailing against the tide, we believe in the wind. Are we thus witnessing to the power of the HOLY GHOST?

4. Or take the brotherhood of the Church. The Church was meant to be the most happy and glorious brotherhood that the world has ever seen. To a great extent it has been a failure in impressing the world that it is so. The world believes that it is an ecclesiastical organisation which exists for its own purposes. Am I, are you, a good witness to the

## Why Am I Here?

brotherhood of the Church—a brotherhood in which rich and poor are all on a level, all equal in the sight of GOD, and which does not exist for itself at all, but for the service and good of the world ? Are we witnesses to that ?

Let us try, then, in four ways to be better witnesses. First, in our daily life, in the home, in the office and in the club. Secondly, by our lips. It is all very well to talk of the reserve of Englishmen— and GOD grant that we may always keep that reserve !—but it is a very different thing to let the natural reserve of Englishmen be the excuse for blank cowardice when we ought to speak out ; and I believe if a man was to take his courage in both hands, and speak out much more than he does about what he really believes—the ordinary layman I am speaking of—it would be astonishing what good he would do. He might nerve the courage of some boy who finds his faith wavering when he sees men not standing up for their colours. St. Andrew's Brotherhood in America and over here have a rule that a true witness ought to find some opportunity, in the course of each week, to speak a word for what he believes to some one. Thirdly, we should bear witness by our worship. How can a man who spends every weekend at the golf-links be expected to impress people with the idea that he really believes in these things ? If he was in church with his boys, that would be a visible witness which no one could possibly resist. " As for me and my house, we will serve the LORD." And lastly, by some definite work. If these great things are true, then, besides our professional work, there ought to be something which we can find to

## Why Am I Here?

do; we might take over the accounts of the church in the parish in which we live, if we are business men; or go and work at a boys' club. Women might work among the women and girls in London. "Work, work, while it is day; the night cometh when no man can work."

And so let us take for our lesson one of those lighthouses which stand on our British shores.

> "The startled waves leap over it; the storm
>   Smites it with all the scourges of the rain,
> And steadily against its solid form
>   Press the great shoulders of the hurricane."*

But it stands, the very type of a witness. May we so stand in our generation as faithful witnesses, and may we bring many a storm-tossed vessel into the haven where it would be!

\* Longfellow, "The Lighthouse."

# WESTMINSTER ABBEY

*WEDNESDAY MORNING*

## III

### WHAT DOES GOD THINK OF ME ?

"WHAT am I ?" "Why am I here ?" "What does GOD think of me ?" I cannot ask and answer that question without thinking of one of whom I heard to-day, who has at last been brought face to face with that question as he is about to meet almost certain death ; and I want you to put yourselves, and I want to put myself, in his place, and ask it with the same deadly reality with which he is saying to himself, " What does GOD think of me ?" We must remember three or four things if we ask that question properly.

First, every one stands absolutely distinct to the eye of GOD. There is a completely wrong individualism in religion, as we saw yesterday, but, at any rate, there is a true individualism, and we have not learnt the solemnity of religion yet unless we realise that every one stands perfectly clear to the eye of GOD, as if there was not another living person in the world.

Secondly, each of us differs completely from the rest ; there never has been anyone at all like what you are ; although there are so many millions of

## What does God Think of Me?

people now alive or who will live in this world, you are a thought of GOD absolutely different from anyone else. There has never been anyone really like you since the world began.

Thirdly, each of us has the whole of GOD to attend to him. I am certain that many of us slip into the belief that, there being so many of us, we have only a millionth or a ten-millionth part of GOD's attention. The awful and glorious truth is this: that, GOD being infinite, each of us has the whole of GOD to attend to him; that when we pray, we have the whole of GOD's attention. We have all His care, as if there was not another living person to look to. And we have not realised the momentous meaning of the question, "What does GOD think of me?" unless we realise that we stand distinct like that before GOD, and have the whole of GOD to care for us, and to watch us.

Fourthly, whether our lives are long or short, sad or merry, they all end in one way; and I think one of the most awful statements in Holy Scripture is the simple statement: "Every man shall give an account of himself to GOD."

Bearing, then, those facts in mind, let us ask ourselves, "What has GOD been doing for us?" before we ask what He thinks of us.

What has He been doing for us? I stand here, as we saw, though a dying man, an undying spirit; and when I ask myself that question I know that my spirit came from GOD. He is the FATHER of spirits.

> "Not in entire forgetfulness,
> And not in utter nakedness,
> But trailing clouds of glory do we come
> From GOD, who is our home."

## *What does God Think of Me?*

The first thing that He has done for me is that He has given me life and light and love. I stand here to-day a living spirit created by GOD. Is that all He has done ? No ; I look round, and I find He has warmed the atmosphere in which I am to live and breathe here ; He has given me that home, He has given me those friends, He has given me that dear mother ; He has given others wife and children, everything they have that has warmed life and makes it happy. GOD has done that for you and me.

I look a little further. Has He done anything else ? And I remember that cross upon my brow, or I know that it was placed there, though I was unconscious at the time, in my Baptism. And not in vain was that cross placed upon my brow, because it tells me that GOD has redeemed me, that He has bought me back, that I am a member of a ransomed Church ; I am one of the redeemed, if I allow myself to be so.

I look again. Is that all that GOD has done for me ? No ; my conscience tells me that He has been trying to sanctify me all my life, that He has been warning me through the lips of friends, that He has been encouraging me through the lips of other friends. He has answered my boyish prayers ; besides baptizing me, He has confirmed me ; He has given me the strengthening power of the HOLY SPIRIT in Confirmation ; I have even been allowed to be a communicant ; and He has been trying in the closest, dearest way to sanctify me.

Has He finished ? Is that all that He has done ? Is the work stopped ? Not at all. I find to-day this glorious sunshine in which He wraps me in my

## *What does God Think of Me?*

earthly home. I know that He has given me the breath which I breathe and by which I live. I know that into my soul, if only I am responsive, He is ready to pour His grace every day; He is watching with loving care to see where I shall be likely to go wrong, and that I am at this moment in the care of undying love. And what I know of myself I know of every one of you. Ask yourselves, then, as I ask myself, this question: " What is GOD doing for me, and what has He done for me ?" And every one, if he is honest, though, perhaps, in different terms and in different language, and suiting his language to his life, would acknowledge: " This hath GOD done for me; this is He doing for me."

When we believe that, and understand it, then comes the awful question, After all this has been done, and after all this that is being done, what does GOD think of me ? What does He think of me as a child of His ? After all this care and all these many gifts, what does He think of me as a child ? Am I a responsive, loving, trustful child, looking to Him every day for help and guidance, trying to please Him, trying to work with Him, as He tries to work with me, opening every avenue of my soul, that He may use me more for His loving purposes ? "What does He think of me as a child ?" I urge you to ask yourselves that question. What is your response as a child of GOD to GOD ? What does He think of me as an example which He hoped I should be to others, an influence upon the other brothers and sisters of the family, an influence on the boys and girls and the men and women He might bring within my sphere of influence ? What am I ? Is He dis-

## What does God Think of Me?

appointed in me ? Am I bracing others to bear their temptations more bravely ? Am I, in the office or in the school, or in the home, making it easier for others to live and serve GOD ? Or is my influence bad ? Do the boys find it harder to be good where I am ? I am bound to ask that question. What does GOD think of me as an example ? What does He think of me as a witness ? And we must ask that with the thoughts of yesterday fresh in our minds. Have I stood firm against unpopularity when the tide was all dead against me ? Have I stood firm, or have I been blown about by every wind of vain doctrine that may blow ? Has the light gone out in the lighthouse and the ship gone on the rocks, whereas if the light had been there it would have sailed into the right haven ? What does GOD think of me as one of His lighthouses in the world ? What does GOD think of me as a sentinel ? " I have put watchmen on thy walls, O Jerusalem, which shall never hold their peace day nor night. Ye that are of the LORD'S remembrancers, take ye no rest, and give Him no rest, till He establish and till He make Jerusalem a praise in the earth." As GOD looks down and expects to see the sentinel pacing up and down the walls of His city guarding, watching, raising up holy hands as the LORD'S remembrancer, praying for the poor, praying for the helpless, praying for the peace of Jerusalem, praying for the Kingdom, what does He think of me as one of His sentinels whom He has placed on the walls of Jerusalem ? How much have I watched and guarded ? Have I blown the trumpet, or been afraid to blow the trumpet ? If so, the blood is on the watchman's head. Have I held up my hands,

## *What does God Think of Me?*

not for myself only, but for others ? Have I been interceding as one of the LORD'S remembrancers day by day ? What does He think of me as one of His remembrancers and intercessors ? What does GOD think of me as one of His soldiers who is to keep the place in the square ? As one of our great poets reminds us :

> "There's a battle to fight, ere the guerdon be gained,
> The reward of it all."\*

I was baptized, in common, probably, with every one of you, that I might be " a faithful soldier and servant until my life's end." Am I fighting as a good soldier of JESUS CHRIST ? Am I fighting and enduring hardships in the battle ? How much have I fought against all the wrong in London, in my set, in the tone of society ? How much have I fought during the last year ? What does GOD think of me this morning ? And as I ask it, I must be careful to distinguish that question from " What does the world think of me ?" There may be a man here very high up in his profession, very much written about in the papers, thought a great deal of by his generation; but GOD may think very little of him. Still more must we guard and distinguish it from " What do my friends think of me ?" Nothing so blinds a soul to its true state as the false estimate of friends. " I cannot be such a very bad man if my friends or my family are so fond of me." But do they know everything ? That is the question. Would they think quite so highly of me if they knew everything, if they knew all that GOD knows ? Oh, let us not,

\* Browning.

## What does God Think of Me?

in asking this question, be blinded by the thought that we are so popular at the club, that we are so popular with our relations. They do not know all about us like GOD. What does GOD think of me?

I only know one way to find out. I must go down on my knees. I cannot discover it in a moment. I must go down on my knees; I must take the Holy Commandments of GOD one by one in all their real meaning, and all the searching meaning given by the SON of GOD when He came, in my home life, in my private life, in my moral life, my life in the world. I must not shirk it, but must take these Commandments one by one, and press them home upon my conscience. Am I making a false image of GOD, and picturing Him to my mind as a cruel, a harsh tyrant? Then I am breaking the second Commandment. Am I quite sincere in my religion, or am I really a hypocrite? If so, I am breaking the third. How do I spend my Sundays? What is my home life like? Am I pure in thought and word and deed? Am I honest and straightforward in all my dealings? Am I coveting to get rich at any cost? Press home these Commandments of GOD, right down into the inmost thoughts of the heart.

That is the first way. But it is only the first. It must be at the foot of the Cross. Only the Cross tells me what my sin is. Why was it that CHRIST, humanly speaking, was put to death at all? It was because a perfectly pure, true life met the tone of the world, and the tone of the world, when He met it quite bravely, killed Him. And it is not too much to say that they do kill Him again to-day. Suppose you see a man really standing up against the tone of

## *What does God Think of Me?*

his office; suppose you see him really standing up for honesty in his business against the rest of the firm; suppose you see him really standing up against his set for strict morality and the possibility of a pure life—I have seen that man crucified before now, and CHRIST is crucified again in him. Look at the Cross then; we must do so if we are to see what our pride, our prejudice, our sloth, our selfishness, is really doing.

And then, lastly, use the light of the HOLY SPIRIT. The HOLY SPIRIT comes to convict the world of sin. And if I want to know what GOD does think of me, I must press home His Commandments at the foot of the Cross, and by the light of the HOLY SPIRIT, and take time to do it; and it will be a surprise if I do not end my meditation with the prayer, "GOD be merciful to me a sinner." And, having begun with that prayer, let my resolution be: "GOD thinks that of me; now I see it; GOD helping me, I will be a better child, I will be a better example, a better witness, a better sentinel, a better soldier, that some day He may say, ' This is My beloved son, in whom I am well pleased.' "

# WESTMINSTER ABBEY

*THURSDAY MORNING*

## IV

### WHERE AM I GOING ?

WE can hardly ask this question without remembering that ancient story which comes down from such distant times in our land, of one of the old heathen chiefs who, when the Christian missionary arrived in this country, pointed to the bird that passed through the tent—came in, and then went out—and said : " The human soul is like that bird ; it comes for a passing time, stays here for a while, and then passes on. If this missionary can tell us where the soul comes from and whither the soul is going, let us listen to what he says." And certainly we are now facing the greatest mystery of all. We can appreciate what a man is stated to have said when about to be blown from the guns—" Now I shall know the great secret." And when we sometimes, perhaps, think life monotonous and unromantic, we can have little real imagination if we fail to realise the tremendous question, " Whither am I going when I have left this tent and gone out into the darkness ?"

First of all, let us quite frankly lay aside three questions which I have been asked constantly during

## *Where Am I Going?*

this Mission, and to which I do not pretend to be able to give a full answer. First, why we are not told more about the other world. "Can you tell me, Bishop," a boy asked me once when he was dying, "a little about where I am going to?" I do not pretend to explain the awful silence after death—the blank. "There is no voice, nor any that answers, nor any that regards." And as we try and picture what the dear wife or sister or brother may be doing, it is very hard to picture it to ourselves at all; and all we can feel certain about is this: that, if it had been wise to tell us more, and if we had had the faculty to understand that other life, we should have been told more. I threw myself back, when the boy asked me that question, upon the SAVIOUR'S words: "In My FATHER'S house are many mansions; if it were not so, I would have told you." "He that believeth, though he were dead, yet shall he live, and whosoever liveth and believeth in Me shall never die."

And so, again, I leave unexplained all those mysterious questions about the length or the nature of the punishment of unrepentant souls. When self-will ceases hell ceases, says a great writer; but will self-will cease? What are the meanings of those awful sentences which our LORD used Himself? Is He not warning us that the will may be so bent that it cannot turn? Is not that the danger which He is pointing out to us? And when people ask me that question I come back to the love of GOD. GOD never ceases to love any soul which He has made; GOD must follow with infinite love every soul always. Or, again, am I in my teaching to set myself up to be

## Where Am I Going?

more merciful than JESUS CHRIST ? JESUS CHRIST died for me, and He died for every living soul in the world. I can trust Him then to do His best for every soul.

And so once again I leave on one side another question, which is asked by many a mother: " How can I ever be happy if my darling boy is not with me ?" I can only say that, deeply as that mother loves her boy, GOD loves him more ; and if punishment—stern punishment—is the best for him, she will look at things from the point of view of GOD in the other world. GOD will not allow punishment for a single one of His children if it is not best for him. And therefore the mother's love, as part of GOD's love, will look at things always from the point of view of GOD.

And so I leave those questions, acknowledging them to be difficulties, and simply state what light I can see in the darkness.

I come now to three facts as to where I am going which I believe to be solid facts which we do know.

1. The first is that the place to which we are going is bound by a law which nothing can break to what our character is now. Judas " went to his own place " —to the place, that is to say, the inevitable place whatever that was, which he had prepared all the time for himself. He could have gone to no other place. If one of us left this world to-day, by a spiritual law which nothing could alter, we should go to our own place—our own place, whatever that was, which we had prepared for ourselves, taking into consideration all our judgments, all our penitence, all our acceptance of the great deliverance from the Cross, all that makes

## *Where Am I Going?*

up the person that you are and that I am ; we must go to our own places.

2. Secondly, what is Heaven to one soul is hell to another. "Go thou and serve." Two souls received the same sentence.

> "Go thou and serve—
>   Across the face there fell
> A darkened shadow, and I heard
> A muttered groan of—Hell !
> Go thou and serve, the same voice said.
> \* \* \* \* \*
> I saw a rapture-lighted face
> Too blessed to answer—Heaven !"

What was Hell to one was Heaven to another. What we are too apt to forget is this : that even GOD Himself cannot make Heaven Heaven to an unrepentant soul ; that even GOD cannot change the longings and the love and the tastes of a soul which has free will, so that in a moment it could pass from loving one thing to loving its opposite without a complete change of character. What is Heaven to one is Hell to the other.

3. Thirdly, Heaven and hell begin now; we carry Heaven and hell about with us. "Surely," says Bacon, in his stately way, "surely it is Heaven upon earth when a man's mind rests in Providence, moves in charity, and turns upon the poles of truth." Surely it is Heaven upon earth. And do not some know what hell on earth is ? I have had some letters, which, if I read them to you, would lead you to say that there are some souls in hell on earth ; and I ask your prayers that I may have, by GOD's grace, the wisdom to liberate some of those souls from

## Where Am I Going?

hell. Heaven and hell, then, begin now. "This is life eternal to grow to know" (as the particular tense means), " to go on knowing Thee, the only true GOD, and JESUS CHRIST Whom Thou hast sent."

What, then, does our question come to be? "Where am I going?" comes to mean, "What is my character every day becoming? What am I learning to enjoy? What am I really loving? What is my ideal? What am I becoming?" I do not think any story ever went home so strongly to the consciences of men as "Dr. Jekyll and Mr. Hyde." There, you will remember, was painted before us with the skill of a great writer the benevolent physician so well known and respected in the town, thought to be a model of philanthropy and a pattern of good works, by day, and in the same town there were rumours of an ugly and mischievous dwarf named Mr. Hyde, who did horrible deeds of cruelty and sensuality, by night; and the awful moral of the story was this, as you may remember: Dr. Jekyll and Mr. Hyde were the same person—Dr. Jekyll by day, and Mr. Hyde by night. What he really enjoyed was what he did as Mr. Hyde; the appearance he kept up before the world was what he was as Dr. Jekyll. We must carry on our self-examination by pressing home with ruthless courage the question, " What do I enjoy— what do I really enjoy?"—not what is the appearance I must keep up in the office; not what is the reputation I must sustain in society, but what do I really enjoy in my soul? what do I love? what do I want to be like? what do my thoughts turn to when I am by myself? That is the man. And it is on that

## Where Am I Going?

fact, what the man is, that the answer to the question Where am I going? depends. That man will go to his own place, and not any other.

And therefore do let us reset our ideals. It has been said that GOD loves us for what we are becoming. We are saved in CHRIST if we accept the salvation, but forgiveness means ultimate reformation. We are forgiven for what we are capable of becoming. The penitent thief is forgiven in a moment, but it is on the understanding that if he lived he would be the reformed thief. Let us not then be discouraged by feeling how far short we all of us are from our ideal, but let us be certain that our ideal, what we are longing to be, what we love, what we are setting before ourselves, is the highest. Our ideal ought to be to become like JESUS CHRIST; I want to have His spirit in me; I want to have His purity of soul; I want to have His unselfishness in my life; and if I grow more like JESUS CHRIST, then I may have a hope that I may one day follow Him where He has gone before. But the whole question is, Am I wanting to be like Him? or is my ideal the popular man in the club, or the successful merchant, or the clever man of the world? It is what I want to be that decides my character— what I persistently want to be.

And so let us leave on one side those puzzling questions which only disturb the true aim of the soul. "LORD, are there few that be saved?" they asked our Master; and what was His answer? "Strive to enter in at the strait gate yourself." "Are they few that be saved?" men ask to-day. The answer is the same: "Strive to enter in at the strait

## *Where Am I Going?*

gate—agonise to enter in, for many shall seek" (a different word) " to enter in and shall not be able." Agonise to enter in. It wants all the power of the soul, all the resolution of the will, all the force of prayer, all the means of grace—Confirmation and Communion ; it demands them all, if under the stress of temptation, and with all the blinding snares of the world, we may attain. " For I intend "—that must be each soul's firm resolve—

> " For I intend to get to GOD,
>   It is to GOD I speed so fast,
> And on GOD'S breast, my own abode,
>   Those shoals of dazzling glory past,
>   I'll lay my spirit down at last."*

\* Browning, "Johannes Agricola."

# ADDRESSES TO MEN

# I

# WHAT THE YOUNG MEN OF THE DAY COULD BE AND DO IN LONDON

### AN ADDRESS TO OLD PUBLIC SCHOOL AND UNIVERSITY MEN AT LONDON HOUSE *

I DARE say you are a little inclined to wonder why you are asked to come in this way to London House. I want to be perfectly frank, and explain to you how the whole thing has come about in my mind. First of all, the idea of this gathering, and I hope of many subsequent gatherings, comes from those great meetings at which some of you were present in Oxford and Cambridge when I used to come down to the University. I shall never forget those meetings at the Corn Exchange at Oxford and Cambridge—the Oxford ones were more numerous because I was better known there—when we had about a thousand men present; and we had four or five hundred also in Christ Church Hall, when I gave a more intimate talk. The question has often occurred to me, What happens to these men? About one in forty are ordained, and I meet them afterwards in my diocese or in other dioceses. What has happened to the great majority of those men who used to come and sit for half an hour listening to my simple

\* About one hundred were present.

## To Public School Men

talk year after year? Every year there were these numbers of men present, and then afterwards no very visible result. I wonder what happens to them. I thought I would make an attempt, if I could, to find out whether there are any of that class of men in my diocese.

Then another thing—and all these points come out just as they lie in my mind—stirred me up to call you together: I find on Boards and Committees in my diocese none but practically old men. I go to the Bishop of London's Fund Board, and I find old men sitting there who were sitting there in Bishop Jackson's time. All honour to them; but I do ask for just a few young men. When these old men die, who is going to take their places? It is the same everywhere I go in this diocese. There seem to be no young men coming to take the places of the men who have borne the heat and burden of the day. I honour them with all my soul; but why only old men? Or again—and this is a third reason—to put it in a humorous way, there are too many bald heads in church. That is to say, as I preach in church after church in London, I find, on looking down, a good many men in some churches—the majority are women—but these men are nearly all grey-headed or bald. Where are the young men with hair on their heads? What has happened to them? When they were at their public schools they were confirmed and went to their Communions, with earnestness, no doubt, at Harrow, Eton, Marlborough, Rugby, and so on. I want to find out what has happened to them.

Then, again, I look round, and I find all kinds of

## To Public School Men

things here in London simply waiting for young men to come and do them. Take, for instance, a successful experiment, such as we started about ten years ago—the Borstal Committee. There was an idea abroad that there was no work in London for young men except to read the Bible to old women; so we formed a body of about sixty young men who gave their names, and, with the leave of the Prison Commissioners, used to go to the Borstal Prison and visit the prisoners. They found out why the prisoners were there, found places for them when they came out, took those fellows up and saw them through, and over and over again set them up for life. That work still lies waiting to be done. I find Settlements wanting men; certainly Oxford House is very full now, but it often is not, and wants constant supplies. Cambridge House has only seven or eight men. Every one of the College Missions wants laymen's work. Eton and Harrow have built houses for laymen, but very often I find no laymen in them at all. Then I find the Friends of the Poor, connected with the Church Army, wanting men. I have lately been seeing an energetic person connected with it, and she said: " We can manage the girls and women, but what are we to do with all these young men who come in ?" They simply want a man to come in and help them. This person said: " If one man would take up one of our men connected with the Friends of the Poor, we could do something to give those men hope." Therefore, you see, as I look first at the Oxford and Cambridge Settlements, then at the Church, and then at my Boards and Committees; as I look again and see all the work—Boys' Clubs and

## To Public School Men

Church Lads' Brigades, almost languishing for want of men—I thought I would try an experiment, and see whether the men whom I used to know at Oxford and Cambridge, and who had now come to London, could not be rallied into a sort of Bishop's Band, a sort of body-guard, on whom I could rely, if necessary, to go down to clubs or Church Lads' Brigades, or for any sort of work for which I wanted them. I have got two bands of girls—the Girls' Diocesan Association and the Lend a Hand Club, together numbering a thousand. They are in society; they have all got their home duties. They have an orchestra, as good as any in London, which goes round and plays in poor districts, and they visit invalid cases in children's hospitals. They have a very efficient secretary, but I personally am able to see very little of them or their work. A band of young men I could myself superintend, and could be in the thick of the work with them. We could have gatherings at Fulham in the summer, and we could have lawn tennis together, and we should get to know each other. You could write and tell me if you wanted, as some men do, more spiritual help yourselves, and I might suggest to you lectures or services which you might attend; and you might really become a band of friends—nay, brothers—in this diocese, on whom I could depend. We should require to talk over what one could do and what another could do. It is quite true that many of you have a great deal of business, and I have no doubt that you are tired after your work in the City all day. Then come and help me on some of my Committees and Boards. It is a matter of arrangement. The point is, can I have a band of

## To Public School Men

young men who will rally round me in the work of this diocese? That is what I have summoned you together to ask.

I know what some people would say, and have said already—that the young men of the day have really given up religion, that they look on it as out of date, that we are going through a sort of backwater in service because modern ideas have altered people's religious views. I do not believe it. In a committee which we had here to arrange this meeting, consisting of about twenty men, three or four weeks ago, one man said: " What we feel is that we are not enough in touch with the Church." A young man in lonely lodgings, constantly out, might honestly say, " It is three or four years since I saw a parson near me," but he might want to be put in touch with the Church, and does not want to give up religion at all.

Others, of course, say that the young men of the day are too selfish; they love pleasure too much. A leading statesman expressed that opinion to me the other day very strongly. It was at the time I was making an effort in the West End Mission among girls. He said: " I wish you would do something among young men; I believe they only care for amusing themselves and having a good time." Of course, if I had believed that, I should not have asked you to come here. I believe there are hundreds of fellows in this diocese who not only want help themselves, but who want to have something definite shown them to do, some man's work they can do. If I believed that the young men from our public schools were too selfish to lift a finger to do anything for anybody else, I should feel that our system of education had landed us into a complete failure ; but I do not believe it for a moment. Down in the City, among the clerk class, I saw a thousand young men the other day in one meeting got up by Canon Newbolt's Guild. He has seventy or eighty young men around him, gathered chiefly from the business houses in the City, and all enthusiastic workers.

Then, of course, others say that the young men of the day are too shy to come out in any sort of definite way. Personally I do not believe that is true. I think we are shy in talking about our religion. I remember how difficult it was to me even to think I should be able to preach, and we all know that, as Englishmen, we are shy of saying anything definite, or committing ourselves to anything definite on this matter ; but I want to put before you one or two considerations to think over. Do not commit yourselves to-day to anything. I will tell you presently what I want you to do to-day, but think over these points now :

1. The standard of a layman, according to the New Testament, is, as a matter of fact, precisely the same as the standard of a clergyman. That may seem a startling thing to say, but I am perfectly certain it is true. If you read the New Testament, you will see there is no difference between the standard of life expected from a layman and that expected from a clergyman. Many a man, I think, when he has decided not to be ordained, really at the bottom of his mind thinks : " I can just settle down now ; I shall not have so high a standard to live up to." It is a pure mistake. There is only one High Priest, JESUS CHRIST Himself, but we are a body of baptized people.

## To Public School Men

Therefore, as being the body of the great High Priest, the whole Church is holy. We who come out to be ordained are the organs of the priestly body, but the *whole* body is priestly. There is no justification at all—and I speak to you frankly, as I used to speak to those of you who were at Oxford and Cambridge —for that limited view. Every Christian must have quite as high a standard of conduct as a clergyman.

2. Then, of course, there is the statement of CHRIST : " He that is not with Me is against Me, and He that gathereth not with Me scattereth." This does not apply only to those who are ordained, but to everybody who names the name of CHRIST. It seems very difficult for anyone who is thinking about it at all, and wants to get his life right, to do nothing for CHRIST in the light of a statement like that. Are we really standing out on His side in the club, in the regiment, in the office, by going to church ? Are we on His side, or are we on the other side ? Are we gathering or are we scattering ? If we bring one person into the great Kingdom, then, according to our LORD, we are gathering ; but if we are not, then " He that is not with Me is against Me, and he that gathereth not scattereth." You cannot get out of it.

3. Then there is another thing which I think is a very serious consideration. How very easily selfishness grows over all of us ! A selfish middle-aged man is bad enough ; a sort of moss grows over him, and he loses all enthusiasm and initiative ; but a selfish young man is far worse. And yet it is extraordinary how easily, even when young, we may slip into a self-centred, selfish way, thinking so much of

our little comforts, and losing all the hardness of a good soldier of JESUS CHRIST. I really think this should be carefully guarded against. Nearly all of you have pretty comfortable lives. You may do hard work, but you have a comfortable home or flat; and it is extraordinary how this quiet selfishness will grow over a man who might have done something if he had started fairly young. I believe this to be a real danger for us all.

4. And then we cannot deny that this is a most glorious time in which to live. I was struck by a remark made by one of my fellow-workers in the Public Morality work, who has done fine work all over the world in stopping the white slave traffic. He is about sixty, and he said: " I tell you, Bishop, it is a glorious thing to be alive in the world to-day." This came from a man who had been working for the last forty years. He had known London intimately all his life, and he said that he had never known such a change come over London as had taken place during the last ten or fifteen years from the moral point of view. The forces of evil are falling back before the forces of GOD. The closing of bad houses, the looking after the girls in the streets, the efforts of the police, and of public bodies, men's meetings, and rescue societies, are really having a telling effect on the morality of London. That was his reason for the remark. I can see the issue of battle trembling in the balance, and it wants another firm charge to beat back the forces of evil. There never was a time when opportunities were so great, and when every effort would tell so strongly. There are openings on all sides for work, and one almost seems to hear the old

## To Public School Men

doom pronounced: "Curse ye Meroz, saith the angel of the LORD, curse ye bitterly the inhabitants thereof, because they came not to the help of the LORD against the mighty."

There is, then, truly a wonderful opportunity for men's work and men's influence. Some people think of Christian work as walking up and down the streets with a bundle of tracts. That is not my idea at all of what you are necessarily to do. My idea is that you should take a firm stand in your own set, to start with, and then, if you have time, also begin some work in such ways as I have already described.

Those are the four considerations I want you to think of: the standard of a layman's life; the very strong language of our LORD about those who do nothing; the ease with which one slips into becoming a selfish being that one does not really want to be; and then the great opportunities which there are of doing the reverse, and really finding a man's joy in work.

"We will think over those things," perhaps you say, " but what do they drive us to? Bring your remarks to a point, Bishop." I am going to try.

1. I will take the moral question. I feel that the Bishop has got a right to ask a body of men like you to be sound on the moral question. I do not mean only with regard to yourselves. I do not suppose anyone here has himself done anything very wrong morally, but it does not follow that you are therefore sound. I have had, I must say, several rather discouraging bits of evidence that some of our public school men and 'Varsity men are not sound on it at all. They really drift into the view that such "things

## To Public School Men

must go on, and it is only human nature." I think we have a right to expect more than that from men like you. I am not speaking individually; I am talking of the class you represent. If you have had to go into the Lock Hospital and seen poor girls breathing out their lives at twenty-six or twenty-seven years of age, you would simply have nothing to do with the moral evil at all. If you saw the numbers of men drinking waters abroad in some hotels, trying to get back the vitality that was sapped away when they were your age, you would have nothing to do with it. You ought to see—I hope you do see—that really the man who enjoys life, who has got a cheery laugh, a clear eye, a good hand at games, is the man who has kept himself straight morally. He is the happy man; the other is not. I have seen it so often. One is happy and can look the world in the face; the other is conscious of some guilty secret, and is ashamed of himself. If nothing else, I feel I have a right to expect a body of men like you to be sound on the moral question, and if you hear talk of this kind, to stand up against it, and to put in a word on the other side, so that younger men may feel that "Anyhow, that fellow does not go in for the thing." I remember a poor man who was led astray, himself a great football player, now very penitent for the past, who said how much they had all admired the captain of the team, because, as he said, "He never came along with us at all. He was always jolly and nice, but he never would mix up with it in any way. And, in looking back, I honour that man more than I can say." That is the kind of respect one wants every one here to earn from those younger than themselves.

## To Public School Men

2. So again I think I have a right to expect, as your Bishop, that you will stand round me in your own religious life. I was talking to the Bishop of Stepney about this gathering. Of course, he takes an interest in it, and in this experiment we are making; and he said : " Well, I feel that such men would do a real work if they would bear their witness by going regularly to church." I do not underrate that at all. In a day when so many spend their Sunday going away for week-ends to the golf-links, or going into the country, but never going to church, people would think much of the young man in the country house for the week-end who goes off to church. They expect the girls and women to go, but if the man goes he no doubt bears a stronger witness. If they believe still what they learnt and professed at their Confirmation, young men of the day should have the pluck and perseverance and courage to bear witness in that way, and to be on the side of the Church to which they belong.

3. Now we come to openings for work. I shall be able to point out to those who give their names to me many parishes which are simply languishing for want of help, and many poor clergy breaking down in despair. A little help once a week puts new life into them. At Westminster three men are wanted to-morrow at a club. This is carried on by Mr. Pilkington, an old Etonian, who has for twenty-five years been working every night for the good of others, just as Mr. Douglas Eyre has done at the Oxford House. Some men might like to do the Borstal work, or might join the Friends of the Poor, or the Church Lads' Brigade. We want some men who know their drill ; we shall

## To Public School Men

not ask Army men to do this work—they have plenty of it. Then I want some men to sit on my various Committees. On the Public Morality Committee I want to have some young men. There is not a single young man who sits on that Board. We want young men on the Committee connected with the rescue work, to back up the women who every night in Piccadilly and Regent Street are rescuing friendless girls from the streets of London. I want more young men for the Bishop of London's Fund. A man who has his own establishment and his own people to look to cannot be going out every night; but if he came to the Bishop of London's Fund Board once a month, it would be something. I mention this only to show how varied the work may be, according to what a man's tastes and capabilities are. All I want you to do to-day is to make up your minds, and then write to me and say: "Well, Bishop, I should like you to have my name and address for your body-guard. I do not know whether I can be of any use; I do not know whether I have any time for anything, but I should like to have a talk with you or somebody, and find out whether I could be of any use." Another might say: "I would like to know whether I can get a little spiritual help myself for my Easter Communion." I should then put you in touch with Liddon House, because you would find two very nice men there—Mr. Trevelyan and Mr. Matthews. That has been established entirely for such young men as you are. The particular man who wrote and said he wanted spiritual help I should put in touch with this House. If, again, a man felt inclined to say, " I have never quite taken

## To Public School Men

to going to a club or a boys' brigade, but I could sit on one of your Boards," let him send in his name for that. When I get your letters and your names and addresses, I should know what kind of start we can make. Our meeting to-day may develope into the most effective movement that we have ever yet had in London. A thing begins in a small way, and gets to be a big thing. Write direct to me at London House, and if you do not hear from me in my own hand, that will be because I have not time to write myself. But I shall read your letters. I shall be President of the Band, if you do not turn me out. I simply ask you to make up your minds as to whether or not you will help me to make it a success.

I hope I have been clear as to my meaning and the object of it all, and I hope you will stand by me in my effort. At any rate, forgive me for having bored you for an hour, and I thank you for accepting my invitation.

# St. Michael's, Cornhill

*MONDAY MORNING*

TO CITY MEN*

## II

## THE PROBLEM OF LONDON

" And should not I spare Nineveh, that great city, wherein are more than six score thousand persons that cannot discern between their right hand and their left hand ?"—JONAH iv. 11.

THE idea of this service originated from the service held in the summer of 1907 in Wall Street, New York. When people read of that service, which aroused some interest, not only in America, but in this country, they asked me : " Will not your own men rally round you ? Is it impossible to speak a message to the heart of the City of London ?" I said : " No, GOD helping, it is a possible thing, and men in London will rally round me if I ask them, as the men in New York have done." And this great and representative congregation is the answer. And what I want in GOD'S name to put before you is what London means. There never was such a problem in the history of the whole world as London. When

* At this service 500 of the leading men of the City were present by invitation, including the Lord Mayor and Sheriffs.

## The Problem of London

you see what they considered a large city in the old days, and reckon out what Nineveh was, it comes to only about a sixth of London : " Six score thousand souls ; that great city "—and we have at least our six millions. And it is not merely that London is so great already, but no one knows better than the Bishop of London how London grows : forty thousand a year is the increase in my own diocese, and that only takes in a little under four millions. And then there is not only the great and the growing size, but also the division into rich and poor. As you know, for nine of the best years of my life I lived among the poor, and what always struck me as one of our great problems was the awful division between rich and poor, like two cities—two cities in one—one rich and the other poor. As most of you—I am not blaming you—go off to where you live among the well-to-do and the rich, down by trams and the buses or walking, into my old East London district pour the thousands and thousands of the poor. As I used to go in the afternoon up little narrow staircases to the garrets in Bethnal Green and Whitechapel, nothing stirred me more than the separation between the city of the poor and the city of the rich, and it is one of our great problems to-day which we have got to face. It is a great problem to feed London, to get a good milk-supply for London, to get a good water-supply ; but the problem which I have called you together to face with me is the problem which lies on my conscience and on my soul every day, as Bishop of London, and it is the spiritual problem. What is that ? It is how to bring the love of GOD home to every living child in London ;

## The Problem of London

how to give every child a chance. The belief which I am carrying round in this Central London Mission is this: that every single living soul is loved by GOD the FATHER, saved by GOD the SON, and is being sanctified, or may be sanctified, by GOD the SPIRIT. And we have not even begun our work yet until we give every child a chance in Whitechapel, Bethnal Green, and those great growing districts, Edmonton, Tottenham, and Willesden, of loving GOD, and knowing that they are loved by GOD, and having their lives expanding in the love of GOD, as they can do, and were meant to do. We have not faced it unless we realise that GOD has a place in Heaven—if only they will have it and reach it, and we will let them reach it—for every little child born in the poorest part of our great city. When we know that, and when we know that there are children, as has been forcibly yet awfully said, " damned into the world," without a chance at present—children of drunken parents, children whom we cannot reach; when I think that every night there are hundreds of boys and girls, born, born capable of being good men and women, a credit to the city and the Church, and fit for Heaven, not only tempted, but fatally tempted, every night that we live; when I know that, in spite of all our efforts, appealing, begging, day after day, we cannot supply a church and Sunday-school for the children as they pour into London, and cannot reach the boys and girls—then I say it is time that the Christian men and women—and especially the Christian men of this great city—met together and faced the question of what we are going to do.

Now, on whom—this is the first question—does the

## The Problem of London

chief responsibility rest ? Whom will GOD look to— whom does He look to as the people who are to remedy this ? You notice in the Bible that GOD always uses men ; He does not do things directly : He does them indirectly. The very reason why the Church exists is that He uses men to reach men. I have a great responsibility in this matter. If I did not work from morning to night, if I did not give every penny I possess, I should not be doing my duty as Bishop of London. I must give myself and all I have before I ask another living person to help me ; and that, thank GOD, I can say I do. And then I come to you, and I believe, before GOD, that the people whom, next to the Bishop of London, He looks to as most responsible for this are the very men to whom I speak now—the very men.

1. The first thing that He asks is yourselves. I cannot have you here and ask for anything except yourselves. My mission is to tell you this, as I told the congregation in St. Martin's-in-the-Fields : that GOD the FATHER knows you by name, knows you individually, and that He loves you with an everlasting love ; that you have the grace of our LORD JESUS CHRIST and the Fellowship of the HOLY GHOST, and that GOD demands you before He asks for a single thing you possess. I was kneeling only an hour ago by, I suppose, one of the richest women in England, who is to pass through an operation for her life tomorrow morning ; and as I knelt by her and prepared her for the operation, lately arrived from her home in the country to face the chance of life or death, I could not help feeling what a little difference the two millions that she possessed made to her to-day. I gave

her, as I would a woman in Bethnal Green, a text to think of : " Thou shalt keep him in perfect peace whose mind is stayed on Thee." And that was incomparably more than all her millions—just the question, did she steadily believe in GOD ? was GOD near to her ? what did GOD think of her ? what was her trust in GOD worth ? That was worth everything this morning, more than the millions she possessed. And I would like you to face that inquiry to-day about yourselves : " How do I myself stand with GOD ? what does GOD think of me ?" That is the only thing that would matter if you were face to face with, perhaps, a fatal operation this afternoon or to-morrow morning. It matters nothing when death comes how much money you are going to leave behind; but are you, the individual person, the immortal soul created by GOD —are you right with GOD ? Are you honourable in your business, pure in your private life ? Do you pray ? Do you love GOD ? How do you stand with regard to Him ? I beg you, before I say a word about what you do with your possessions, give yourselves first to GOD.

" My GOD, I give myself to Thee,
Thine only, ever Thine, to be."

2. And then I come to the second responsibility, and that is what I dwelt upon in New York. We are solely stewards of what we have, absolutely and entirely stewards. Life is a stewardship, and not an ownership; not a penny that we have belongs to ourselves; and, as GOD looks down, having given this one, perhaps, so many thousands, and this one so many more, we are not facing the real facts if we do not

## The Problem of London

realise that GOD has lent us that to administer for Him, for His poor and for His people. I have lately buried one of my parish priests, one of the most faithful parish priests of London, and I have already told in the course of this Mission a story that I would not tell you if he were alive, because he would have hated it.\*
Regularly his £400 or £500 a year that he did not want for his board and lodging came to me as representing JESUS CHRIST. And as I spoke over his dead body to his people, I thought to myself: " Here is the man who really believed himself to be a steward. He had to take, quite rightly, what he needed for the supply of his bodily health and food and clothing; after that, he said 'O JESUS CHRIST, it is Thy money; take it; I spend it for Thee.'" Now, is not that man with his few hundreds a lesson to those who have thousands ? And I would ask you, in all love, to ask yourselves this question: " Am I like that man, looking upon myself literally as a steward ?" You say, " I must put by against a time of adversity; I must lay by for my children "—rightly so—" I must make provision for my family." But are you regarding yourself as a steward who may have to answer to-morrow to GOD for what He lent you ? Are you administering what He lent you for the good of the people ? Surely you who employ these people, you whose great businesses have brought this multitude together, are the first people to see that their souls are cared for. And I put the appeal to you at a time like Lent, when we remember One Who, " though He was rich, yet for our sakes became poor "—and I may ask in passing, When was

\* See page 18.

## The Problem of London

JESUS CHRIST a rich man ? When people try to persuade me that JESUS CHRIST was only a good man, I reply : " St. Paul did not think so." " Though He was rich," he said, " yet for our sakes He became poor." You, then, who are Christians in the full sense, believe that what we commemorate on Good Friday is the sacrifice of GOD Himself ; that He left all His glory, all His omnipotence, all His greatness in Heaven, and died the death of a slave on a gallows —the Cross which we see on St. Paul's Cathedral is the old gallows—died for the children whom He loved. If you believe this with earnest, humble faith, is it not a great chance to do something like He did ? Enter into the spirit of the sacrifice of GOD, and be like JESUS CHRIST, " Who, though He was rich, yet for our sakes became poor."

If you do answer that appeal—and I am keeping very strictly to the time, because you trusted me about your time this busy day—if you do answer to that appeal ; if you say, " Bishop, we will stand by you now in a way we have never done before ; we will make our City Association for the Bishop of London's Fund a first charge upon our funds ; we see the awful problem, and we will stand by you in it "—let me tell you, as business men, how we try to administer that fund in the name of GOD, and for the sake of the people, in as businesslike a way as possible. We do not trust it to one or two individuals. We have a body of laymen and clergymen, some of the most experienced in London, and we have the best financial advice. We study every parish ; we have an expert knowledge of every district where a church is wanted ; and by these means during the last forty

## The Problem of London

years we have built 220 churches in the growing parts of London, and without those London would, from a Church point of view, be a pagan place. Therefore, you need not be afraid that your money would be wasted. We must be businesslike; "Be good bankers until I come" is the literal translation of one of our LORD's sayings, and we do not think it unspiritual, but actually spiritual, to see that not a penny should be wasted of the LORD's money in fostering those spiritual centres, which are the hope of London to-day.

My last word is that this is very hopeful work. If only you could come down with me and see some of those churches we have erected among the working people, with the Sunday-schools around them, with the children in them, with the young people brought up in virtue and in religion, loving their church, and praising GOD in it, you would see that if we take GOD at His word the work is very hopeful, and GOD helps us when we give what we can for Him.

So I leave my appeal with you; I appeal to you personally as your Bishop to stand round me; I appeal to you in the name of GOD to be fellow-workers with Him. Think of His love, think of His mission, think of His sufferings, think of His self-sacrifice; and if you join, in this little span of life, in this work, you take part in the greatest work that can be done in the world; and when you go to meet Him, as perhaps that rich sister of ours may have to do this week, He will look into your face and will say to you, knowing you have taken part in His work: "Rejoice with Me, rejoice with Me, for I have found the child which I had lost."

# University College

*TUESDAY EVENING*

ADDRESS TO STUDENTS

## III

## FAITH

I HAD to think over what would be an appropriate subject for this address. On the whole, I decided that the best thing was to speak to you on the subject of " Faith," because faith may not appear to you to be quite of the same importance at your age as it is to me in middle life; and I cannot conceal the fact that I am fifty, because it has been stated in every paper in England. As I think over what is felt about faith by young men, I know it sometimes seems, in the first place, an unnecessary thing. Scientific knowledge, getting on well in the schools, and fifty other things, to say nothing of athletics—these seem of the most primary importance to us at your age; but faith seems an unnecessary thing—at any rate, not as important as other things. It is opposed to reason—that is often thought—and not founded upon certain facts, like those a man relies on in business life, or in science. And it is supposed that it has very little effect upon a man's life. I am going to give a flat contradiction to all this; I am

## *Faith*

going to try to prove that all these ideas are perfectly wrong. I am going to prove to you, if I can, that, in the first place, when you really understand what life is, faith is the most essential thing in the world ; secondly, that it is not the least opposed to reason ; thirdly, that it is founded upon perfectly certain facts, on which you can lay your hands ; and fourthly, that it makes the whole difference to your life for the next thirty years, and right on, whether you have faith or not.

1. Let me take the first point. We live in a diocese, in a city, in which some one dies every eight minutes, day and night. Looking to this fact alone, we feel how essential faith is. In one week I was with one of my clergy, holding his hand while he died in the prime of life ; I went about eighty miles to see another dying of cancer ; and one of my most able clergy died on another day in that week : in one week three men, one not fifty, one about fifty, and one a little over fifty, in my own little circle ! This is going on all over this great London ; every eight minutes, day and night, somebody dies. Think what that means in human suffering and mourning and anxiety beforehand, to say nothing of the actual death ; and ask yourselves what you are going to say to the mourners —how are you to comfort that wife and those children who have lost their mother ; I could not go through my present life for a week if I had no faith. Where are you going to find out from science, or from anything you learn in your classes, how to comfort those people ? I am not going to speak in a depreciatory way about science. I have the greatest respect for it. But when you come to the vital things of life in

## Faith

such a place as London, you want faith. Nothing you can learn from science will help you.

It is the old question asked by our ancestors in old days in England. They were discussing whether they should listen to the missionary or not. One chieftain said : " A bird flies into the tent on one side, and flies out on the other side, and the soul of man comes in and goes out; but if this missionary can tell us where it comes from and where it goes to, for GOD'S sake let us listen to him." That is one ot fhe earliest stories of our race in England, and it is true now. People forget that. You have no answer, however clever you may be. We are still where our ancestors were. We do not know more than they knew on this question.

My first point, then, is the *necessity of faith*. Let us go a little further, to a more scientific point of view. I was, the other day, reading an interesting book called " The Agnostic's Progress," by Mr. Scott Palmer. It is well worth your reading; he points out among other things that, when we inquire into astronomy—as, for instance, how Neptune was discovered—we learn that it was by the deflections which were made upon the planet Uranus. And if you ask what was the cause of those aberrations of Uranus, you might equally say Uranus was the cause of the discovery of Neptune, or Neptune the cause of the aberrations of Uranus ; but when you ask a philosopher what is the real cause of both of them, why they are there at all, and why they are moving, the man of science answers, " It is force which is the cause." And when you go a little further and ask, " But where does that force come from ?" as Mr. Scott Palmer

## *Faith*

truly says, we have got no answer as mere students of science. We have one or two learned scientific men present, and I am certain that they would say the same thing. All they can say is, " It is matter and force." But if, as religious and philosophical men, we want to know where that force comes from, there is no answer in science at all. You might hold the view that there is no answer to the question, but if somebody else says it comes from GOD, life comes from Life, force comes from Force, there is nothing in science which can contradict him. Science takes you up to a certain point and leaves you there, but there is nothing whatever in science which contradicts a further belief which rests on other grounds. I believe that force comes from Force, and that there is a GOD of Force ; and just as a man swinging a stone round with his hand has to keep the stone moving, so, as Herschel, the great astronomer, said, every law of Nature requires the continued application of force ; and if we believe on other grounds that it is GOD'S force, we are not contradicting science in the slightest ; only science cannot tell us so itself.

Further, looking at the world—I am treating you as philosophers—I ask you, What are we making towards ? Is there any reason to suppose that we are progressing ? We hear very often about the " hopeful tone of science," but when you say to yourself, " I am a hopeful person ; I put my trust in science for my hope," you will have to read Huxley's Romanes Lecture at Oxford. That outspoken man in his Romanes Lecture at Oxford pointed out that those who were putting their hopes for the progress of

## *Faith*

the human race simply in science were trusting in something that did not give them hope at all. He said that all that he could learn from biology was that, in all probability, the world would wax and wane—I believe those are the actual words he uses. And it was really, from the point of view of science, the only answer that could be given. It is quite true, as he looked those hundreds of men in the face, he felt he could not leave them there. As a human being, he said something about a noble end which might be attained; his heart was too big for his head, but his friends pointed out that he was saying something which was entirely unjustified by his premises.

Therefore, my point is: if you want to look hopefully at the world, if you want to believe in progress, in some future for yourself and every one you know, you have no certainty of such progress from science. It tells us what happens, but Huxley derived no hope from it whatever.

I have tried, then, to prove in a simple way—I do not pretend to give a learned argument—that from the point of view of death, you want faith; and from the point of view of getting a real answer as to what is behind everything, what is at the centre, you want faith. You get no answer from anything else. And when you come to ask what will be the end of everything, you want faith. At no point can we do without it. The short-sighted person, the shallow-minded man, who really acquiesces in the belief that faith is a sort of harmless accessory to life, may think it is not very important. My point is, if you think deeply at all, if you are what we call a philo-

## *Faith*

sopher—we ought to be philosophers—you must have faith.

2. Now I come to my second point. I want to meet the idea that faith is contrary to reason. It is very commonly considered to be so by young men who have not thought the matter out; and they very commonly imagine, from reading certain magazine articles, that this is the case. I am going to prove to you that, whatever else it is, faith is not in the least opposed to reason. Let me take, for instance, the question of whether or not there is such a person as GOD. I like to recommend books, especially those that have helped me. I was for a time in much perplexity and doubt about these things; therefore, it is a labour of love when I am at Oxford and Cambridge every year, as well as when I am here, to try to put considerations before people who may be in the same state of mind as I was. I want to mention Professor Flint's book on Theism. You could not read a clearer book on that subject. If you read it, you will see that, so far from putting your reason behind your back when you believe in GOD, it is just the other way, and that your reason drives you to a GOD. I do not say it carries you all the way, but it drives you towards a belief in GOD. He says, for instance—I remember it after these twenty-five years—that we know GOD as we know our fellow-men. We know our fellow-man through his manifestations; we hear what he says, we see what he does, and from that we make a rapid inference as to his character. He says that we know GOD in just this same way: we know Him through His manifestations. We do not see our fellow-man,

## *Faith*

but we know him. And he takes such an illustration as this : He says (I am paraphrasing his words) : I look at the heavens on a beautiful, clear night, and I say to myself, What is the explanation of that ? I am on one of the planets going through space, and there are twenty million flaming suns we call stars, all in perfect order, and there is an atmosphere round the earth. These are facts which I can see ; what do they prove to me ? Without putting my reason behind my back, what does my reason tell me ? It tells me this : that, just as it would be absurd to suppose that a box of letters could form themselves into a play of Shakespeare, which it certainly could not, so it is equally absurd to say that the atoms of the universe threw themselves into the universe, because there is the mark of mind in the play, and that ordered pageant or play which we see on a starry night affords just as much evidence to my reason of the existence of mind as the play of ' Hamlet ' affords to the existence of the mind which produced it. The box of letters could just as easily form ' Hamlet ' as the atoms could form the universe. He goes on : I look inside myself, and I find in my breast, and in the breasts of other men I know, something which tells me the difference between right and wrong; it has got the power of discerning right and wrong, just as the eye has power to see the difference between black and white. I must not say much about the eye in the presence of experts on that subject, but the eye certainly sees the difference between black and white, however slowly it has been evolved. Therefore, conscience in the breast of every one is an evidence that the Person

*Faith*

Who made us, and the Person Who presumably made the stars and the world, has a character; besides being wise and clever, He has a character; and He would not have put what Dr. Chalmers called " a reclaiming witness against Himself " in the breast of everybody if He was not righteous. Just as the stars are evidence of the power and wisdom of GOD, so the conscience in everyone is a witness to the righteousness of GOD. It was Kant himself who said : " Two things fill me with awe and wonder—the starry heavens without and the moral law within." And therefore, without going against your reason, you say : " This Being Who made the stars is also righteous, for He made me and everyone I know with a conscience. The existence of a conscience is a sign to my reason of the righteousness of GOD."

Let us go a little further. You say : " Do you know anything more ?" You might say : " So far, Bishop, we follow you ; it is common sense ; do you know anything else about this Person ?" That wholly depends on whether you believe in Christianity or not. " Is He a loving Person ? Is there any sense in talking about the love of GOD ? Is there any use in praying in the morning ? Does He care about us ?" That depends upon the truth or otherwise of the Christian religion. As I look at Nature, and simply consider it from the point of view of natural religion, there are certain things that tell on both sides. There is the sunshine, there are the birds, the happy summer day, the sea, and so on ; the beauties of Nature all speak a message about the love of the Creator. But, on the other hand, there is another side : the animals prey upon one another. It is very difficult to under-

## *Faith*

stand that, and to reconcile it with love. Then there were those 160 children lately crushed or burned to death—a holocaust of 160 children! You have got a great number of facts which seem to tell on the other side. If I had not had a demonstration of love, a vindication of love, my faith would not be strong enough to enable me to believe that this righteous and wise Person was also loving; I should not be sure of it, and I could not go from death-bed to death-bed every day, as I do now. But the point is that my reason drives me on to believe, at any rate, that there is a GOD, that He is wise, and that He is righteous; and if I believe the Christian religion (to which I am coming in a moment), it drives me to believe that He is also loving. And if I have wisdom, righteousness, and love as characteristics of the Power behind the world, He must be a Person. Anyone who is wise and righteous and loving is a person, a personality. Without putting my reason behind my back for a single moment, then, I believe in a GOD. But perhaps you answer me, and say: " Yes; but you believe much more than that: you believe that GOD revealed Himself to man, and that He had power over Nature which we call miracles, and that He raised the dead." I am coming to the grounds of this belief. My present point is that there is nothing in reason against it; there is no reason in the world why that Person should not have revealed Himself to man if He wished; there is no reason why, when He was here, He should not have had more power over Nature than I have. It would puzzle me if He had not. There is no reason why what we call the laws of Nature, which are the observed uniform-

## *Faith*

ities in Nature, should not be superseded when the LORD of life comes Himself by something which is not against law, but which cuts our laws at an angle different from what we are accustomed to see. No one says this more clearly than Huxley. He says: "The miracles that I see in Nature are ordinary phenomena to the naturalist, and the miracles of Nature make the miracles of religion seem child's play."

My first point was that faith was really necessary if you are a philosopher; my second, is that it is not opposed to reason, but that reason pushes you on to faith; (3) and now I come to my third, which is that our faith as Christians stands upon certain historic facts, as certain as the facts on which any business man erects his plans.

Whether, then, people agree with us or not, they cannot say that we are foolish people. (a) The first certain fact is, that there was a widespread expectation throughout the whole of the ancient world for centuries that some great One was coming. Of course, we know what the Jews thought, from their writings; but if you read Plato or any of the philosophers of the old Greeks, you see that there was a great expectation in the Gentile world too. You will read in Plato that we are like men on a raft—that is his idea, that we are really like sailors on a raft on the sea of truth—" unless," he said, " there be some word from GOD which may more safely carry us." And he guesses that if the Perfect Man should ever come, he would probably be put to death, as He was. When it is put into our LORD's mouth in the book of Revelation—" I am the root and the offspring of

## *Faith*

David, and the bright and the morning star "—He is claiming to be the fulfilment of both lines of prophecy : the offspring of David, for the Jews ; the bright and the morning star looked for by the wise men from the East. The first fact, then, is that there was this widespread expectation of a great coming One in both sections of the human race.

(*b*) Then I come to another certain fact—that this Person whom we call JESUS CHRIST did come. I remember I once thought that it might be a dream that JESUS CHRIST ever was here at all, and it was a relief to see in the prosaic account of Tacitus : " JESUS CHRIST was put to death in the reign of Tiberius, when Pontius Pilate was Procurator in Judea." This is a solid fact in Roman history, not carrying us a very long way, but, so far as it goes, a piece of Roman history. He was an historical Person, at any rate, whatever might be thought of Him, and whatever theory we might erect on the facts of His life.

(*c*) Then I come to a further fact, and I find it is also a certain one : that this Person has attained such a position to-day, in modern Europe, that I do not think that anyone here would deny the statement when I say that He holds ten million times over more power than any Emperor or statesman in the world. Napoleon said : " I know what men can do. I have to be present to exercise power ; JESUS CHRIST holds the human soul as an appanage of His own, and millions would die for Him, Whom, having not seen, they love." He is a Power in the world, this Person ; He has an influence even in progressive Europe a million times more

## *Faith*

powerful than any other person. Every year we see hundreds of thousands throughout the world converted to a belief in Him.

(*d*) Fourthly, of this Person John Stuart Mill said: " Live so that He will approve of your life "—that is his advice to young men—" make Him the ideal of your life ;" and Mr. Lecky says : " The records of these short years have done more to regenerate mankind than all the disquisitions of philosophers and all the plans of statesmen." Taking their verdicts as those of impartial men of the world, I look to see what this ideal Person says about Himself. It is a certain fact that He makes the most astounding claims about Himself. He was humble and sincere, but He says : " I am the Light of the world "; " before Me shall be gathered all nations, and I will separate them one from the other as a shepherd divideth the sheep from the goats." " I am the bread of life." And when pushed, as it were, to say what all these assertions mean, and what He was claiming to be, He claimed to be GOD Himself. " He that hath seen Me hath seen the FATHER." " Before Abraham was, I am." " I and My FATHER are one thing." It is a certain fact that this perfect ideal of humility and sincerity, love and strength, said these things about Himself.

(*e*) I go a little further. I believe it to be a certain fact that He attested these things by His Resurrection from the dead. I want to know from anyone who doubts it how the Cross came to be at the top of St. Paul's Cathedral. I notice it is so ; I ask myself, " Why should a gallows be taken and waved in triumph over a cathedral in the biggest city in the

## *Faith*

world ? How did it get there ?" Personally, I know of no answer to that question except that something happened to change the old object of shame, the Cross, into a sign of triumph; and there is no historical explanation how it came to be a sign of triumph, unless the death was transfigured in some marvellous way by His subsequent Resurrection from the dead. I know no answer, except the fact of the Resurrection, to the question why on a day called Sunday all work stops; why is it not on Saturday ? Our friends down in Whitechapel keep the sacred day on the Saturday. Quite right; they always have. Why did a body of Jews, the most conservative people in the world, change their sacred day from Saturday to Sunday—not to Friday, which was the day their Master died—but Sunday, when nothing whatever happened, unless the Resurrection took place ?

(*f*) Or take another historical fact, a service we call " the Holy Communion." I am saying nothing for the moment about the spiritual value of it, although I find in it the greatest spiritual help, but I am speaking of it as an historical fact, and I ask myself how this service has lasted, as no one denies that it has, without intermission for nearly two thousand years. No one denies that it was instituted by JESUS CHRIST Himself. Why are the tokens of a shameful death enshrined in a triumphant and glorious service ? Why in the Eucharist—the Thanksgiving —should there be tokens of a shameful death, the body broken and the blood shed, unless that shameful death was transfigured by a glorious fact which changed it into a great cause for thanksgiving ? I want to

*Faith*

know what happened to the body of JESUS CHRIST if He did not rise with it. Only two sets of people could have had it—either the Jews or the disciples. If the disciples had it, and went about stating that He was risen, they were impostors of a terrible character; but not a critic in Germany believes that they were deliberate impostors. If the Jews had it, they would naturally have produced it, and confounded the story of the disciples. They would have said: "Here is the body which you say is risen." There never has been any answer that I have ever heard to satisfy my mind, but that it must have been the same body glorified and transfigured which convinced even Thomas of its reality, and was seen by five hundred people on a mountain. I hold it as an unassailable fact that this same JESUS CHRIST not only had that character and gave that teaching, but sealed it by His Resurrection from the dead; also that during His lifetime He raised other people from the dead and healed the sick. These lesser miracles fall into place if once you believe in the great miracle of His Resurrection from the dead.

When this Person with claims so great, Who has had these claims attested by His Resurrection, looks me in the face and says, "What think ye of CHRIST; whose SON is He?"—I answer back, not putting my reason aside at all, but with my mind and reason as well as with my heart, "Thou art the King of glory, O CHRIST; Thou art the everlasting SON of the FATHER," as the Christian Church has answered ever since. And if anyone supposes that this is some later faith, turn to the undisputed Epistles of St. Paul—to the Galatians, the two

## *Faith*

to the Corinthians, and the one to the Romans. These four Epistles have convinced many and many a man that, whether right or wrong, St. Paul held the belief held by the Church to-day. " GOD sent forth His SON, made of a woman, made under the law " (in Galatians); " Declared to be the SON of GOD with power" (Romans); " Through Whom [JESUS CHRIST] are all things" (1 Corinthians); "Who, though He was rich, yet for our sakes He became poor " (2 Corinthians)—when was He rich as man ?

We have, then, these unassailable facts upon which to rest our faith. I shall not have time to ask you personally if I have convinced you that JESUS CHRIST, this historical character, was the revelation of the FATHER and was the everlasting SON of GOD. But I am not afraid. I have, of course, had a life of controversy; I have defended my faith for twenty years, in the open air, in great mass meetings, and in the lecture-halls, and have been heckled afterwards for an hour and a half on every single point of it. Although it is quite true that the mind has to make an act of faith, and there must be something in each person which has to respond to this evidence, yet at the same time I am not ashamed to look you in the face and say that our Christian faith rests on as certain facts as any business in the whole world.

4. This brings me to my last question, and that is, Is it true that the presence or absence of faith makes no difference to your life ? I do not believe that any single thing in the world is more vital to your happiness and strength and usefulness in life in the long run, as whether you have faith or not.

## *Faith*

Should you live thirty or forty years, nothing in the world will make more difference ; if you have faith, you will be strong people, happy people, useful people, and will leave a mark on your generation ; but if you have no faith, however clever you may be, however much you may be known for your professional work, you will not leave the mark which the man of faith will leave. If you are with a mother who has lost her child, and you have faith enough to convince the mother that the child is not dead, but that the Good Shepherd has taken it in His arms to Paradise —and I have had to try and do this in countless cases—you have done a work for that mother which no scientific argument could do. Sir Oliver Lodge has helped us very much. He believes that, from the point of view of science, he is driven to believe that life goes on. I am only too thankful to anyone who can help people to believe. Personally, unless I believed in JESUS CHRIST, Who said, "In My FATHER'S house are many mansions ; if it were not so, I would have told you," and then sealed His message by what I have described, I should not have had faith strong enough to convince those mourners. We should, however, take whatever help we can get, and Sir Oliver Lodge has helped us so far as he can. But if faith gives you power to comfort people in the hour of death and mourning, so also faith makes all the difference in the time of your temptations. Faith gives strength to the belief that GOD will stand by you as you try to struggle with dark thoughts and with the temptations of youth. If a young man believes he has a source of strength which nothing else can give him, he will go back to his lodgings to fight his lonely battle with new

## *Faith*

strength. It makes all the difference in the world to the man who is lonely. If he believes this truth, he hears a Voice saying, " Lo, I am with you alway, even to the end of the world " ; it means having this living Person with you all the days to the end of the world. The lonely man can say, " I am not alone, because my SAVIOUR, my Master is with me." Look round in the City : to whom do men on the Stock Exchange go when they are in trouble ? They go to the man of faith. Nurses in hospital go to the woman of faith. A strong influence is exerted in a college, at Oxford or Cambridge, by the young man of faith, the man who has got something to give, some strength of character to stiffen up the moral tone. Faith is power and strength. You are, then, making the mistake of your lives if you imagine it makes no practical difference to your future life whether or not you have faith. I venture to say it makes the whole difference, and that faith will be the secret of your power.

What keeps men back from faith ? (1) These doubts of which I have spoken. If you are in the middle of them, do not be discouraged, do not be disheartened. Remember how kind our LORD was to Thomas. " They that will to do His will, shall know of the doctrine, whether it be of GOD." Live up to what light you have ; pray on, and you will come out of your doubts if you stay with the Church and do not go away, and do not give up your religious practices. Thomas stayed with the Church, and he said finally, " My LORD and my GOD !"

2. Secondly, there may be some moral flaw. Again and again I have found that the young men who

*Faith*

have come to me in doubt, and even young women, have had something take place in their lives which has upset their character : a moral flaw has come into the spiritual eye. " If thine eye be single, thy whole body shall be full of light ; but if thine eye be evil, thy whole body shall be full of darkness." Every one should ask himself, " Is there something in me—am I doing something against my conscience which has dulled my spiritual eye ?" Faith and morals go closely together. It is the pure in heart that shall see GOD, and it is the pure in heart to whom these things become clear.

3. Sometimes it is simple carelessness : there are so many interests in life. I put this lately to a great body of men—and it seemed to strike them more than anything else I said, as they told the chaplain afterwards—" If this is true, it is either everything or it is nothing ; " either this Christian religion, such as I have tried to put before you, is the revelation of the truth of GOD or the greatest imposture which has disgraced the world. Therefore, to treat it with apathetic carelessness, to be indifferent about the whole thing, is not common sense ; it is not the part of reasonable men. This story is the most astonishing thing in the world, and people who get so accustomed to it that they become Gospelhardened are simply not using their imagination. It is not the reason that fails ; it is the imagination that fails. Do not, then, let simple carelessness and indifference rob you of your Christian faith.

Faith is a most necessary thing ; faith is not opposed to reason ; faith is founded upon unassailable facts ; faith makes all the difference to life.

## *Faith*

What ought to be the issue of all this? To my mind, it ought to be just the simple prayer of the disciples: "LORD, increase our faith; LORD, increase our faith." If any man here has faith like a grain of mustard-seed, that little grain will grow and grow, if he will take the trouble with it, until the fowls of the air will lodge in the branches of it—other souls will come and shelter under his faith. A boy or young man who thinks his faith so puny, and is in despair about it, does not realise that twenty years after many people may be sheltering under it until they get a faith of their own. Therefore, "LORD, increase our faith" should be our prayer. Take time for thought; pray to be guided right; read what books will help you; by all means, study the other side; think over these things, and study them to their depths; do not be afraid of any investigation at all; and, please GOD, in the years to come there will be many of you who will not only live, but work by your faith.

# St. Anne's, Soho

*SUNDAY AFTERNOON*

TO MEN CHIEFLY*

## IV

### HOPE

"The GOD of Hope fill you with all joy and peace in believing, that ye may abound in hope, through the power of the HOLY GHOST."—ROM. xv. 13.

I AM going to begin by reading to you one of the most despairing letters which I have received during the Mission. It runs thus: "I have been reading your Mission addresses in the papers, and I try, as far as I know, to live a right life; and now GOD has utterly forsaken me. If I have done anything wrong I try hard to repent, and I confess it to GOD several times. I kept to Communion, but I got no comfort at all. I was taught all those stories about the early Christians, and about those forty men†. My thorough Christian teaching has brought me to poverty, misery, and desolation. I am terrified at the thought of death, for I fear I shall have a dreadful death. I try to say the twenty-third Psalm, but it seems no good. I have known what it is to feel that GOD did love me, and He allowed me in

\* Women were present in the gallery.    † See pp. 34, 35.

## *Hope*

times past to work for Him ; but He has now cast me aside. I have seen clergy and others who worked for Him allowed to come to a dreadful end. It seems hard to believe that GOD is love. When I have heard the note of the lark, I have had a little hope ; but my life is full of terror, and all my friends have forsaken me. Why is it that so many become lunatics, and suffer long years of torture ?" and so on.

That gives me my text for what I want to say, and that is that there is not the slightest doubt that no rose-water Gospel will suit the facts of life. There is no doubt that there is a good deal of despair in the world. One of the saddest things about this London of ours is the number of souls who are in despair—some from poverty, not knowing where to get the next meal ; some from having yielded to temptation, like those poor girls in London whom we strive to win back in our rescue work, and find at the very depths of despair again and again. Young men of London come to me in their troubles, and I find some poor lad all by himself struggling against some sin of which no one knows, and again and again he is despairing, or almost in despair. We have to face the fact that people do not get their deserts in this life. Some poor man will struggle on as best he can against adversity, and he seems borne down at the last, and he says, " GOD has forsaken me, and man won't help me." I have seen such despair often in East London ; and we have to face the fact that if we are to look to the world as it is to-day for evidence—certain evidence—that there is a good GOD, Who is in this world righting everything, we do not find it. And therefore it is that I want to face with you what

## *Hope*

I call the despair of the world; I want to preach a message of hope to every despairing soul—to that young man who is struggling on with his great temptation; to some poor lonely soul here despairing, battered down into the workhouse,* perhaps from no fault of his own at all. And I want to face these things with you quite frankly—with the men of London especially—and to help you with your difficulties. Are we to take that despairing note of the letter, and say that, as some one expressed it the other day, it is an "out-of-hand world," and there is no GOD Who rules it at all?

Now, the first point which makes us pause is finding a man like St. Paul, who at every point was subject to the same temptations and despair, uttering the words which we have taken for our text. He was battered and persecuted, although he tried, like the writer of the letter quoted, to do what he thought right. He did not get his deserts in this world, and yet he gives us from his prison and out of his poverty and out of his persecution this glorious message of hope: "The GOD of Hope fill you with all joy and peace in believing . . . through the power of the HOLY GHOST." And when we look a little further, and watch the life of JESUS CHRIST Himself—I want you especially to think of this who imagine, because times are hard, that therefore GOD has forsaken you altogether—when we watch His life, and see Him on the Cross—

> "Mocked of men, of GOD forsaken,
> Left in death's last hour to fail,"

---

\* Some of the members of the local workhouse were present by special invitation.

## Hope

as the poet says—let us remember that over His head all the time there is the ringing approbation of GOD: "This is My beloved SON, in Whom I am well pleased." And therefore your judgment of the world, and your idea that, if there is a GOD, every one must have his deserts in this life; that, if not, GOD must have forsaken you; that you cannot be loved by GOD because you are poor and tempted—that must be wrong, unless CHRIST was wrong. And, as I have said again and again in the Mission, and in preaching about this diocese, my whole faith centres in the Incarnation. If JESUS CHRIST was not the Eternal SON of GOD, if GOD did not come into the heart of the suffering and pain and bear it Himself—" See the blood blind My eyes, the scourge fall on Me "—I have no answer whatever to give you in your doubts and difficulties. I could not believe in any rose-crowned Apollo who never dipped his finger in the world's anguish: I can love and I can follow a "Man of sorrows and acquainted with grief." And therefore I take this sentence from our LORD'S great servant, which rings down the ages; I take it as a message of hope: "The GOD of Hope fill you with all joy and peace in believing, that ye may abound in hope, through the power of the HOLY GHOST."

1. And I want you to look first of all at hope as a great Christian virtue. I shall show you in a few moments on what it is founded. I know some people are apt to imagine that we are either of a hopeful disposition or not, and they think that, while it is right enough to have this or that— right enough to have, for instance, purity and virtue—it is a matter almost of temperament whether

## *Hope*

we are hopeful or not. One thing we want in London is strong men. To be strong men, to be useful men, is to have more hope—hope for the slums, hope for our rescue work, hope for the men of London dragged down by sin, hope for the poor girl or woman who has such wretched wages that very often she is driven to vice. Hope is what we want, and I summon you men and women to be fellow-workers with me in trying to help London to put on the helmet of salvation. Hope is a strong, active Christian virtue.

2. Secondly, it is a great duty. When the problem of being Bishop of London seems almost too hard for me, when I find strong forces against me, when I find all the organised power which there is in the actual traffic in vice alone in this city, when I find the carelessness of public opinion that has got accustomed to wrongs, when I am most conscious of my own weakness and frailty, I rouse myself in the morning and say, " I *must* have hope ; hope is a duty ; O GOD of Hope, give me hope ; O GOD of Hope—a very glorious title of GOD—give me hope for the day ; let me be hopeful from one day to the other, from one service to another, from one problem to another !" I must have hope, or I shall fail in my duty. And what I say to myself I say to you. You fail in your duty if you fail in hope. I had just now before me one of those terrible things which damp hope when they happen. A man who had taken to drink, whom I had had to remove from a place of trust because of his drinking habits, whom I had tested for nearly two years most carefully, and whom I had allowed at last again to do a

## *Hope*

little responsible work—that man this afternoon is dead drunk. And if I speak now, perhaps, with unusual emotion, it is because such things go to the very bottom of one's soul—when you see talented, able, brilliant men dragged down by a sin like that, and you have hoped and trusted in them in vain. But again I say to myself, "That must not make me despair." If some of you are standing by a wife, or sister, or friend, and you are beginning to despair about them, or beginning to despair about yourself, and saying, "I cannot conquer that temper, I cannot conquer that habit of drink, I cannot conquer the dominion of the lusts of the flesh over me," remember that Hope is a duty. "The GOD of Hope fill you with all joy and peace in believing." I bring you a message of hope, and tell you that hope is a duty. "GOD shall forgive thee all but thy despair."

3. Thirdly, hope is the strongest influence that you can exercise over another man or another woman, or boy or girl. I have often repeated the story, because I think it is a very telling story, of the little boy who believed intensely in his grandfather. The grandfather was a selfish, niggardly, mean old man, but the little boy thought that he was a kind, benevolent, and generous man. He came to stay with his grandfather, and kept saying to the old man, "What a kind old man you are! You are always so generous and loving. How fond everybody must be of you!" The mean old man could not stand the praise of the little grandson, and the pretty part of the story —"Little Lord Fauntleroy"—is the telling how the old man became what the boy thought he was:

## *Hope*

he was melted by the praise of the boy. That is what I call the influence of hope on character. And when you look round the world, next to the direct grace of GOD, you find that nothing has so much effect upon you as people trusting you. " I cannot disappoint my mother "—this thought will keep straight a boy in lonely lodgings in London—" I cannot disappoint my old mother at home ; she believes in me." " I cannot look my sister in the face if I do that." Or some girl here working in some of these great shops may say to herself, " I cannot give up altogether my Church and my Communion. There is that friend of mine ; she believes in me." And as you look round and see what influences people I think you will find out that, next, as I say, to the direct grace of GOD, the strongest thing of all is hope—somebody's hope in them, somebody's trust in them. And if that is the case with ourselves, do we not see it is the strongest influence we can exercise upon anyone else ? Why I feel so keenly what has happened in regard to that man is because I had exercised hope on him and trusted him. And, although certainly for reasons which we never can tell, it does seem to fail from time to time in individual cases, yet it may succeed another time, though not in the same way. But what I want to get out of you is the power of hope that there is in you for the good of London. I am told that there are some of our police force present here to-day. There is no body of men for whom I have a greater honour and respect. I have seen them over and over again—so tender to the poor little child at the crossing ; so strong, so

## *Hope*

firm, and yet so gentle, in the way they exercise their duties. I should like them to take this special part of the message home, and to have hope for perhaps the worst and most abandoned with whom they have to deal. Do not let the sight of the seamy side of life stamp out their hope. Hope on in human nature; you see the worst of it, but still by your generous hope, by perhaps your word of warning to a poor giddy girl in the hour of her trial, or a word of encouragement to the poor boy whom you have to drag off to prison, you may save many a boy or girl from going wrong again.

4. I come, then, to ask you to-day, What is it that manufactures hope? I have put to you hope as a great virtue, hope as a great duty, hope as the strongest influence we can exercise over our fellows. What is the factory of hope? How are we to make it? This the Apostle tells us. He says, " May the GOD of Hope fill you with all joy and peace in believing, that ye may abound in hope, through the power of the HOLY GHOST." In other words, you cannot have hope—and I believe this to be literally true—you cannot have hope unless you have joy and peace in believing. And that is why we have these Mission services in church after church. We are manufacturing; they are the spiritual factories in which we are forging this great Christian virtue. We must have joy and peace in believing if we are to have hope. Now, the point is, What is it we are to believe? I believe you will find five things which you are bound to believe if you are to have the strong virtue of hope—at least, I cannot see myself any single one in the five that could be

## *Hope*

left out and yet leave me personally hopeful in my work.

(*a*) The first is, you must believe in GOD ; you must believe in a Great Power behind the world. If once you imagine that the world has really slipped out of GOD's hands, if you once get to believe, from reading books of science, that this world is simply spinning through space, leading a kind of devil's dance without any object at all, and no power for good behind —well, what hope can you have ? If you want to see what that leads to, read the last writing of that perfectly straightforward and honest man, Professor Huxley. In his Romanes Lecture—the last lecture he gave at Oxford before he died—he describes with perfect accuracy—as of course he would—the world of Nature as he observed it ; how everything gradually waxed and then waned again. He said : " I hear some people " (I am only giving the substance of his words) " talk about the hopeful note of science. Well," he said, " all that science reveals to you is the processes of things, and, as I observe it, Nature gradually waxes and gradually wanes again." And the whole keynote of that lecture, until you get to the end, was one of blank despair—I mean, it gives you nothing to encourage you. It is quite true that we discover electric light, the properties of radium, and so on—all most interesting ; but when you come to living and dying men and women, and their hopes and fears, and their consciences, I should like to know what hope there is merely in science. There is none at all. No one honours science more than I do, but it merely describes to you exactly what happens. There is no progress, in the sense of

## *Hope*

certain hope for the human race, in science at all. If you are to be hopeful men and women, you must believe in GOD behind everything—a GOD of hope, a Power working through this world towards something. This world will probably disappear into the sun; the Bible prophecy, "The world and all that is therein shall be burnt up," is probably exactly what will happen; when the resistance gets gradually less, the earth will be drawn into the sun. If we are believers in GOD, this will make no difference to us, because the real permanent things—the things that are not seen—are eternal. The bodies of the thousand people who are listening to me may be burnt up with the earth and disappear; but the person, the immortal soul, which looks through your eyes into mine this afternoon, that cannot die, that will be with GOD. It will have gone to its account, for it will have passed out of this body here. If, then, you want to have hope in this world, you must be working on for something that will last. There is nothing more hopeless than building on something that will not last. All our work is useless, the Bible is a perfectly meaningless book, if people do not go on living after death; its warnings and its promises are equally empty unless spoken to immortal souls.

If we are to have hope, then, we must believe in a GOD behind. I gave reasons for this belief early in the Mission; I cannot repeat now the reasons which drive us to believe in GOD. We do not believe, as I have often said, that a box of letters can throw itself into a play of Shakespeare, because there is the mark of mind in the play; neither can the atoms of the universe throw themselves into the universe.

## *Hope*

Any person, however foolish, can see that there is the mark of mind in it. Those twenty million blazing suns all moving in perfect order ; the extraordinary care with which the earth is placed, the presence of the atmosphere which surrounds it to stop the friction—all this shows the mark of mind. And every man has a conscience, which is the mark not only of a great and clever GOD, but also of a righteous GOD. I assume at every church that my hearers have been driven by their reason to believe in a GOD. What I say this afternoon is that the first principle of hope is belief in a GOD Who has everything in hand: " and no man shall be able to pluck them out of My FATHER's hand." The poor soul, whoever he is, who writes this letter is not out of his FATHER's hand at all. I admit that in this life he may not have got his deserts, as hundreds of others have not, in common with St. Paul, in common with JESUS CHRIST. But I say that no man can finally pluck that soul, or any other, out of the FATHER's hands. That is the first thing to believe.

(*b*) The second thing is that you must believe that GOD will, in the long run, be justified in His saying and clear when He is judged—in other words, that, however slowly it may be in working out, GOD is going to make good win ; that

> " There is a land of pure delight,
> Where saints immortal reign " ;

that all the sufferings and all the trials of life here are only for our probation ; and that for the poor men in the workhouse, who go on patiently bearing what they have to bear, and trying their best to be Chris-

## *Hope*

tians in the workhouse, there is a glorious life to come. GOD loves the man in the workhouse just as He loves a prince or the King on his throne; there is no difference whatever in the eyes of GOD. Although we cannot understand, and I do not profess to explain, why one has a harder life than the other, in the long run GOD wishes all His children to have eternal happiness; He has a place in Heaven for every one, "a bright home above, where the sun never sets." The poor lonely boy on London Bridge, selling matches in the pouring rain, was heard saying to himself, "I could not bear it but for thinking of the golden gates." Although it is quite possible to press that side of the Gospel out of proportion—and I, for one, believe the Christian Church has to try and give everybody a good time here; not to talk about everything happening afterwards: a Christian is not doing his duty unless he is trying to rescue people from drink, to establish a land of righteousness, a city of sobriety, to provide a decent home for every working man, and give a chance to every boy and girl — yet I believe we should go on preaching at the same time the gospel of a glorious Home in the world to come where all shall be happy and bright.

(c) As a pledge of this you must believe—I am not going to press this in detail again—that GOD gave His only-begotten SON. Unless GOD has done something, we have no pledge that He cares; unless He has borne something, we have no certainty that He feels; if He is

". . . On the hills, like gods together,
Careless of mankind,"

## Hope

then what pledge have we that He loves men with an absolute love ? We must believe in the Incarnation.

(*d*) Fourthly, I feel that we must believe in the HOLY GHOST. If I did not believe that there was a Power in the heart of every one battling with the evil, that while the Evil One comes with lustful, bad, dark thoughts, stirring up hatred, as he certainly does—if I did not believe that there was a Power working against him, pulling back the erring, trying to make the life pure, I should have no more hope for you than for myself ; but what a difference when we believe that

> ". . . every virtue we possess,
> And every conquest won,
> And every thought of holiness,
> Are His alone."

The fourth secret of having hope is " joy and peace in believing in the HOLY GHOST." " Come, HOLY GHOST, our souls inspire," ought to be the daily prayer of every Christian.

(*e*) Then, fifthly, I feel we can have no hope unless we believe in what has always been called the " Holy Catholic Church," unless we believe in a Divine society which is to draw the best out of us, and to use us for the good of others—unless we believe, in other words, that the Church was sent into the world to be the most glorious brotherhood the world has ever seen. I may be speaking to some who hate the Church—hate the very name of the Church—who were brought up, perhaps, to believe that the Church is a narrow-minded body which simply works for its own ends ; and that all these Church things, like

## *Hope*

Baptism, Confirmation, and Holy Communion, are mere outward signs which stand between the soul and GOD. If you never hear it again, listen as I put before you how I understand the Church. JESUS CHRIST wanted to have a witness to Himself until He came again—something which would remind the world of Him, and bring His SPIRIT into the world; something which would be as hands and feet as He gathered in the lost and strayed. He formed this Divine society to be united—and GOD help us to be more united than we are!—to be a living, united band of brothers, to go out into the world in His name, preach the Gospel, and gather in the lost and strayed. The world was to believe that the FATHER sent Him, by the visible unity of the Church— " That they all may be one, as Thou, FATHER, art in Me, and I in Thee." Baptism is JESUS CHRIST standing by the font, and saying, " Suffer the little children to come unto Me, and forbid them not." Confirmation is the living JESUS breathing on them, and saying, " Receive ye the HOLY GHOST." The Holy Communion is the living CHRIST standing and saying, " Here is the Bread of Life for you to eat, and here for you the Wine of Love to drink." There was no idea of these outward signs getting between the soul and CHRIST. The Church is nothing unless the living CHRIST walks up and down in it, and everything done in it is done in His name and by Him. If He is not in the Church, the Church is dead. The Church lives by His life, and we preach the living society of a living CHRIST, in which everybody is equal—rich and poor. Unless you believe in that, unless you believe that He sent that living

## *Hope*

society to break down class distinctions and establish brotherhood again, what hope can you have for the world ?

Now do you believe in all this ? Do you believe in GOD, or do you listen to the sceptical arguments of some shallow friend ? and are you giving up religion altogether ? Do you believe in the other world, or do you think you are going to end at death ? Do you believe in the Eternal SON of GOD, or is somebody persuading you that Christianity is all an idle tale ? Do you believe in the HOLY GHOST ? Are you, as a matter of fact, a faithful, living, working member of the Holy Catholic Church ? I ask you these questions; I want you to answer them to yourself. If not, then I do not wonder that you have no hope. If not, I do not wonder you are not the strong, active, living men and women you ought to be, whom we want to see rally round the standard of JESUS CHRIST. But I come here not to reproach you : I come to rally you ; I come to say, in the name of GOD, that these things are true, and that there is joy and peace in believing them. You, too, may have hope. " The GOD of Hope fill you with all joy and peace in believing, that ye may abound in hope, through the power of the HOLY GHOST." Why should you not have it ? There is no single argument that will hold water for a moment against the truth of every one of them. Read Sir Oliver Lodge, if you prefer to follow a scientific man rather than a clergyman ; he will lead you on some distance in belief in these things. What I feel perfectly certain is that either the public opinion of your world, or carelessness in life, or simple disinclination to prayer and religion, is what has robbed

## *Hope*

you of your hope and strength. I do urge you not to let the tone of your office, or the tone of your warehouse, or the tone of your street, pull you down. "If any man shall be ashamed of Me and of My words, of him shall the SON of man be ashamed when He shall come in the glory of the FATHER and His holy angels." Our great glory is that we have to change the world, to be faithful in a faithless generation. See to it that you are. I do urge you to come back to your prayer again, come back to your Church, come back to your Communion, put yourself in touch with the powers of the world to come; and it will be the happiest day you ever spent in your life if you do.

> "Return, O wanderer, to thy home;
> Thy FATHER waits for thee."

We sang that right through East London, and many a soul heard the cry and came back; and if with humility and with repentance, and with a humble trust in GOD's goodness, you come back to the old religion—in other words, come back to GOD—not only will you have joy and peace in believing, beyond expression, but you shall abound in hope through the power of the HOLY GHOST.

# ALL SAINTS', MARGARET STREET

*SUNDAY AFTERNOON*

TO MEN ONLY

## V

## WORK

" Son, go work to-day in my vineyard."—ST. MATT. xxi. 28.

WE have taken, during this Mission, for the men's services, Wonder, Faith, Purity, Hope; and now I am going to speak on Work.

1. I am going first to carry your minds with me to a scene which I had before my eyes at about one o'clock this morning. We started in Westminster about eleven o'clock last night with a band and a long procession with torches, and we walked for an hour and a quarter through all the poorest parts of Westminster, and held little services at the corners of the streets ; and when the public-houses closed we drew in with us at the end a large band of men, some quite drunk, some half drunk, and all the worse for drink ; so at half-past twelve I had before me in two rooms about the number of men, or nearly the number of men, who are in this church now. And I want to picture to you what it is to look down upon 200 drunken men. They were, many of them, young—

## *Work*

very few over forty—many of them having the signs about them of men who might have been so different. We began with hymns; all the shouting and the joking with one another calmed quietly down, and at the end of twenty minutes of singing and of quieting down—which the excellent Church Army workers know so well how to carry out—I spoke to those men in as dead a silence—except for two, who questioned what I was saying, as often used to be done in the East End—as that in which you listen to me. But here was every one of these men, created by GOD, redeemed by JESUS CHRIST, capable of being sanctified by the HOLY SPIRIT, with a place for him in Heaven, and a place meant for him of useful work and happiness on earth—every one of them, or practically every one of them, gathered within a mile, dragged down by this curse. And when I thought that if I had the same band and the same torches and the same organisation as I had last night, I could have filled in every mile of poor London every mission-room with the same number of men, I realised myself the first thing that I want you to realise now—that there are tens of thousands of our brothers who are like that in London every Saturday night between eleven and twelve. I must say it was very touching, the way in which they, even in that half-drunken state, showed the good there was in them. As they got quieter towards one o'clock, many of them came forward and thanked me heartily for what I had said to them, and spoke to me about themselves. Many of them said, " Bishop, if you will just sign the bottom of the card, I think I could take the pledge and keep it after to-night." All of them

## *Work*

looked on the whole visit as a mark of brotherhood and love, and you felt that, if only there was power enough in London, and if only the whole Church could rise, and the State could rise, to wipe away the curse with a loving and yet stronger hand, thousands of these brothers of ours, who are like that every Saturday night, might be saved for GOD.

2. Then I ask you to come to another scene—and you will see in a moment how all this applies to yourselves. At the same time there would not be far off another, even sadder, gathering, into which the noble women who every night of their lives go out, when we go to bed, into the streets—Piccadilly, Piccadilly Circus, Regent Street, and the Strand—have collected women gathered off the streets of London. You might see them, as I have seen them, not in such gatherings, but in the Lock hospital, with their youthful beauty all gone in their youth, like flowers crushed to pieces ; girls and women who might have been happy mothers or wives ; somebody's daughters, one perhaps sent up by some poor woman in the country—her only child—to make her living in London. You might look down on 100 or 150 faces like that ; of course, there are some men who do not seem to feel anything : they are so wrapped up in their own comfort that you may tell them the most piteous story, and it is to them a tale of little meaning. As I was warning a gathering of Oxford and Cambridge graduates and public-school men * a few days ago, there is a great danger that there may grow over us a horrible moss of selfishness ; we get so accustomed to our comforts and little ways that the cry of a

* See p. 253.

## *Work*

whole universe would not rouse us. But if you are not like that—and it is one of my objects in speaking to you to prevent you and myself from getting like that—if you were to see that little band of girls, and knew that there were thousands, and perhaps tens of thousands, of women and girls like that in London, you would have the second thing that I want you to think of. I will return to both these pictures in a moment. " Is it nothing to you, ye who pass by ? Is there any sorrow like unto My sorrow ?" On Passion Sunday we are obliged to listen to that question ; I believe that our LORD JESUS CHRIST looks down with sorrow upon both those sights. What do *we* feel about it ? That state of things is not what was meant by GOD at all. When that poor girl was born and sent into the world, she was not meant for that. That poor fellow, looking up at me—a nice-looking lad he must have been once—with seams all down his face made by drink, was not meant for that.

3. And then I look again to a more cheerful sight and one that I have very often seen—500 boys who might have been like those young fellows I saw last night, in some great airy boys' club, vaulting over the wooden horse, or engaged in other gymnastic exercises, or playing draughts, or up in a quiet room reading a book, or on Saturday afternoon playing football or cricket, or running races in competition through the streets at night, as you must often have seen them in the City, or in the East End, or in the poorer parts of North London. I know that one club like that has saved, out of the numbers which it contains, hundreds of young fellows during

## *Work*

the last twenty years; through its work the loving hand of the Church of England has come down in time and said, " No, my lad; that is not what you are meant for. This is the boy's true life—home, recreation, amusement, by all means plenty of it. The mind is not meant to read the garbage of the streets; read good books. The body is not meant for that sensual self-indulgence; it should have exercise in healthy games. The spirit is not meant to be quenched out; it should have good food given it; come to our Mission service." And at such a service you can speak where such work is going on, as I have done time after time, and these lads—who might have been what the world would call hooligans—will listen so quietly that one could hear a pin drop: not a word is said. And you find in the districts where this sort of work is going on that there is no hooliganism, no horseplay, such as that in which a man is sometimes killed by the use of those terrible belts of which you have heard; while in the next district, where there is no such work going on, hooliganism reigns supreme. I have seen forty hooligans up in the gallery of a hall where the " Messiah " was being performed by boys and girls from their own district of Bethnal Green, listening to the " Messiah " for an hour and a half, having paid their money to come in, and softened by the beauty of the message spoken by the music.

4. Or take another scene, and you will see in a moment how it applies to you. It is one of those starry nights which are so beautiful by the seaside ! there are 400 London boys about to sleep in the surrounding tents. It is prayer-time before they go

## *Work*

to quarters, and they are drawn up for me to speak to them for five minutes before they go to bed. After this was done one night I spoke to one of the officers —for 400 boys there are some fifty officers, chiefly young clerks from London, who work in the great business houses—and I said: " You followed just now what I said about GOD'S love, the great infinite love which looks down from the stars, as the poet says so beautifully—you believe all that, don't you ?" " Yes," he said, " but I tell you, Bishop, what made me believe it—I will tell you what made my religion real to me; it was not so before." I said, " What ?" " Why, the Church Lads' Brigade. Being an officer in the Church Lads' Brigade has changed my life. I never did anything before, and religion was far away from me. Now I have worked for these lads, and have learnt to love them, and I have given up a week of my holiday regularly for them for years. I understand now about the love of GOD ; I believe in love, and I understand about the love of CHRIST. That made my religion real." So he said to me under the stars.

5. And one more scene. I should like you to picture the Church Army workers, men who, many of them, have given up a good wage for about twenty-five shillings a week—which is the minimum which will keep them—men who very often, when they were carpenters and joiners, cared nothing about religion, but who were converted, and converted so thoroughly that they wanted to work for GOD Who had saved them. There they are, a noble band of men. The more I see them at work, the more I admire them ; and the members of the Women's Department are as fine and noble a body of women as work for the

## Work

Church in any quarter of the world. I have just heard that for the first time they are short of workers; for the first time the class from which they are recruited, which is more the working class than any other, has failed to supply enough of them to come forward and work. These are the men who, under GOD, are saving for us the victims of drink and helping to save the outcast women in London.

II. Now I want to come to yourselves. I speak to myself just as I speak to you. Come back to that night scene. (1) Have you and I anything whatever to do with it? I dare say—in fact, I am sure—that many Socialists—so-called Socialists—would look upon me as not at all a thorough-going Socialist; and I speak, therefore, simply as a Christian when I say this: If it is true that we are members one of another, if it is true that the State is one body, and we are responsible for one another; if it is true that the Church is one body, and every member is responsible for the other, you and I have got to face those two rooms full of drunkards. You have to ask yourselves, first of all, whether we make them drunk. I know perfectly well I speak to people who have probably never themselves been drunk in their lives; they may have been, like myself, teetotallers for five-and-twenty years, but I say I am bound to ask myself—and I did last night—" Am I responsible, as a citizen, by the arrangements which I have countenanced in my country—am I responsible, by the teaching or the carelessness and want of teaching of my Church, for the state of those men, and thousands like them, who would fill every mission-room on Saturday night in London? I am perfectly certain that, when we face GOD, He will not take the

## *Work*

excuse that we are not responsible. " Where is thy brother Abel ?" was the question which sounded long ago from Heaven; and it is impossible for us to live our little limited lives and cut ourselves off from the others. I am bound to see if I am investing my money in such a way as to help to bring about this state of things. I can imagine men here who are living on some invested savings yielding a constant income; but how is your money, that income, produced ? I always thank the Christian Social Union for teaching me this twenty years ago. You are part-owner of the business from which your money comes, as much as if there was no other owner; you are responsible for the labour that is sweated; you are responsible if that man cannot get enough, or if that girl cannot get enough for an honest living. We cannot put the responsibility off on others at all. And therefore, quite apart from what we are doing to rescue them, I do put it to you—I never thought of this myself twenty-five years ago—that you cannot divest yourself of responsibility as citizen or member of the Church—as to whether every boy has a good or a bad chance. I may not pray only " My FATHER"; GOD is not only " *my* FATHER," He is " *Our* FATHER," and when I say " Our FATHER," I kneel beside the worst drunkard or the most abandoned girl in London. If I say " Our FATHER," I kneel by my brother and my sister when I say it. The man who pays no attention to the question how they came there, the man who thinks he has got nothing to do with it—that man, I venture to say, has not yet prayed " Our FATHER " in the right spirit. And, as a member of the nation—I am introducing no controversial subjects, because I think it most

## *Work*

unfair to do so in the pulpit, as there is no right of reply—as a citizen, we have to ask ourselves this question—not now especially, but at any time—" Am I working among my friends, in my County Council, in my parish, so that the poorest brother and the weakest brother there shall have a better chance because of me ?"

2. And then I have got to ask myself a further question: " What am I going to do to help the man now ?" It is not enough to recognise our responsibility for a man's conditions of labour or the conditions of his home ; but when he is down we must ask—and when I saw those young men in that condition I said to myself what I say to you—" What are you doing to save him ?" If we had an army of men—men who understood what the work was—we could save them in thousands. What each wants is a brother-man to devote himself almost individually to him. It is astonishing what can be done in that way. In the Church Army there is an organisation called " The Friends of the Poor," and every one who gives in his name to be a Friend of the Poor has only one case given him, one family or one man, and he is that man's friend—he is devoted to that man. He may be busy (and many of them are), but that is his friend, that is his brother, that is the family which belongs to him. When, some ten years ago, there was started what is called " The Borstal Prison Committee," and some sixty young men in London gave in their names to go and visit the prisoners, we gave them only one man each, but he was to be his brother, and he had to see him through—find work for him when he came out, go and see how he was getting on, and show a brotherly sympathy with him. That is

## *Work*

the way numbers of lives are brought back from dishonesty and vice, before it is too late, to lives of honest work.

And again I say, What are you doing? whom are you helping? have you ever brought anyone back? I am conscious, as I speak, how much more I ought to have done. I have tried my best. I am not reproaching you, but I ask myself and you, Who is the better for my being in the world? Where is Abel, thy brother? It is not enough to say, " I had a good home, and I was taught not to drink or gamble by my parents; I am in a business house now, and I try to keep straight." That is not anything like enough. We are responsible for the others, and unless we can say, when we face GOD, " Here am I, by Thy mercy, and here is Abel, my brother," we have much to learn still about the Christian Gospel.

3. Or take that other sight, and see if you have any responsibility about that. To me as a man it sometimes seems an awful thought that here is an army of good women trying to undo what we men, as a class, have done. And that is why we have those great meetings of men in hall after hall right through London. Perhaps there are some here who came out from them; fifty came out at one meeting, and became stewards for the next meeting. But we have hardly touched the fringe of the problem yet. We have to make every man in London realise that if he has part or lot in tampering with one of these children of GOD he has incurred the wrath of the Lamb. The wrath of the Lamb is so awful because it is the wrath of the most gentle being in the world; the wrath of the Lamb is so awful because it is the love of the Lamb for the victim that is turned against the

## *Work*

betrayer. And therefore we must face the question whether we have incurred it. There may be some of you who have to face it for yourselves; and if it is possible that any one of you has even kicked lower down the ladder one already half down, you must go down on your knees, if you are to be saved, if you are to be forgiven, and say, " GOD be merciful to me, a sinner!" There must be no beating about the bush, no excuse made of what is said in the office, no " All the men do this," and so on. That is not the standard which will be the standard at the Day of Judgment. It will be, " What is GOD's moral law ? Did GOD love His child or not ? Did you help her, or did you help to damn her ?" And I charge you not to let this Mission pass without going down on your knees before it is too late, and asking GOD to be merciful to you a sinner, and saying to yourself : " I never realised what I was doing; I see how awful it is now, how cruel to others and how destructive of myself; and, GOD helping me, I will return to pure life again."

4. But even that is not enough. What about the bad jokes in the office, the talk which sometimes goes on eternally where men gather on one subject, the sneer about virtue and chivalry ? Which side do you take ? You may have been saved from the worst sin, but on which side are you ? " He that is not with Me is against Me, and he that gathereth not with Me scattereth." " Son, go work to-day in My vineyard." And the first work you have got to do is to be a man, to stand up and say you will not have this talk in your place of business. Many a young man has put the whole thing down by his single example and courage. And if you are busy from morning to night, and have

## *Work*

no time to go out and do other things, at least that is your work. " Work to-day in My vineyard." And the first work you have to do is to take your part with the boys in the office, and see that they do not hear bad jokes or filthy conversation from the older men; stand up for them as they try to keep straight and live up to what they are taught at home. The man who does not do that is not worth the name of Christian. " He that is ashamed of Me and of My word, of him shall the SON of man be ashamed when He shall come in the glory of the FATHER and the holy angels."

5. Or take these happier scenes: the bright boys' clubs full of happy boys, those glorious seaside camps, this Church Army work. Why, as a fine old man said the other day, " I tell you, Bishop, it is a glorious thing to be alive in the world to-day: there never were such opportunities of doing good; there never was such a change of public opinion coming so rapidly on the moral question, on the temperance question; there never was such a growing conviction that everybody—the richest man—must do something; that he is only rich that he may do work for others; that the selfish idler of Piccadilly is as much one of the unemployed as a man of the lower class." Some of the hardest workers in England are the noblest in family and the richest men. What are we doing? Why should not some of you young men become officers in the Church Lads' Brigade, or go down once a week to some boys' club in a poor part of London and taste the great happiness and the new reality of religion, as that young officer did who spoke to me under the stars? Why not *you*,

## Work

and *you*, and *you*? " Son, go work to-day in My vineyard," that is what GOD says. And if some of you older men here say, " Well, Bishop, I am up in the City all day; when I go home my family naturally expect to see something of me in the evening," then I agree that this is not your work: home must come first; you have got your home to think of. But how many a poor clergyman in London is breaking down for want of men who will come to him and say, " I do know something about figures; I will deal with your parish accounts for you, Vicar." Or you might help to start and work a branch of the Church of England Men's Society in the district, which can be done on Saturday afternoons or largely on Sundays. That would be quite compatible with the duties of a man with family ties.

Now, it is not a question of my going on and showing you the work that is waiting. There is an old proverb, " Where there is a will there is a way," and it is the will I want to claim for GOD. I want you to feel that there will be no reproach so great as the reproach of the man who has let the battle go by default because he would not fight; who sees his day go by, the most glorious day, when untold opportunities are at hand, and does nothing. " Some work of noble note may yet be done." I would rally you round me, as I try to superintend and carry on the work of GOD in this great diocese. It is GOD who says to you and to me, " Son, go work to-day in My vineyard"; and even if up to now you have refused to listen to His voice, be like the man in the story—" afterwards he repented and went."

# St. Marylebone

*SUNDAY AFTERNOON*

TO MEN ONLY

## VI

## PRAISE

"O praise God in His holiness; praise Him in the firmament of His power; praise Him in His noble acts; praise Him according to His excellent greatness."—Ps. cl. 1, 2 (Prayer Book Version).

WE have already* faced in this Mission the questions, "What am I? A dying man, and yet a man who cannot die; a man who will be the same five minutes after death as he is five minutes before; a man with a will and a mind and a conscience and an undying spirit." "Why am I here? For what end was I born, and for what cause came I into the world? Not to enjoy myself, not to get rich, not to be popular; but to this end was I born, and for this cause came I into the world, to bear witness to the truth. And if I am not doing that, I am a perfect failure, whether I am a bishop, priest, or layman." What does God think of me?—the only question which will be worth anything five minutes after death. What does God think of me—

* See p. 211 *et seq.*

## *Praise*

the GOD Who made me, and under whose eye I stand as clear and distinct as if there was not another living person in the whole world ? GOD being infinite, GOD is wholly with us; we have the whole of GOD to attend to our prayers. What does GOD think of me ? What does He think of me as His child ? What does He think of me as a witness ? What does He think of me as His sentinel ? What does He think of me as His soldier ?—the only questions which will matter at all one day, and therefore the only questions which matter to-day. "Where am I going, when it is all over, when I die, as more than two or three younger than myself whom I knew will have died in the last week ? When I die, whither am I going ?—a question you would think that every man must ask unless he is a very foolish man. You realise how quickly life goes; what comes afterwards ? Whither am I going ? We have seen that when you translated that into other language it was, Which way am I going ? Heaven is character, and Heaven depends on character. Am I going uphill or downhill ? The whole terror of death is that it is no change, that death only lifts off the weights, and I go to my own place, like Judas. You go to your own place. You cannot alter it then ; you go to the place you have prepared by your life. There is no miracle at the last moment, unless it is a conversion so complete as to turn the whole character. But, roughly speaking, we go to our own place, the place which we have prepared for ourselves. Which place am I going to ?"

We pushed those questions home as we knelt in silence, and it has been very touching since then to

*Praise*

see the number of letters I have received from the men and the women who were present at those midday meditations in Westminster Abbey.

Then I am bringing to a close the Mission which has been held in the different churches. If you believe in this, if I am this undying and yet dying man, and if the love of the TRINITY is so great for me, what ought my response to be? We have taken Wonder, we have taken Faith, we have taken Hope, we have taken Work, and on this last Sunday of the Mission it was a great question with me as to what the last should be. But there cannot be any doubt really—there cannot be any doubt when we look at the Bible and read the Psalms, what it must be. It must be Praise. The man who does not praise is an unconverted man; the man who does not praise is the man who has not taken in, at any rate fully, the love of the HOLY TRINITY. And therefore it is that I feel guided to speak to you to-day on Praise as the response of man to the love of the TRINITY. When you look into the question you will find that praise has always been the response. When "the morning stars sang together and all the sons of GOD shouted for joy," praise was the note of creation. When you read the Psalms, they are full of praise. The Psalms are not full of morbid expressions of feelings, like many of our modern devotions; they are full of praise to GOD: " Praise GOD in His holiness; praise Him in the firmament of His power; praise Him in His noble acts; praise Him according to His excellent greatness." What a manly note that is! When the love of the TRINITY was manifested in the Incarnation, the answer was praise; the angels sang, " Glory to GOD in

## *Praise*

the highest, on earth peace, goodwill toward men." When the Apostles were in prison they sang praises unto GOD. And if we take a really helpful work like Bishop Andrewes' " Devotions," by a great and holy man who gives a pattern of what devotion ought to be, it is again praise, praise; the whole thing rings with praise. And therefore my message to-day is this : If we have never praised GOD before, or understood what praise is, there must not be a man among us to-day who does not go away determined to praise GOD for the rest of his life.

And so it is that I want to face with you two or three very searching questions about praise. First, why does GOD want so much to be praised ? A good man does not at all want to be praised ; a good man dislikes it if he is too much praised, especially to his face. Why does GOD want to be praised ? Why is the whole of religion said to be praising GOD ? Why, for instance, in the Ordination prayer is it said, " He [CHRIST] gathered together a great flock in all parts of the world to set forth the eternal praise of Thy holy Name"?—one of the most beautiful sentences in the Ordination Service. Secondly, why is praise the highest part of worship ? why is it the highest part of religion altogether ? Thirdly, " How can I, a man who works from eight in the morning to eight at night every day, in the City, in a business house, who have to go up to the City to look after my business and provide for my family, how can I spend my time in praise ? It is all very well for a Bishop or a member of a Cathedral choir, who has nothing else to do but take part in the service of the Cathedral." Fourthly, what is it that keeps me from praise, or,

## *Praise*

at any rate, what keeps many of us from praise ? Lastly, what is my resolution to be on the last Sunday of this Mission ?

1. Now, let me begin quite frankly with the first. I can remember when I was a young man that this was a real difficulty to me. I could not understand why it was. It seemed almost selfishness on the part of GOD to want so much praise. Let us look that straight in the face. My belief is that we do not face these things directly enough, and that is why our religion is so often unreal. In order to answer that, I want you to call to mind a picture which seems to me one of the most inspired ever painted. You have probably seen it, or seen representations of it. It is called " The Triumph of Love." It is one of Watts's pictures, and it represents a slim and beautiful figure trampling upon apparently dead bodies, with outstretched hands and upturned face to GOD. I ask myself, what is the meaning of that picture ? Here, clearly, is a figure in praise. Love has triumphed, and Love praises. Is GOD a selfish GOD Who simply craves for congratulations ? See what the painter-poet meant. What he pictured was this : pure love struggling down here against all its foes, with vice and drink and gambling and malice and hatred, all against it. Love finds the battle very hard, beset on all sides, almost trampled down, just as you see to-day some good man almost trampled down by the forces against him ; or some man almost sneered out of his religion in the City office ; or a boy laughed at for being firm, who almost gives up his religion altogether ; or a reformer in London trying to get rid of drink, gambling, vice,

## *Praise*

profligacy, who goes down sometimes under the organised force against him. But Love is struggling like that always, and just when Love is almost conquered, Love finds a power come down from Heaven and enter into him, finds new strength put into him, finds hope in his heart, finds his faith burning again, finds a strength not his own as he grapples with those enemies against which he fights, and at last, to his intense relief and to his glorious triumph, he conquers in a strength which is not his own. These foes of the human race have gone under his feet, and he knows that something is tingling in his veins which is not his own; a will not his own has grasped his; a heart not his own has warmed his; he hears in his ears a voice not his own, and he is all triumph, and he looks up and he praises. Is that selfishness on the part of GOD ? Why, GOD has been in the thick of the battle; GOD came down on the Cross, and bore the worst for love—GOD was the Love Who was slain. It is, then, for our sake we have to praise, and not for GOD's sake. GOD wants His child to love Him; He wants His child's response, as any father does, but it is for our sake that He wants us to praise. It is the child who does not praise who does not believe; it is the man who does not praise who has not had his soul expanded with the love of the TRINITY. That is why we are to praise, and that is why He longs that every man here shall begin to praise. Have you taken in all that we have spoken of during these six weeks ? That the love of the TRINITY is with you in answer to your prayers; that when you kneel down there is GOD the FATHER with His hands full of gifts ready to give you—" Ask, and ye shall receive;

## *Praise*

seek, and ye shall find; knock, and it shall be opened to you"; that GOD the SON is kneeling by your side and saying, "Simon, Simon, Satan desires to have thee that he may sift thee as wheat, but I will pray for thee"; that GOD the HOLY GHOST comes and prays in us with groanings that cannot be uttered. Have you taken in what the Incarnation is, or do you imagine that the Christian religion is about a good Man named JESUS CHRIST Who once lived on earth? No wonder you do not praise; but, if you have taken in what the Incarnation and what the Atonement are, that they formed part of a great plan of the HOLY TRINITY for the salvation of mankind, that GOD the FATHER gave His SON, that GOD the SON came, that GOD the HOLY SPIRIT was the agent of the Incarnation, and that JESUS CHRIST, through the Eternal SPIRIT, offered Himself without sin to GOD, and that, as a matter of fact, GOD the FATHER, GOD the SON, and GOD the HOLY GHOST have been pouring Their love out upon you every single day of your life and of my life—if you believed that, you could not help praising. My answer, then, to the question why GOD wants praise is, Because it is only when His son praises that His son is at his best; it is only when His son praises that His son believes in GOD the FATHER, GOD the SON, and GOD the HOLY GHOST, and in the love of the TRINITY; and if you never hear that again between now and the day you meet GOD, remember you were told it now. What does GOD think of me? The answer depends upon whether or not I praise.

2. And that brings me to the second question, Why praise is the highest thing in our religion. I may be speaking to some man who says his prayers, who

## *Praise*

when he has been very sick and prayed, and has recovered, gives thanks—sometimes, anyhow—but who does not ever praise GOD in His holiness, or " praise Him in the firmament of His power." Now, why is it that praise is the highest thing ? First of all, because praise demands the whole man. We kneel to pray, we stand to praise, because the whole man has to be offered in praise. It demands our mind, that we may know and understand who GOD is, and what He has done, and be able to face such questions as I have asked already ; and yet how many thousands of men never think of them at all. It demands our conscience. It is impossible to praise GOD if there is anything on our conscience ; and it may be the very reason that there are some of us who never praise ; there is something between us and GOD on our conscience—that is why we cannot praise. It demands our hearts ; the love of the TRINITY demands the love of the human heart. And it demands our bodies. There is nothing wrong in the body. We have seen that in service after service of the Mission. You cannot ever say, " It is my passions, or the instincts of my body, which make me sin." Nothing of the kind. There is nothing sinful in the body at all. CHRIST wore the human body without sin at all. There is nothing wicked but a wicked will. And therefore this wonderful thing called the body which we have all got, made by GOD, part of the manifestation of the love of the TRINITY, is to be offered in praise, a living sacrifice. And I would like to ask you whether you are even attempting to do that. Are there some saying, " It is all very well, but it is the body that drags me down ; it is the lusts of the flesh, and the

## *Praise*

temptation of the devil"? "I have been," a man here says, "led to drink, and I have been dragged down from my ideals by my passions." All I can say is, What is the good of a Mission if it does not teach you that you can be forgiven for that, if you stop now? there may be a day when you cannot stop. I have had men brought to me in Missions who were so dominated by drink or by lust that, humanly speaking, it seemed impossible for them to turn. That is what our LORD warned us of when He spoke about " the worm that dieth not, and the fire that is not quenched." He uses the strongest language in warning us that we may so twist our wills that we cannot turn. Thank GOD it is not so to-day. I am able to summon myself and every one of my brothers up to the highest act of Christian worship ; and I say praise is the highest act, because it demands my conscience, my heart, my will, my body. Is there one here who will refuse to offer himself a living sacrifice? You must purge the conscience, break off the sins of the body, and make that body pure and true again.

3. But then you say, "Yes, but how about that third question of yours? How can we business men, worried in the City, worried on the Stock Exchange, worried by ceaseless work from half-past eight in the morning till half-past eight in the evening in some great business house—how can we praise, even if we wanted to? How can we offer a life of praise?" I do not think there is anything I am more keen about than that the standard of the layman is the same as the standard of the clergyman—that I have no possibility of praising GOD any better than you have, Just as Aholiab and Bezaleel consecrated their skill

## *Praise*

and art to GOD; just as many of the great saints have had to earn their own living; just as Brother Lawrence was working in the kitchen of the monastery when he wrote those beautiful "Meditations," so can you dedicate your life, and offer it as a sacrifice to GOD. You can do it as well as any clergyman or Sister of Mercy or Bishop in the world. There is only a difference of functions, and not a difference of standard of religion. You are called to be holy, and you have the opportunity of being as holy as anyone in the whole world. Do you remember that beautiful story in Browning, where the little cobbler boy—I used to tell this story in Bethnal Green, where there were so many cobbler boys—worked all day at his trade, but—

> "Morning, evening, noon and night,
> 'Praise GOD!' sang Theocrite"?

Borrow a Browning, and look out that story. All the time he worked, "Praise GOD!" said Theocrite. And when, as the story went on, this little boy was spirited away, GOD listened from Heaven, and said:

> "I miss my little human praise."

Among all the voices that came up from the world, that voice GOD missed. Now, I believe that to be one of the most beautiful truths in the whole world, that GOD misses the voice of every one of His sons whom He does not hear praising in the morning; and that the man who starts his day with praise in the morning, sings his song of praise, utters his praise by his prayer-desk or by his bedside, consecrates all that worrying day in the City, all the time asking GOD to keep him

## *Praise*

straight and true, does his duty, offers the day to GOD —that man is helped by GOD, is living a life as acceptable to GOD, as well-pleasing to GOD as when he comes on Sunday and consecrates the whole week at the Holy Eucharist in the morning, and at church afterwards. That man is living a life as acceptable to GOD as any ordained person in the world. That is my answer to the question, " How can we busy men of London live a life of praise ?" I say, if your hearts are pure, your hands are clean, and your souls are humble, you may live a life of praise as glorious and acceptable to GOD as anyone else. If there is nothing in that business which you cannot own, and nothing in the accounts are wrong, and nothing in the manner of carrying it on which is harsh to others, and if your soul is humble, so that you say, " What have I that I have not received ? If I am blessed, GOD blessed me ; I am only a steward of what I have ; it does not belong to me "—then your life is a noble life to offer to GOD.

4. And that brings me straight on to my fourth question : What is it that holds us back from praise ? Why is it that as I have spoken to you I am certain that many a one in his conscience has answered : " Oh, this is all above us to-day. We understand the straight talk about the body, gambling, and drink—we can keep clear of these ; but it is impossible for ordinary men like ourselves to live a life of praise " ? Now, what is it that keeps us back ?

First, being engrossed with self. The reason that praise is so ennobling is that we forget self when we praise. There may be something selfish even about prayer, or about thanksgiving, but there is nothing

## *Praise*

selfish in praise. We simply look up and "praise GOD in His holiness." Are any of us being kept from praising by being engrossed with our little cares or our little life ? We have to look away from them up to the glorious love of GOD.

Sloth keeps us back too. We are too lazy to get up in the morning and praise GOD. We are too tired to come to church on Sunday at all. We are too indolent to say our prayers in the evening or sing our praises.

Sin keeps us back. We have had this past week so many souls who have been kept back from a life of religion by some sin, which had not been confessed for years and years ; and, if you had seen the peace that comes into the face of a man or woman who has had a sin on his or her conscience for years, and then told GOD all about it, and put out the hand of faith and taken the peace of forgiveness, then you would understand the keenness with which I look into your face and say, If you want to spend Easter in peace, if you want to sing a song of praise on Easter Day—and what day more glorious is there for praise ?—you must get rid of that old haunting sin before Easter. Confess it—some habit never confessed up to now, something in your life of which you are ashamed ; perhaps already discontinued, but never confessed to GOD. I do again and again say to you, if that is keeping you back from happy and glorious praise, even if it be like cutting off the right hand or plucking out the right eye, do it before Easter, and it will be the best Easter you have ever spent.

Lastly, why should I not—I, this living man, who am also a dying man ; I, who have been created by

## *Praise*

GOD, redeemed by JESUS CHRIST, and sanctified, or with the possibility of being sanctified, by the HOLY GHOST, Who is always ready to do it—why should I not offer my life back in praise ? It would give me an unselfish happiness in life, and it would prepare me for a life of praise beyond the grave. Is there any answer to that ? If you were to look up in my face and say, " Tell me, Bishop, what I am born for ; tell me what is it I could do most pleasing to GOD ?" I should say, " You were born to praise, and you could not please GOD more than by living a life of praise in return."

Let us kneel down together then, humbly grateful to the GOD who made us ; let us resolve every Sunday without fail to join in the praises of GOD's holy Church on earth ; and then, when this life is over, we shall be allowed to join in that song of praise ever ascending in Heaven : " Worthy art Thou to receive glory and honour and power, for Thou hast created all things, and for Thy pleasure they are and were created !"


**THE END**

www.ingramcontent.com/pod-product-compliance
Lightning Source LLC
Chambersburg PA
CBHW050836230426
43667CB00012B/2023